FOOD ✕ SWAP

FOOD SWAP

Specialty Recipes **for Bartering, Sharing** & **Giving**

Including the World's Best Salted Caramel Sauce

EMILY PASTER

Storey Publishing

The mission of Storey Publishing is to serve our customers by publishing practical information that encourages personal independence in harmony with the environment.

EDITED BY Margaret Sutherland, Lisa Hiley, and Corey Cusson

ART DIRECTION AND BOOK DESIGN BY Michaela Jebb

INDEXED BY Samantha Miller

COVER PHOTOGRAPHY BY © Michael Piazza Photography, except © Doug McGoldrick (author) and John Polak (back flap)

INTERIOR PHOTOGRAPHY BY © Jasmine Pulley, 9, 10, 12, 16, 19, 21 (top), 25, 26 (middle), 36, 42 (top), 43, 46, 52, 56, 57 (top), 61, 62, 67; John Polak, 75, ribbon (102 and throughout); Mars Vilaubi, 13, 14, 15, 18, 20, 21 (middle & bottom), 26 (top & bottom), 28, 29, 31, 37, 38, 40, 47, 51 (top), 53, 54, 55, 57 (bottom), 58–59, 60, 65, 68, 69, 70, 74, 76, 78, 79, 82, 83, 89, 96, 101, 115, 116, 131, 138, 147, 161, 165, 174–177, 186, 196, 197, 201, 210, 228, 233, 236; © Michael Piazza Photography, 1–7, 22–24, 34, 35, 72, 73, 77, 80, 86–87, 88, 90, 91, 93, 94, 97, 99, 104, 107–109, 119 (top), 123, 124, 132, 135, 141–145, 150, 155, 159, 160, 162, 167–172, 180–185, 187, 188, 194, 203, 208, 219, 223, 224, 227, 230; Michaela Jebb, 11, 30, 32–33, 39 (bottom), 42 (bottom), 44, 48–49, 63, 66, 84–85, 173, 192, 198–201, 213; © Picture Partners/iStockphoto.com, 207; © stockcam/iStockphoto.com, paper texture (39 and throughout)

ILLUSTRATIONS BY © Sara Mulvanny

Storey Publishing
210 MASS MoCA Way
North Adams, MA 01247
www.storey.com

Printed in China by R.R. Donnelley
10 9 8 7 6 5 4 3 2 1

Library of Congress Cataloging-in-Publication Data

Names: Paster, Emily, author.
Title: Food swap : specialty recipes for bartering, sharing & giving—including the world's best salted caramel sauce / Emily Paster.
Description: North Adams, Massachusetts : Storey Publishing, [2016] | Includes index.
Identifiers: LCCN 2015044862| ISBN 9781612125633 (pbk. : alk. paper) | ISBN 9781612125640 (ebooks)
Subjects: LCSH: Cooking. | Barter. | Food cooperatives. | LCGFT: Cookbooks.
Classification: LCC TX714 .P3776 2016 | DDC 641.5—dc23
LC record available at http://lccn.loc.gov/2015044862

In memory of **my beloved father, Howard George Paster, the one true grown-up.**

Contents

Foreword

HAD YOU TOLD ME ABOUT THE TIDAL WAVE OF INTEREST that would burst forth from packing my 900-square-foot apartment in Brooklyn with 26 eager food swappers, I might have laughed. Had you shown me that an event that began with a Twitter exchange then blossomed into plans for a low-key swap party while sipping drinks with Meg at Roberta's in Bushwick would become a worldwide movement, I'd have laughed again and asked if you wanted to trade me for some marmalade. That very first BK Swappers was rooted in the blossoming DIY food scene of 2010; friends, friends of friends, and even strangers flocked to bring the sharing economy back to food as we knew it. We moved the furniture out of the living room, set up a tea station in the kitchen, popped open the snacks and samples, and had a wonderful time sharing and swapping in the neighborly and communal fashion that I was so hungry for living in a big impersonal city.

Trading food is as old as agriculture, animal husbandry, and communities themselves. Bartering, specialization, and gatherings surrounding food are at the core of human civilization. A modern forum for allowing people to bring what they have and swap items one for one with each other connects us not only with each other, but also with the ingenuity (and necessity) of our ancestors. Modern food swapping allows us to share with each other in the midst of a capitalism-centered economy.

Many of our swappers in Austin, where I returned at the end of 2010, have launched food businesses and now sell their wares, but their roots in the swap run deep. There's something amazing about not attaching monetary value to everything we do. By valuing the products we create in our home kitchens and acknowledging the inherent value in taking time to make items from scratch, we begin to feel more connected to a larger sharing economy. Those foods are consumed with the knowledge that someone put special care into them, someone you (now) know did work that you did not have to do yourself in order to eat a homemade item.

As I traveled across the country in 2011, touring for my first book, *Hip Girl's Guide to Homemaking,* I was delighted to receive invites from all the new food swaps that were popping up. I attended swaps in Portland; Los Angeles; upstate New York; San Francisco; Minneapolis; Coventry, Connecticut; Bellingham, Washington; and many others. At each swap, though they differed in size, set-up, and city-related mores, the same people were drawn to this grand sharing event. The people who attend food swaps are seeking the community that is supposed to surround food.

Fast forward to now, with many of our founding swaps at or approaching their five-year birthdays, when my good friend and co-creator of Food Swap Network, Emily Han, admits new swaps weekly to the network. Swaps are taking place in the UK, the Netherlands, France, Canada, and of course all over the United States. As you explore these pages, open your mind and your pantry to the community connectivity and deliciousness in store from simply swapping.

Kate Payne
Author of *The Hip Girl's Guide to Homemaking*
Cofounder of the Food Swap Network

Introduction

WHILE THE IDEA OF TRADING FOOD is as old as agriculture itself — if one neighbor had a cow and the other neighbor had chickens, trading milk for eggs just made good sense — how did this ancient form of commerce get revived in the twenty-first century?

Kate Payne and Megan Paska unwittingly launched modern food swapping in 2010, at the intersection of the artisanal, DIY food movement and social media. At the time, Kate, the author of the popular blog and book *The Hip Girl's Guide to Homemaking*, lived in a 600-square-foot Brooklyn apartment and was obsessed with making marmalade. Running out of room for all her jars, Kate mentioned on Twitter that she would be willing to trade some of her stash for other homemade foods. Megan Paska, who blogs at *Farmer Meg's Digest* and has written a book on urban beekeeping, was also living in Brooklyn, where she kept backyard chickens and maintained a rooftop beehive.

Megan responded to Kate's Tweet about trading marmalade, which led to an email exchange and then a meeting at a local restaurant where Megan swapped honey and eggs for Kate's marmalade. At that meeting, Megan mentioned how much fun it would be to have a larger exchange; they both knew plenty of others just like them in Brooklyn making and producing their own food. And thus the food swap movement was born.

Kate and Megan hosted the first group food swap in March 2010 in Kate's small apartment. They set up tables for sampling and swapping, and served snacks and tea. About two dozen people came. Megan came up with the idea for swap sheets, which have been a staple of food swaps ever since, as a way to organize the actual swapping. (For that first swap, Kate and Megan hand-wrote the swap cards as people were arriving.) Everyone had so much fun that Kate and Megan knew it had to become a regular thing. They began hosting food swaps under the guise of BK Swappers every other month.

A Growing Trend

BK SWAPPERS QUICKLY ATTRACTED media attention, and when homemade food enthusiasts in other cities learned about the concept of swapping food, they wanted in. Portland, Oregon, was the second city to have its own food swap in late 2010, followed shortly by Minneapolis. (The Minneapolis swap, MPLS Swappers, was shut down by the local health authorities in 2011 after less than one year of operation.) The online television show and blog about food and sustainable living, *Cooking Up a Story,* created a video about the first event held by the Portland food swap group, PDX Swappers, which brought the concept of food swapping to an even broader audience.

That video inspired Los Angeles–based food writer Emily Han to start the LA Food Swap in spring of 2011. By this time, Kate Payne had moved to Austin, Texas, where she promptly started another food swap, ATX Swappers. That brought the number of official food swaps to five.

In March 2011, an article about BK Swappers appeared in the *New York Times.* After that, the food swap movement began attracting widespread national attention. Kate, Megan, and Emily were inundated with emails and calls from people wanting to start food swaps in their own cities, something all of the original food swap organizers enthusiastically encouraged. Kate created a private Facebook group for organizers to share tips and best practices. Busy promoting her first book, Kate realized that it would be far more efficient to consolidate all of the food swap organizers' knowledge and expertise in one place than it was for her and the others to constantly answer individual queries. Shortly thereafter, in June 2011, Kate and Emily happened to be in Seattle at the same time and got together to discuss the future of food swapping. That meeting became the foundation of the Food Swap Network.

Kate and Emily created an advisory board that included Kim Christensen and Mandy Ellerton from the Minneapolis food swap, Bethany Rydmark from the Portland group, and Megan Paska as cofounder of BK Swappers.

Together they began creating a website for the Food Swap Network. It took months to get the website off the ground, with Kate and Emily paying for the costs out of their own pockets. The group even launched a community fund-raiser to help pay for a graphic designer to create a logo.

In the fall of 2011, FoodSwapNetwork.com was launched. Food swaps all over the world — by this time, Apples for Eggs had started in the United Kingdom — could submit their information to be listed as part of the Food Swap Network. For food swap organizers, the site was a great way to spread the word about their group. People wanting to join a food swap could search the Food Swap Network's listings for a swap in their area.

And if they did not find one, the Food Swap Network had tips and resources for people wanting to start their own swaps. These resources included a swap tool kit, tip sheets on how to host and how to attend a swap, what to do on the day of a swap, sample swap sheets to download, and answers to other frequently asked questions. With these resources now available for everyone to access, it was easier than ever for cities to get their own food swaps. In just over a year, food swapping had become a bona fide national trend.

The *Chicago* Food Swap

WHEN I STARTED the Chicago Food Swap in late 2011, I had no idea that it would change my life. My interest in starting a food swap was purely selfish: I had a basement full of jams, chutneys, and pickles that I had spent my whole summer canning, much to the bewilderment of my husband and two young children. We had more jams and pickles than any one family could possibly eat — a fact that my husband pointed out every time I returned from the farmers' market with yet another flat of berries or half-bushel of green beans.

The idea that I could trade jam and pickles for homemade foods that my family would want to eat was revelatory — it's hard to make a whole meal out of condiments. A food swap would be a way to justify my obsession with canning, to show off my beautiful homemade creations, and to meet other people who were equally obsessed with DIY kitchen projects. Little did I know that the Chicago Food Swap would become my new passion and help launch my culinary career.

In September 2011, I read a post on my friend Marisa McClellan's award-winning canning blog *Food in Jars* about the first-ever Philly Food Swappers event. Although the food swap movement was well underway at that point, this was my first introduction to the concept. I was enchanted by Marisa's description of the varied offerings at the Philadelphia event, which ranged from the typical (jams, granola, salsa) to the exotic (horseradish-infused vodka, customized tea blends) and of how she traded jam for pumpkin bread and a bacon-chive cheese spread.

I was desperate to participate in such an event. Yet much to my astonishment, there was no Chicago-based food swap. My only option for participating in an event of this kind, it seemed, was to start one myself. But I was more than a little intimidated by the prospect. Marisa had

The idea that I could trade jam and pickles for homemade foods that my family would want to eat was revelatory – it's hard to make a whole meal out of condiments.

started the Philly Food Swappers with three other food-obsessed friends, and she encouraged me to find some partners, particularly other bloggers, both to help share the work and to help spread the word about the swap. I reached out to several, including my neighbor and friend Vanessa Druckman, author of the popular *Chefdruck Musings* blog. Despite the fact that Vanessa had given birth to her fourth child only a few months before, she and I began meeting to discuss how to get the Chicago Food Swap off the ground.

Finding *a Spot*

THE BIGGEST CHALLENGES in starting a new food swap are typically finding a location and finding participants. This was certainly true for the Chicago Food Swap. As bloggers, Vanessa and I felt confident that we could spread the word about the Chicago Food Swap when the time came, but finding a location was more difficult. Because we didn't plan to charge admission (see To Fee or Not to Fee, page 64), we needed a location that we could use without paying any rental fees. As we would already be out of pocket for expenses such as printing, name tags, and other supplies, we wanted to minimize our financial burden.

We initially explored noncommercial sites such as church basements, libraries, and community centers, which food swap founders in other areas had recommended. But none of these options worked for us, either because they charged a fee or because they were squeamish about events with food, particularly home-cooked food that was not subject to any inspections or prepared in a licensed facility. (This may not be true in your area, and anyone interested in starting a food swap should certainly explore these kinds of sites.)

It occurred to me that we needed a location that (a) would derive some benefit, other than a straight rental fee, by hosting our event and (b) shared our interest in, and passion for, handmade goods. In that spirit, I identified a store in a nearby town that billed itself as an "alternative craft boutique." Pretty Little Things in Forest Park, Illinois — which has since closed its doors — sold only handmade items, ranging from clothes to notecards. I thought that the owners of such a store might appreciate the philosophy of a food swap, which is all about showcasing homemade foods. And because Pretty Little Things did not sell any food items, a food swap would not be taking money out of the store's pocket.

Lastly, I thought that a small, independent store might be grateful for an opportunity to bring people through its door. I dashed off an email to the owners explaining what a food swap was and asking if they might be willing to host one. To my surprise and delight, they were very interested, and furthermore, they had a large, empty basement that would be perfect for such an event.

Vanessa and I met with the owners of Pretty Little Things in the late fall of 2011. We discussed how the event would work and figured out a mutually convenient date for the first swap. We chose a Sunday afternoon because the shop closed early on Sundays. (As it has turned out, this somewhat haphazard choice established a pattern: almost all of our succeeding swaps have been on Sunday afternoons. It seems to be a good time for many host sites: either they are closed or, if they are open, it is a slow time.) Once we had a location and a date, our next task was publicity.

THE MOTHER OF ALL FOOD SWAPS, BK Swappers was started by Kate Payne and Megan Paska in 2010. Jane Lerner, a freelance writer who attended the very first BK Swappers event, now runs the swap with her co-organizer, Margaret Spring.

BK Swappers puts on approximately four events a year, with an average of 35 to 40 attendees. Jane believes this is the ideal number of swappers to create a bustling, lively event without overwhelming anyone. The swaps fill to capacity, with a long waiting list. People come from Manhattan, Long Island, and even northern New Jersey.

Because it is Brooklyn, there is a misconception that those who attend BK Swappers events are hipsters making pickles in mason jars and riding fixie bikes, but Jane insists that it is not really like that. The people are nice, unpretentious, and from all different backgrounds who would not normally get to interact if not for the swap.

Jane is constantly amazed by the swappers' creativity. Just when she thinks she has seen it all, someone brings something that she never imagined making at home. While the swap items vary widely, more than anything they reflect the seasons. Winter brings more sweets and baked goods, and summer more fruits and veggies. Brooklyn is home to many artisanal food businesses, and indeed there are some swappers who started their businesses as a result of the swap.

Every time Jane opens her refrigerator, she sees proof of how amazing the swap is; she uses something she got from a swap every day. While the food is exceptional, for Jane the true joy of BK Swappers is the community. She jokes that running a food swap is like throwing a party for 40 strangers, but it is not really true. The swappers are no longer strangers.

Because it is Brooklyn, there is a misconception that those who attend BK Swappers events are hipsters making pickles in mason jars and riding fixie bikes.

Jane is extremely proud that BK Swappers kicked off the national food swap movement. For Jane, food swapping is a wonderful symbol of our time. Something that is organized online has created real, in-person communities. The fact that food swaps have spread organically to cities around the world speaks to humans' desire to connect through food. Food swaps create a framework for strangers to come together to share food.

Spreading *the Word*

ONE OF THE CHARMING THINGS about food swaps is that they are in-person events that are inevitably organized on the Internet and social media. Vanessa quickly created a basic website for the Chicago Food Swap, while I created a Facebook page. We pressed our own blogs and social media networks into service to help spread the word. We used Eventbrite — a ticketing website that doesn't charge the organizers for free events — to register people and borrowed heavily from descriptions of other food swaps for our event. Being fairly social-media-savvy to begin with was one of the keys to our success in getting the Chicago Food Swap off the ground.

The Chicago Food Swap started small, as do most new food swaps. Despite all of our efforts, we had only a dozen people at the first exchange, and most of those were people we knew. But that was enough to make me want to do it again. I managed to trade a few jars of jam and pickles for delicious cookies, bread, and a drink syrup — none of which I would have made on my own. Moreover, people admired my jars and coveted them. Having spent the past few years alone in my kitchen mastering the art of water-bath canning, it was thrilling to get some recognition for my efforts from people outside my own family. Everyone else seemed to have a great time as well, and Vanessa and I were gung ho to do it again in a few months.

The second swap attracted about 20 participants. That was enough to give it a real swap feel — not everyone could swap with everyone else, and some items were in much higher demand than others. Also, there was a greater variety of items. Instead of mostly baked goods, as was the case with the first swap, there were more savory and shelf-stable items. Everyone had a great time and came away inspired. Several of the participants in the second swap were also bloggers, and they wrote about their experiences on their sites. The presence of bloggers at Chicago Food Swap events from that second swap on has been one of the factors that enabled us to grow into such a large community.

Growing Up

FOR THE NEXT YEAR, Vanessa and I held swaps every other month at sites around the Chicago area. Those events ranged in size from 30 to 50 people, depending on the location. The August 2012 swap, which featured an appearance from Marisa McClellan, in town to promote her first cookbook, titled *Food in Jars* after her blog, was particularly popular. By late 2012, our swaps were filling up, sometimes within days of registration opening, and long waiting lists began to form. Each event was a mix of returning swappers, some of whom had become quite religious about not missing an event, and newcomers.

When I had the chance, I always asked new participants how they heard about the Chicago Food Swap. Some had heard about it through word of mouth, blog posts, or friends; others had read about the larger food swap movement in the press and were intrigued. Fortunately for us, a Google search for "Chicago food swap" or "food swap Chicago" led these folks right to our virtual door.

A strategic partnership with one of the darlings of the Chicago artisanal food scene, a chocolate company called Katherine Anne Confections, elevated the profile of the Chicago Food Swap even further. Katherine Duncan, the owner of Katherine Anne Confections, heard about the Chicago Food Swap from a mutual friend. She had recently opened up her first storefront in Chicago's trendy Logan Square neighborhood. Katherine contacted me and Vanessa in early 2013 about the possibility of hosting a swap at her cozy shop. Although space was tight, Katherine made it work, even allowing us to use the kitchen area for people to set up their swap items.

Katherine's background made her especially keen to support the Chicago Food Swap. She never attended culinary school but began making truffles and caramels as a hobby and over time turned her passion into a thriving business.

The presence of bloggers at Chicago Food Swap events from that second swap on has been one of the factors that enabled us to grow into such a large community.

As a result, Katherine felt a kinship with the members of the Chicago Food Swap community. Some devoted swappers who dreamed of opening their own food businesses someday used the swap as a bit of a laboratory. Katherine was living proof that those dreams could come true.

Vanessa and I were thrilled that someone as well known in the Chicago food scene as Katherine Duncan wanted to host a swap. What we did not realize, although we certainly should have, was that our association would lead to even greater exposure. The week before the February swap, the Chicago edition of *Tasting Table* — a well-regarded online food publication — recommended the Chicago Food Swap as one of its foodie events for the weekend.

Tasting Table was our first press mention, and it exposed the Chicago Food Swap to a much wider audience. After a flurry of last-minute sign-ups, the shop was packed to the gills, and

the room had a certain buzz and energy like we were all in *the* place to be for that afternoon, which was, in fact, Super Bowl Sunday. Although we did not know it at the time, that event was a turning point — after its success, the demand to attend a swap went through the roof.

The April swap, which had already been planned, was going to be small by necessity; the host site was a craft boutique called Local Goods Chicago. The number of people on the waiting list for that event was greater than the number of spots we had available. People who were not able to get a spot at the April swap, which included some of our regulars, complained about being shut out. They didn't want to wait two months to swap again, and we didn't want to let this momentum fizzle out.

Establishing an
Ongoing Presence

BY NOW WE WERE HOLDING SWAPS mostly in local businesses, and the largest group that most of these spaces could accommodate — leaving room for tables to display the swap items of course — was 40, maybe 50, people. Because we were limited in the size of the swap, the only way to meet the growing demand to participate was to swap more frequently. At that point, we decided to start holding swaps every month.

The Chicago Food Swap began meeting on a monthly basis in May 2013, at which time my partner Vanessa gracefully bowed out. With four kids ranging in age from eleven to one and a successful blog, Vanessa no longer had time to devote to running the swap, which was turning into a part-time job, albeit an unpaid one.

Running the swap consumed 10 or 12 hours each week. Although I was slightly overwhelmed by the amount of work required, I was extremely gratified and excited by the success of this little organization. Food swapping was growing as a national trend. The Chicago Food

Swap was generating a lot of buzz and excitement locally. Running the events gave me a place in the Chicago food scene among those who were seeking to promote home food preservation, edible gardening, eating locally, and artisanal food production. The food swap became my entrée into this broader culinary world. This was certainly not my original intention, but now that it was happening, I was ecstatic.

Moreover, the community that had developed out of the swap was genuinely heartwarming. I met and formed relationships with other food bloggers, regular people who were as crazy about food as I was, and even some culinary professionals. (Several professionally trained chefs and people in the food industry are swap regulars.) Participants in the swap raved about how much they loved it and expressed their gratitude for all my hard work. Friendships formed among swappers, and people began meeting for meals and going on foodie excursions to markets and trendy restaurants. It was humbling to think that something I started on a whim had touched so many people.

I was especially proud of the diversity of the group that we attracted. There were swappers of all ages, from teenagers to grandparents. Some were bloggers who Tweeted and Instagrammed everything they saw, and some were people who barely checked their email. Swappers came from all racial and ethnic groups, and many brought traditional foods: amaranth candies and farmer's cheese from Poland, fiery habanero salsa from Mexico, kimchi from Korea, and purple yam buns and lumpia from the Philippines. Given Chicago's ethnic diversity, one might have expected this, but I never took it for granted.

People came from all over the greater Chicago area: young, urban swappers sharing lovingly crafted bitters and exurban, homesteading mamas with fresh eggs and foraged mulberries. We had vegan swappers and gluten-free swappers. In short, the swap brought together groups of people who might not otherwise have had any reason to meet, let alone to trade food and stories. The only thing that we all shared was a love of homemade, or homegrown, food. In a society where we tend to spend most of our time with other people just like us, the Chicago Food Swap was breaking through those walls and tearing down those silos. And it was all because of *food*.

The other characteristic of the Chicago Food Swap that was important to me was the way it recognized the efforts, and expertise, of home cooks. As a home cook who spent years learning to bake bread, make caramels and fresh pasta, and can jams and pickles, I often felt that my efforts were akin to a tree falling in the forest with no one to hear it. What was the point of it other than to amuse myself and enrich my friends' tables? Food swapping changed that. It gives home cooks a community beyond our immediate circle that appreciates our skills and expertise. A food swap garners recognition — and something of tangible value — for home cooks who make exceptional food.

After a year of organizing monthly swaps by myself, I was worn out. The biggest challenge, by far, was coming up with a location every month. Needless to say, when the possibility of a permanent home for Chicago Food Swap events presented itself in the spring of 2014, about the same time that I began to work on this book, I was thrilled. A local community gardening nonprofit, the Peterson Garden Project, announced that it had taken over the lease of a large teaching kitchen on the far north side of Chicago.

The goal was to offer cooking classes and other events in that space as a benefit to the local community. All I could think was: what a perfect place to hold a food swap.

Finding a
Permanent Home

THE PETERSON GARDEN PROJECT, founded by the dynamic and tireless LaManda Joy, is known throughout Chicago for its incredible success in teaching city residents how to grow their own fruits and vegetables in community garden sites all over the city's north side. After several years of this, the next logical step was to teach people how to cook what they had grown. Thus in 2014, LaManda and her staff sought to take over the pristine and unused commercial kitchen, now dubbed the Community Cooking School, at the Park District's enormous facility at the Broadway Armory Field House.

The Chicago Food Swap was already well known to the folks at the Peterson Garden Project. Many regular Chicago Food Swap participants had plots in Peterson Garden Project

sites, and the organization had hosted two earlier food swaps in their cozy office. LaManda felt that the mission of the Chicago Food Swap, namely to encourage homemade and homegrown food, aligned closely with her mission to promote edible gardening.

In the end, I didn't even need to ask; LaManda offered the space as a permanent home for the Chicago Food Swap. It was a godsend. No more looking for a space each month; no more scouting new locations; no more spots that weren't quite big enough or didn't have quite enough display space. The Community Cooking School is enormous and has plenty of counter and display space. The Peterson Garden Project, with its impressive email list and connections to the Chicago food community, was a perfect partner, and hosting the swap fulfilled its mission of offering events that benefit the local community and helped get the word out about its classes. With the opening of the Community Cooking School in the fall of 2014, the Chicago Food Swap had greater stability and growth potential than ever before.

Since September 2014, the Chicago Food Swap has held the majority of its events at the Community Cooking School. I occasionally move the swap around to different locations, including some of our past favorites, when there is a conflict or just to mix things up. But that is the exception. The stability of having a permanent location has allowed me to focus my efforts on other things that will help strengthen the Chicago Food Swap, such as reaching out to the press and continuing to spread the word about food swapping.

The community enjoys the familiarity of a known location. Partnering with the Peterson Garden Project has also benefited the Chicago Food Swap by expanding our audience. The Chicago Food Swap continues to grow and expand, becoming an important part of the local food scene in its hometown.

Why has the Chicago Food Swap been so successful? Organizers of smaller swaps ask me this question over and over again. Food swap organizers have come from as far away as Columbus, Ohio; Ames, Iowa; and St. Louis, Missouri, to attend Chicago Food Swap events in the hopes of re-creating its energy in their own cities. Although it is hard to pinpoint exactly, I attribute our success to a combination of the city's intense food culture; a few well-timed lucky breaks; effective use of social media and networking; and hard-core food swap evangelism. (The organizers of some successful swaps in other cities and towns identify different "cocktails" as the secret to their success.)

The point is, interest in food swapping has no geographic limitations. Every region of the country and every kind of setting, from urban to rural, boasts a successful food swap. Wherever you may be located, you can be part of the food swap movement.

1

What Is A FOOD SWAP?

Do you love to grow your own food, cook from scratch, or make the kinds of food — jam, pickles, ketchup, cheese — that most people usually buy? Do you ever find yourself with more garden produce or homemade food than you and your family can eat? Have you ever given away food that you grew or made to neighbors or friends? Do you want to meet other people in your community who share your love of homemade food? If you answered yes to any of these questions, then you might be ready to join the growing international food swap movement.

At a food swap, home cooks, bakers, canners, gardeners, and foragers get together to trade their homemade and homegrown food items. No money changes hands among the participants. Indeed, you cannot come to a food swap with cash in hand hoping to buy a jar of homemade jam or a head of kale from someone's garden. If you want to participate in a food swap, you have to come bearing something you made, grew, raised, or foraged yourself and trade it for items brought by the other participants.

How *Does* a Food Swap Work?

THE MODERN FOOD SWAP MOVEMENT began in — where else? — Brooklyn, New York, in 2010. Since then, it has spread to every corner of the United States, Canada, Europe, and even South America and the Antipodes. There are food swaps in every large American city and in many small towns and rural areas. Some food swaps meet once a month; some meet only a few times a year. Some food swaps have 50 participants and some have a dozen. Swaps are held in all kinds of locations, from church basements, parks, and community centers to stores and cooking schools. Some swaps charge admission and some are free.

In short, food swaps take many forms, but they all have the following common elements, many of which the founders of the modern food swap movement, Kate Payne and Megan Paska, established at that first 2010 swap.

No money changes hands. Trading, not buying, is what the food swap movement is about. A food swap is intended to be a more personal alternative to the commercial food marketplace. There is also a less romantic and more practical reason for this requirement: food that is to be sold is subject to various health and safety regulations. In many states, for example, food that is intended for retail sale must be prepared in a licensed kitchen by someone who has taken required sanitation training, and labeled according to industry standards.

Some states, California being a prime example, have more lenient cottage food laws, but even then, if one prepares food for sale in a home kitchen, that kitchen is subject to inspection by state health regulators. I will discuss the legalities of food swapping in more detail a little later, but for now, the key point is that by swapping rather than selling food, participants in a food swap can avoid triggering this kind of regulation and government scrutiny.

All items must be made or grown by the participants. You cannot buy something in a store or at a market and bring it to a food swap to trade. You must bring something homemade or homegrown. Most swappers are hobbyists: home cooks and gardeners who love to grow and prepare homemade food. Some participants may be culinary professionals or farmers, but even they must trade what they bring.

What people bring to food swaps varies widely but can include baked goods, candies, condiments, preserved fruits and vegetables, cheese, fermented foods, drink syrups, alcoholic infusions, hand-milled flours, herbs and produce from vegetable gardens, eggs from backyard chickens, foraged fruits, and so on. I will talk more about what makes a good swap item — and give you plenty of recipes for same — but as you can imagine, the best swap items are things that are portable, not highly perishable, distinctive and delicious.

The requirement that the swap items be homemade or homegrown is just as important as the first requirement about no money changing hands. The point of the food swap movement is to celebrate the growing, raising, and making of food. (I say food here, but sometimes people do bring non-food homemade items, such as dog treats, candles, notecards, or health and beauty products. Whether that is permitted and where to draw the line on what kind of items are allowed is up to the organizer of each individual swap.)

The food swap movement is the natural outgrowth of the DIY revolution that has led cooks everywhere to try their hands at making the kinds of foods that most people buy: foods like cheese, charcuterie, jams, pickles, condiments, and candy. At some point, all those homemade enthusiasts found themselves alone in their kitchens with too much of whatever they liked to make. The food swap movement gets those people out of their kitchens and creates a marketplace, albeit an informal one, for those homemade foods. In short, what makes a food swap a food swap is this: people trading items that they made or grew themselves.

A *Typical* Event

WHILE EACH INDIVIDUAL food swap is different, food swap events tend to follow a similar timeline. First, the organizer of the swap usually asks people to register in advance. This is important for logistical reasons, but it may also be important for legal reasons, as I will explain later. On the day of the swap, the participants arrive at the designated time, check in with the host, and stake out a spot to display their swap items.

Swappers put on name tags to allow them to find one another. For each different item they bring — not multiples of the same item — people complete a swap card that lists what the item is, who brought it, the ingredients, and how to use the item (if it is not obvious). The swap cards also have a space where other swappers can make an offer for the item. While these offers are not binding, they are a helpful starting point for negotiations.

For the first part of the event, the participants mingle, sample one another's swap items, and make offers on the swap cards. Once everyone has had sufficient opportunity to look around, the host announces that it is time to swap, and that is when the action begins. The swapping itself can be chaotic. Some people stand by their items and field offers; others grab their items and go out in search of trades. Everyone has to decide on a strategy.

All trades are negotiated by the participants themselves — the host does not get involved — and naturally not every offer is accepted. Saying no is part of the process, and most of the participants understand that. Once everyone has swapped their items, the event begins to wind down. Some folks pack up their stuff and leave right away; others may linger. The hours and days following a swap may see a lot of activity on social media as the swappers post pictures of their haul, compliment one another's cooking, and ask questions.

Why Participate in a Food Swap?

IF YOUR FIRST THOUGHT upon reading my description of a food swap was "Why on earth would anyone want to trade homemade food with strangers?" then this may not be the book for you. But I hope the fact that you have read this far means that you are intrigued by the idea of food swapping. The truth is that there are many good reasons to participate in a food swap. Here are four that I find particularly compelling.

It increases your options. Participating in a food swap allows you to diversify your pantry with different kinds of homemade or homegrown food. Whether you are a gardener, a passionate baker, a home food preservation expert, or just a DIY enthusiast, you probably end up with a lot of the same kinds of food. Gardeners invariably find themselves, at some point in the summer, drowning in tomatoes or zucchini. Backyard chicken keepers can never eat all the eggs they collect. And how many cookies or cupcakes can your coworkers eat as you perfect that recipe? By joining a food swap, you can trade your excess homemade or homegrown food for items that you would have never made or grown on your own. And that allows you to eat more homemade food, which is a wonderful thing.

In my years of running the Chicago Food Swap, I have found that even outstanding home cooks have their area of expertise and their phobias. For example, I love to can, but I have a black thumb. (No, really: I killed mint.) I also used to be afraid of yeast doughs after some bad experiences with dough not rising. This seems perfectly logical to me, but when I go to the food swap with my homemade jams and pickles, I meet amazing gardeners and gifted bread bakers who tell me how terrified they are of canning! I am working to overcome my fear of yeast, but until that happens, I can go to the food swap and trade my preserved fruits and vegetables for wonderful homegrown produce or artisan breads.

It's a sustainable practice. Trading excess food cuts down on food waste, which is an environmental catastrophe. According to the United Nations Environmental Program, the vast amounts of food that end up in landfills in the developed world are a major contributor to global warming. Food loss and waste also squander the resources — water, fertilizer, fuel — that were used to produce that food. Joining a food swap is a way to eat more seasonally and locally, practices that cut down on the resources that are used to grow food.

And by swapping excess food, be it garden produce, eggs, or prepared foods, you not only receive some value for that food, but you also prevent its waste. Of course, those organizing food swaps should make an effort to ensure that their events are sustainable by encouraging participants to package items in reusable containers, recycling, and cutting down on waste.

It will make you a better cook. If you are like me, you love to cook with unfamiliar ingredients and learn new skills in the kitchen. You take cooking classes; pore over cookbooks and food blogs; maybe even create your own original recipes or write a blog. The knowledge that they will be trading food with other skilled home cooks motivates passionate cooks to up their game. Everyone who comes to a food swap wants to make *the* killer item that people are lining up to trade for.

The more you swap food, the more you push yourself to make something unusual, exotic, and impressive to wow your food swap pals. (However, I do want to emphasize that it is truly not necessary to make something particularly exotic or impressive to participate in a food swap. Delicious cupcakes and granola do very well at every food swap I have ever seen.) After a few years of swapping food, you may find that you have acquired a whole new set of skills in the kitchen.

Not only does participating in a food swap motivate you to expand your cooking repertoire, but seeing the foods the other swappers make will inspire you to try new techniques and experiment with unfamiliar ingredients. I cannot tell you how many times I have heard someone at a food swap say, "I didn't know you could make that at home!" If you have never thought of making your own marshmallows or pasta or root beer, you will after coming to a food swap. Food swaps also expose participants to home cooking from many different cultures. At the Chicago Food Swap, I have tried unfamiliar delicacies from all kinds of different cuisines, including South Asian, Polish, Jamaican, and Filipino. These encounters have inspired me to learn more about these global food traditions and to incorporate some of their ingredients and techniques into my own cooking.

Food swaps create communities. The very best reason to participate in a food swap, other than bringing home delicious food, is that you will meet all kinds of people who share your passion for homemade and homegrown food. Joining a food swap gives home cooks and gardeners a new and appreciative audience for the wonderful food they make and grow. At a food swap, no one questions your sanity for making your own cheese or ketchup or charcuterie. Instead, people line up to trade you for something equally yummy and impressive that they made. Swappers trade recipes and gardening tips, network, and form friendships that go beyond the food swap itself. Because food swaps are in-person events that are typically organized online, they tend to attract a diverse group of participants and bring together people who might not have a chance to meet otherwise. That is part of the magic of food swaps: they cut through the barriers that separate us — things like age, class, race, and geography — and connect people who share a love of food.

What Are the *Cons?*

ARE THERE ANY REASONS *not* to participate in a food swap? Certainly. Trading homemade food requires a certain level of trust in the kindness — and cleanliness — of strangers. While a responsible food swap organizer will ask participants to adhere to the highest standards of hygiene when preparing their food swap items, there are no guarantees that they will comply. Participants are trading food made in home kitchens that aren't inspected by anyone, let alone the local health authorities. I will delve into the legalities of food swapping a little later, but if you are uncomfortable eating food that was prepared out of your sight by a home cook, then food swapping may not be for you. It is, in fact, not for everyone.

If you have a serious food allergy or dietary restriction, food swapping poses certain risks. Food swap organizers should remind participants to label items well, but again, there is no guarantee that everyone will comply. Some participants find reassurance in the fact that they are able to talk to the individuals who prepared the food, and many of the items traded are not especially likely to cause food poisoning or other illnesses because they are non-perishable. But again, if you are squeamish about eating food prepared by strangers who are not professional cooks, then you may not be a good fit for a food swap.

Participating in a food swap also requires some amount of willingness to socialize with strangers. Food swaps, are at their heart, social occasions. People mingle, sample the swap items, and ask questions, sometimes for 30 or 45 minutes, before the swapping begins. If you aren't comfortable talking about what you have brought and asking others about what they have brought, then you might not enjoy a food swap. If walking into a roomful of strangers is difficult for you, but you still love the idea of food swapping, consider coming to a food swap with a friend or partner. Many people attend as a couple or group, which certainly makes things easier both socially and logistically.

What if No One Wants My Food?

YOU DO HAVE TO BE OPEN to the possibility that not everyone will want to trade with you. Participating in a food swap requires a willingness to be vulnerable. Please do not think that you have to be an amazing or professional cook to participate in a food swap. This is the biggest misconception about food swapping that I encounter. If you can make one delicious thing, be it chocolate chip cookies or a killer salsa, take it to a food swap and someone will want to trade with you. That being said, you do have to be willing to risk rejection.

First-time swappers always worry that no one will want to trade with them. In my many years of doing this, I have never seen any swapper be completely left out. It is not uncommon for swappers to end up with some items left over or for people to bring two different items and have one of them be more popular than the other. It is best to learn from these experiences and change what you make for the next event. But you cannot take a refusal to trade personally.

Find **a Food Swap**

TO FIND A FOOD SWAP in your area, your first stop should be the Food Swap Network website, which lists over one hundred food swaps organized geographically. If you live in a large American city, chances are that there is already a food swap nearby. The Food Swap Network relies on organizers to submit their events, however, so if the organizer of a food swap has not asked for it to be listed, you will not find it on the website. In other words, if no swap is listed on the Food Swap Network for your area, don't assume that no swap exists.

Your next step should be a simple Internet search. Start with your city or town name plus "food swap." Some food swaps use a city's nickname, so be sure to include those in your search. (For example, I could have called the Chicago Food Swap the "Windy City Swap.") The search may turn up a website or a Facebook page for your local food swap. It may also turn up a blog post recapping a recent (or not-so-recent) event held by your local food swap and written by one of the participants. This would give you the information you need to track down the swap itself, as well as an idea of how that swap works.

If you do find a website or Facebook page for a food swap in your area, the next step is to ensure that the swap is active and open to the public. When I was looking for a food swap in Chicago back in 2011, I did find some evidence that someone had taken preliminary steps toward starting one, such as creating a Facebook page, although they had not held any events. I also found that local food and sustainability groups had held individual swaps or exchanges, but that these either were not recurring events or were only open to the group's members.

If your city has an active food swap that meets regularly, then it should be relatively easy for you to start swapping. With any luck, the food swap in your area has an upcoming event that you can attend. (For tips what to bring to your first swap, check out chapter 3.) Some swaps are extremely popular and fill up quickly, sometimes within a day or two after registration opens. Other swaps always have room for even last-minute attendees. If you live in an area with a popular swap that always sells out, find out the best way to learn about the swap's events. Does the swap organizer make announcements through Facebook? Does the swap have a regular newsletter that you can sign up for?

If the next swap is already full, check if there is a waiting list, and put your name on it. Email the swap organizer expressing your interest and asking any questions that you may have. Most food swap organizers are passionate about their swaps and love to welcome new swappers and reassure them. I respond personally to every inquiry I receive about the Chicago Food Swap.

What if your search reveals that your town does not have a food swap? Then you may just have to start one yourself.

AUSTIN, TEXAS

AS SOON AS BK FOOD SWAPPERS cofounder Kate Payne left Brooklyn for Austin, Texas, she began planning ATX Swappers. Because she was returning to town after some time away, Kate was looking to connect with others who shared her interest in homemade food. As it turned out, some of the people who came to the first few ATX Swappers events have become Kate's closest friends in Austin.

ATX Swappers meets every three to four months. Kate and her cohost, Megan Myers, like to change the time and locations to attract different constituencies. Some of ATX Swappers' locations include swappers' homes, local farms, a zero-waste grocery store, and an eco-hardware store.

Having started two food swaps and attended others across the country, Kate is better able to compare how swaps operate in different places than almost anyone else. Ultimately, she says, the two swaps are not that different. The items people bring in Brooklyn and Austin tend to reflect trends in food, like the boom in ferments and home brewing. The community feel and passion for homemade food is what unites swaps across the nation and overseas.

The biggest difference Kate sees is packaging: swappers in some cities tend toward more elaborate packaging than others. Of course, depending on where you live, transporting your swap items is an important consideration. In Brooklyn, Kate points out, you have to carry your swap items on the subway. In Texas everyone drives, so they do not worry about how heavy their items are.

One thing Kate noticed about ATX Swappers in the early days was a reluctance on the part of participants to say no. Austin is in the South, and a certain politeness is part of the local culture. Kate and Megan have worked hard to create an environment where it is okay to decline a trade.

ATX Swappers' locations include swappers' homes, local farms, a zero-waste grocery store, and an eco-hardware store.

As for the future of the food swap movement, Kate notes that there was a frenzy of activity, with new swaps popping up all over, at the beginning of the movement. As the newness wore off, some swaps fizzled out. The ones that have continued to grow and thrive are the ones where the organizer loves doing it and has managed to integrate the swap into the local food scene.

VARIATION
Make It a Meal Swap

EVEN PEOPLE WHO LOVE to cook can get weary of making dinner every night and find themselves turning to take-out and prepared meals more often than they would like. Those who live alone find it particularly hard to cook for themselves without either wasting food or growing very tired of leftovers. If you fall into either of these categories, consider hosting a monthly meal swap.

I first learned of the idea of a meal swap from Danielle Welke, founder of the Mid-Mitten Homemade food swap in Lansing, Michigan, who organized a bi-monthly meal swap in her community. At a meal swap, a small group of people meet at someone's home on a weekday evening. The host prepares a meal to feed the assembled crowd. Each attendee brings a dish that can serve the number of people in the group, minus him or herself, divided into individual portions. At the end of the night, everyone has enjoyed a lovely home-cooked meal with friends *and* has an array of different home-made meals to bring home. What a terrific concept!

Meal swaps work best for singles or couples, not large families. To start one, find at least three, and up to seven, friends, neighbors, or co-workers who want to partic-ipate. Because most recipes serve four to eight, it is easiest if your group falls within that size. Begin by meeting once a month or perhaps once every other month. If the meal swap is a success, you can always decide to meet more frequently. Hosting duties should rotate among the group.

Because everyone in a meal swap brings home everyone else's meals, it is important to establish guidelines, such as whether the meals should be vegetarian, ahead of time. Indeed, a meal swap may not be ideal for people with significant dietary restrictions unless everyone else in the group shares those same restrictions. (A gluten-free or vegan meal swap might be a wonderful thing, however.)

Ideas for easy-to-divide, crowd-pleasing dishes that would work well for a meal swap include lasagna and baked pastas, enchiladas and tamales, stews and chili, or casseroles. All meals should be suitable for reheating. For a larger group, think also about bringing dishes that freeze well. If each attendee is bringing home seven meals, he or she may not be able to eat all of them within the week and one of the goals of a meal swap is to cut down on food waste, not create more. Speaking of cutting down on waste, encourage participants in your meal swap to reuse the containers in which the meals are packaged.

An excuse to get together with friends *and* several days' worth of delicious, home-cooked dinners? That is a winning combination.

2

Joining the
FOOD SWAP
MOVEMENT

Are you ready to join the food swap movement? There are two ways to become part of this growing trend. First, you can join an existing food swap. (See Find a Food Swap, page 30). If there isn't one in your area, or it doesn't meet your needs, then you can start your own.

$\mathcal{S}tarting$ **a Food Swap**

IF THERE ISN'T AN ACTIVE FOOD SWAP near you, don't despair: you can start one. No professional cooking or event-planning experience is necessary. Most of the food swaps around the country were started by regular people who were enchanted by the idea of trading homemade and homegrown foods. The truth is, while it does require some time and planning, it is easy and inexpensive to get a food swap off the ground.

The first thing you should consider is finding a partner. Many, though certainly not all, food swaps are organized by two or more people. Because food swaps are volunteer efforts, it can be hard for one person to manage all the details, let alone actually run the event. Having a partner spreads out the work. Additionally, having a partner means you can tap into two networks instead of one when looking for locations and spreading the word about your swap.

In looking for a partner, your first instinct may be to ask a friend or someone else you know well who shares your passion for food. While it may more comfortable at first to work with someone you know and trust, it makes sense to reach out to someone whose talents and abilities complement your own. Food swaps appeal to people in many different demographic groups, and you want to attract as many people as possible. Because a passion for food cuts across all kinds of boundaries, such as age, race, class, and geography, your outreach should include all kinds of people who may not fit into the same demographic as you. A well-chosen partner can help with that effort.

On the other hand, I started the Chicago Food Swap with a friend and neighbor who fit into the exact same demographic as I did, and we were nonetheless very successful at reaching people from all over the Chicago area. How did we do it? Many of those people simply found us through a basic Internet search, having heard about food swapping from another source. Another part of our success had to do with the fact that as bloggers, both Vanessa and I had platforms before we started the Chicago Food Swap. An existing platform and social media savvy are two other factors to consider in looking for a partner.

Many of the largest and most active food swaps were started by food writers and bloggers. If you are not a blogger, don't let that stop you. There are plenty of other ways to publicize a swap, but if you don't have a following on social media, you may want to consider partnering with someone who does have an established platform, such as a food-related business, blog, or strong social media presence, as a way of reaching the greatest number of people in your community.

Whether you are working with a partner or not, what do you need to start a food swap?

Location, **Location, Location**

ONE OF THE biggest challenges for food swap organizers is finding locations to hold events. Some organizers have found permanent or semi-permanent homes for their swaps, which frees them from having to look for new locations. Others have a pool of recurring locations among which they rotate events. Still others, especially those in large urban areas, like to move their swaps around because it allows them to reach and appeal to different constituencies. Unless a permanent location falls into your lap early in your swap's history — and if it does, take it — you will have to spend some time and energy finding locations. Here are some ideas on how to do that.

There are two basic categories of places that can host a food swap. The first is a noncommercial location like a church, library, park, or community center. Depending on where you live, it may be possible for you to reserve a space like this for very little or no money. The other option is a commercial location like a store, coworking space, teaching kitchen, or restaurant. In my experience, savvy owners of these types of locations can see the marketing benefits of hosting a food swap.

So what kind of place is good for holding a food swap? The best space is a large room or adjoining rooms with tables or counters on which swappers can display their items. If the room doesn't come with tables, you can always bring them in, although that is yet another task to manage. I have done swaps in completely empty rooms where the participants had to bring their own tables to display swap items (in a pinch, an ironing board works), but it is easier if there are at least some tables or counters already there. You do *not* need chairs — there is no sitting at a food swap, much to the chagrin of my middle-aged knees.

Although you will likely have a small group for your first swap, try to find a space that could accommodate at least 20 or 25 people with tables in the event that you are very successful at getting the word out.

Noncommercial Spaces

MOST FOOD SWAP ORGANIZERS are looking for free or very inexpensive spaces to hold their events. These kind of spaces tend to fall into two categories: (1) public, community spaces, such as libraries, churches, or community centers; and (2) commercial spaces, such as offices and businesses. You should certainly take the time to investigate public spaces in your area, but be forewarned that many of these spaces are either too small to host a decent-sized swap or have prohibitive restrictions that render them useless.

Be very clear with the responsible person at the location about what is involved in the event. Explain that there will be food and sampling — it's really hard to have a food swap without sampling — and that none of the food will have been prepared in a commercial or licensed kitchen. Ask if the location permits alcohol, making it clear that you won't be selling or serving it, but that it is a possible category of trade goods that will be sampled on the premises. (It's not a deal-breaker if the location bans alcohol, but make sure to communicate that to your swappers.)

If the location requires a small fee, you can always ask your swappers to donate a few dollars to cover it. But think twice about doing this if you are unwilling to cover the fee in the event that only a few people show up. I know of a handful of swaps that meet in a church, library, or community center, often for a nominal fee, and that works well for them. But others have found that these types of locations do not work because of high fees or restrictive rules about open food.

Commercial Spaces

THE MAJORITY OF SWAPS meet in some sort of commercial location. To find one, think of a local business whose mission complements that of a food swap, and approach the owner. Small, local businesses may be easier to approach than chains or large corporations. (Don't rule out large chains, however. The Michigan Avenue Sur La Table has hosted a Chicago Food Swap.) These types of locations should not charge a fee, because they will receive a benefit from the collaboration. But as with community locations, be very clear about what a food swap involves and ask about any possible restrictions, such as permitting swap items that contain alcohol. Look for a day and time when the business is usually closed — if the owner is willing to come in at such a time. I have found that weekend afternoons, especially Sundays, are a good fit.

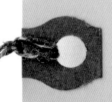

DON'T TRY THIS AT HOME

I believe that you should host your swap at a public place, not a private residence. This opinion is by no means universal among food swap hosts. Some food swaps meet at people's homes and the organizers of those swaps enjoy the intimacy that comes with a private location. I personally feel uncomfortable with swaps meeting in homes unless you plan to invite only people you know. Most food swaps open registration to the general public. As a result, the people in attendance do not necessarily know one another. While food swaps inherently ask us to trust our fellow humans to some extent, which is one of the aspects of food swapping that I love, I believe that hosting the swap in your home is an unnecessary risk. But, ultimately this is a decision that every food swap organizer must make for him- or herself.

When trying to come up with possible locations, think about who might come to your events and what kind of businesses they would be inclined to patronize. Those businesses are the most likely to be open to a pitch about why hosting your swap would be good marketing for them. Take a spice store, for example. If you own a small, independent spice store, wouldn't it be a great marketing opportunity to have 25 or 30 passionate cooks in your store at a time when it is usually closed or business tends to be slow?

Don't underestimate the value of what you have to offer as the organizer of this event. You are hand-delivering a large group of potential customers to their business. These customers are likely not only to spend money at this establishment on the day of the swap and going forward, but they will also provide good word of mouth to their friends and neighbors.

Because food swappers are often tech-savvy, hosting a food swap also generates buzz for local businesses on social media. Every time you post on Facebook or Twitter to promote the event, you necessarily will mention the host as well. And during the swap, you will encourage the swappers to post on Facebook, Twitter, and Instagram, tagging the host all the while. Finally, after the fact, you can expect at least a few recaps of the event on blogs and social media outlets. That's a lot of marketing for the host business with very little cost or effort on their part. With any luck, you'll be able to find businesses in your area that will see these benefits.

Businesses that are related to food and cooking are a natural fit for hosting a food swap so long as your event does not seem like direct competition. Think about cooking schools and specialty food and kitchenware shops. Swappers need to buy their ingredients and cookware from somebody. Food swappers also tend to be interested in gardening and living sustainably — maybe a garden center would be willing to host a

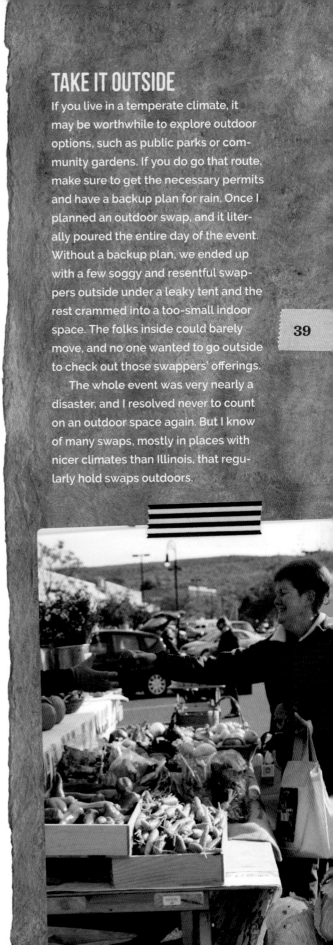

TAKE IT OUTSIDE

If you live in a temperate climate, it may be worthwhile to explore outdoor options, such as public parks or community gardens. If you do go that route, make sure to get the necessary permits and have a backup plan for rain. Once I planned an outdoor swap, and it literally poured the entire day of the event. Without a backup plan, we ended up with a few soggy and resentful swappers outside under a leaky tent and the rest crammed into a too-small indoor space. The folks inside could barely move, and no one wanted to go outside to check out those swappers' offerings.

The whole event was very nearly a disaster, and I resolved never to count on an outdoor space again. But I know of many swaps, mostly in places with nicer climates than Illinois, that regularly hold swaps outdoors.

39

swap? Or think of local businesses with a "green" focus. Swappers need supplies to package their swap items, so maybe they patronize craft stores; there is another potential category of host. I know of some swaps that meet in local breweries, bars, or restaurants as well. Beyond food, think about art galleries, craft boutiques, and other local businesses that share the food swap's focus on handmade and artisanal products.

CHECK OUT COWORKING SPACES

BECAUSE FOOD SWAPPING is part of the new sharing economy, I have found that other participants in this new technology-driven sector are especially open to hosting, specifically coworking spaces. This new type of office, which rents desks and offices on a short-term or open-ended basis to start-ups and freelancers, often has an open, loftlike layout that is ideal for hosting events. I have held food swaps in two different coworking offices in Chicago, and I know of several food swaps in other cities that meet in coworking spaces as well.

These spaces are typically empty on weekends, and the owners often feel that hosting a food swap in their space is both a fun thing to do and good marketing. Given how frequently I have heard of food swaps meeting in coworking spaces, it is worth researching whether there is such a space in your area.

Scouting Locations

WITH LUCK, there may come a time when businesses are contacting you begging to host a food swap at their store or office. Many of the more established swaps have no trouble finding new locations every month or few months, because so many businesses want to host their events. Having potential hosts contact you saves you the trouble of having to find locations, but you will still have to scout that location and meet with the owner or manager.

Finding a willing host is only the first step in the process of choosing a location. The second step is scouting that location. It is imperative that you visit every new possible space prior to committing to holding a swap there. There is no substitute for doing this. You have to assess the size of the space available, how many swappers it can accommodate with tables, and whether you need to bring in any tables or display space.

DON'T GO IT ALONE

By no means should you be expected to find locations to host swaps all by yourself. Recruit your community to help you. Before I found a permanent home for the Chicago Food Swap, I constantly reminded the swappers to think about possible swap locations, and several of our locations came from their suggestions. Call on your personal network as well if you have friends who are business owners. When you are running a food swap, you cannot afford to be shy.

QUESTIONS TO ASK A
Potential Swap Host

How big is the space?

Do you have tables or counters to display swap items?

How many people are you comfortable hosting?

How should we set up the room for the event?

How long before the event begins can I arrive to set up?

Will you be open for business during the swap? If so, is the space where the swap will be private or semiprivate?

Is there parking available nearby? Is the area served by public transportation?

Do you have any restrictions on sampling food? Do you permit alcoholic beverages?

Who from your business will be there during the event?

Would you like to offer a discount to the swappers for purchases made the day of the event? (A 10- to 15-percent discount is typical.)

Would you like an opportunity to speak to the group during the event? How else do you hope to connect with the participants?

Can you share the information about the swap with your mailing list or on social media?

Is there any particular information about your business that you would like me to include when I promote the event?

As the organizer of the food swap, one of your many duties is to ensure that the owner or manager of the host location gets what he or she expected out of hosting the swap. It is to your benefit to leave the host happy so that he or she will invite you back or perhaps recommend you to another business. To that end, be conscientious about mentioning the host as much as possible when promoting the event. Thank the host during the event and give him or her an opportunity to speak to the group. Encourage the swappers to shop there or to sign up for the business's mailing list.

Prior to the day of the swap, be in touch with the owner or manager of the host location to confirm what time you can arrive to set up. Minimize the burden on your host to the extent possible. Be prepared to set everything up and provide all the necessary supplies yourself. Treat the space as if it were your own. Do not plan to leave the location until everything is cleaned up and back to the way it was before your event. Be an appreciative guest, and you may well be asked back.

Establishing a *Permanent* Location

AS I'VE MENTIONED, many food swaps have a permanent or semipermanent home for their events. What should you do if a host offers to let you hold all of your events at its site? While there is an argument for moving a swap around to different locations, especially in large metro areas, if you are lucky enough to find a permanent location, my advice is to take it. If it is a new location for you, I certainly recommend holding at least one event there before committing. But if you know the location and have held a successful swap there in the past, I would accept the offer gratefully.

Imagine how you would set up the room for the swap. Learn where the restrooms are located. How do people get into the space? A ground-floor business with a front door is easy, but what if it is a second-floor office space? Is there a buzzer? Stairs? An elevator? Wheelchair access? If the location is in a large building, is it hard to find? Will you need to post signs or have volunteers directing people where to go? As the organizer, you have to anticipate the experience of your swappers when they arrive at the location carrying their possibly heavy swap items. You need to make sure the space works and determine how to troubleshoot any potential problems before deciding to hold a swap at that location.

Don't neglect to investigate the area around the business. Think about where the swappers will park or whether there is public transportation nearby. Sometimes the neighborhood itself is part of the draw. Is it a hip neighborhood with cool restaurants and boutiques? If so, include that information when you advertise, because it might entice people to come. If the neighborhood is a little sketchy, on the other hand, you may want to have your swap end before dark.

Having a permanent location saves the organizers hours of work. I know some people who would not continue to run their swaps if they had to search for a location each time. Having a familiar location is helpful for the swappers as well. They know how long it takes to get there; they know where to park; they are familiar with the way the room is set up; and so on. Some people naturally feel anxious about traveling to and swapping in a new place, and having a standing location removes that anxiety. If you miss moving the swap around to different parts of your metro area, you can always hold one or two special swaps a year in other locations while keeping the majority at the standing location.

If you are fortunate enough to land a permanent location for your swap, be sure to express your gratitude to the host location, and not just in words. Try to find other ways to support the host as well, especially if it is a business. Encourage your swappers to shop there. Mention the location frequently on social media, and be generous about promoting the location's other events, especially if they are food-related, to your community. If the location is a public space or a nonprofit, try to offer them some financial support. For example, I donate a portion of the proceeds from each swap's ticket sales to the nonprofit that operates the teaching kitchen where the Chicago Food Swap has its permanent home.

Finding and investigating locations is one of a food swap organizer's biggest challenges. But with luck and a little effort, you should be able to find public spaces and businesses in your area that appreciate the mission of a food swap and recognize how hosting such an event would benefit them. Partnering with a great host site can be one of the best parts of organizing a food swap.

What Else Do You Need?

ONCE YOU HAVE FOUND A LOCATION for your first swap and have agreed on a date and time, the most critical thing is to have tables, counters, or other places for swappers to display their items. A 6-foot-long folding table can usually accommodate three to four swappers and an 8-foot one can accommodate four to six, so plan accordingly. If the location lacks tables or does not have enough tables, you can try to borrow some from your friends and neighbors or ask swappers to bring their own. (Not every swapper needs to bring a table, as most tables can accommodate more than one person. And bear in mind that some people may be arriving by public transportation or otherwise cannot bring their own table.) But be forewarned that this creates additional work for you as the organizer.

Food Swap Checklist

A food swap requires little in the way of equipment. Other than tables, you'll need the following supplies:

* Name tags

* Swap cards

* Lots of pens

* Signs directing people where to go (if necessary)

MAKING SWAP CARDS

Swappers fill out a card for each type of item they bring and leave it on the table with their goods. During swap time, interested swappers wander around and make offers, writing on the cards. In this way, the format is similar to a silent auction, but unlike at an auction, the offers on the swap cards are not binding. By suggesting a trade on the swap card, you are not obligated to actually swap with that person if something else catches your eye or you simply cannot connect with the person when the swapping begins.

Here is an example of a sample swap card. Print two to four swap cards on a regular sheet of paper, then cut them out.

Food Swap Card

WHO *(Your Name)*

EMILY PASTER

WHAT *(Your Item)*

SALTED CARAMEL SAUCE

NOTES *(What's in it · How to eat it · What to pair it with · Vegan · Gluten-free · Vegetarian)*

ENJOY on ICE CREAM or POUND CAKE

OFFERS *(Name & Item)*

Erica · Mini Pies
Jean · Kim Chi
Melissa · Lavender Syrup
Michaela · Beet Tahini Dip
Georgia · Peach BBQ Sauce

Beyond tables, you only need a few basic supplies. If you are using folding tables, which might be dirty, or nice tables that need protection, you may want to buy or bring some tablecloths. Plastic disposable ones have the benefit of being inexpensive, but they are an environmental disaster. For a little more money, you can invest in reusable tablecloths. Vinyl ones with flannel backing are inexpensive and easy to wipe clean, or perhaps you or someone in the swap community could hem a few up from a length of sturdy fabric.

Name tags are essential so that swappers can find the people who suggested trades on the swap cards. Although you can ask participants to fill out swap cards in advance, you will certainly need to print and bring extras. Lastly, you will need pens — lots and lots of pens.

As the organizer, it is very possible that you will be out-of-pocket on some of these items. But you should not have to spend more than $20 on all of these supplies combined. If the expense is a concern for you, again, you can ask that swappers donate a few dollars to help defray the costs of running the swap. (See To Fee or Not to Fee, page 64.)

Be sure that you collect email addresses for the attendees. You will need this information to communicate with them before and after the event.

All Publicity *Is Good* Publicity

ONCE YOU HAVE A DATE and a location, your next task is to recruit participants. Begin by creating a registration page. It is imperative that people register for the swap in advance, or planning for the event will be practically impossible. It is also helpful for legal reasons, which I will explain later. Asking people to register in advance is not overly burdensome, because no one walks into a food swap off the street.

There are numerous event-planning websites that are relatively easy to use and typically free for events that don't charge an admission fee. I recommend using a site such as Eventbrite, Brown Paper Tickets, or Ticket Tailor to keep track of the attendees. These sites often have excellent promotional tools as well; some people simply search these sites for interesting events in their area, giving you another way to reach potential swappers. Make sure your event is listed publicly on the site to take advantage of the power of its promotional tools, unless you do not want to be listed publicly for legal reasons.

Another option for registration is to use a Google form on your swap website, but in that case you won't benefit from an event-planning website's reach. Whatever registration tool you use, be sure that you collect email addresses for the attendees. You will need this information to communicate with them before and after the event.

Once you have set up your swap registration, you need to ensure that people hear about your event. To begin, create a Facebook page for your swap and use any other social networking sites that you are comfortable with, such as Twitter. Look for community events calendars, especially ones related to food, and list your swap on as many of those as possible. If you are a blogger, use your blog as a way to reach people. If you do not have your own blog, reach out to food bloggers in your area and ask if they would be willing to promote the food swap to their networks.

Don't be afraid to recruit friends and neighbors. We all have friends who are great cooks, bakers, or gardeners; flatter them by begging them to come to your food swap. The first Chicago Food Swap event was almost exclusively people that Vanessa or I knew personally and had specifically invited — and for our first event, that was just fine.

If there is an existing food swap in a nearby city, ask the organizer if he or she will promote your event to that community. For example, my friend Toni Snearly started a food swap in northwest Indiana after attending a Chicago Food Swap event. She lives two hours away from Chicago, so I certainly understood why she wanted to start a swap closer to home. I was delighted to promote her events to the Chicago Food Swap community for the benefit of those people who live closer to northwest Indiana than to downtown Chicago. Don't hesitate to reach out to other food swap organizers for help — there is no sense in reinventing the wheel.

First Day

WHAT SHOULD YOU expect on the day of your first swap? Nerves, to be sure. And excitement. Think of yourself as the host of the event, and be prepared to be welcoming, gracious, and accommodating, just as you would if you were hosting an event in your home. Try to set up for the swap at least an hour beforehand. In my experience, some swappers will arrive early, especially if they are coming from far away, and you do not want to be caught off-guard. (Although if people do arrive early, do not hesitate to put them to work.)

Set up the tables with plenty of room to circulate around them. Cover them with tablecloths where necessary, and leave plenty of pens on all the surfaces. Set up a small area for check-in with a list of attendees, name tags, and blank swap cards. (You can print a list of attendees, or download an app, available on some event-planning sites, that allows you to check people in on your smartphone. Don't expect that swappers will bring their tickets with them; be prepared to check people off a list.) If you are swapping — and you should be — set up your items with their swap cards well in advance, because you may get caught up checking people in and answering questions and not have another chance to do it.

Once swappers start arriving, you or your cohost should check everyone in, hand out name tags and swap cards, and encourage people to find a spot to set up their items. It is helpful if one of you stays at the front for check-in and the other floats around the room answering questions and troubleshooting. If you want, you can pass out fliers explaining how a food swap works, but this is by no means necessary, and printing fliers is an added expense.

At 15 or 20 minutes past the hour when your swap was supposed to start — once most people have arrived — ask for everyone's attention. Feel free to prepare some bullet points in advance for your opening remarks. You want to (1) welcome everyone; (2) thank your host; (3) remind everyone to get name tags and swap cards; and (4) go over the time line for the event and the rules for swapping. Make clear that people are to mingle and make offers but not to actually begin swapping until you announce that it is time to do so. Make any other announcements, such as a discount offered by the host location, at this time as well.

If you like, encourage people to discuss the event on Twitter and Facebook or share photos on Instagram and tag your swap and the host location where applicable. (For more tips on using social media to promote your food swap, see page 53.)

After your opening announcement, you can then join in with mingling and checking out the items that people have brought. Talk to the swappers, and ask them how they found out about your event — this is great information for future planning. You may have to field questions from anxious swappers and deal with latecomers arriving and needing to be told what to do. Be sure to take plenty of photographs as well.

The amount of time needed for browsing depends on the size of the swap; the more participants you have, the more time people need to see and taste everything. But factor in anywhere from 20 to 40 minutes for browsing and mingling. When you determine that the participants have had enough time to see all the available items, announce that it is time to swap. The actual swapping can be somewhat chaotic and is usually over in 10 to 15 minutes. The event tends to wrap up quickly after the swapping, so be prepared to thank people for coming and ask for feedback when you see people beginning to leave. Once the participants have all left, be sure to stay and clean up until your host is completely satisfied. Remember to thank the host again, and ask for his or her feedback as well.

Following Up

IN THE DAYS following your first swap, it is important to capitalize on the momentum you have generated. Word of mouth is crucial to growing a swap, and the buzz will be at its peak right after a successful event. Encourage attendees to post and comment on your swap's Facebook page. I always ask people to post photographs of their swap hauls, then share those photos with the group. If you have a blog or website, post a recap of the swap as soon as possible with lots of tantalizing pictures. Encourage any attendees who have blogs to do so as well, then share the links to those posts on social media channels.

Be sure to mention and link to your host site as much as possible as a way of acknowledging its hospitality. The host may share a recap and photos on its website or Facebook page as well, and depending on the size of its following, that could be a great way to reach potential swappers.

Now that you have hosted your first swap, what should you do to make your swap bigger and more successful? Perhaps you have been hosting food swaps for several months, or even years, and you are still struggling to find locations and attract participants. What's the key to growing a food swap and turning it into a must-attend event?

VARIATION

Set Up a Soup Swap

Many people who have never heard of the food swap movement have participated in a soup swap. Smaller than a typical food swap, soup swaps are usually limited to friends or neighbors, meaning you can comfortably host one at your home. Soup is a terrific item to exchange because it's easy to make in large quantities and often freezes well. By participating in a soup swap, you can stock your refrigerator and freezer with a delightful variety of easy weeknight meals, making it perfect for busy professionals or young parents.

Invite your guests several weeks in advance so that they have time to prepare. Because of the large quantities involved, people may have to make two batches. Invite at least six guests, but if you can fit more in your house, do so. Twelve or fifteen guests is probably the largest group that you want to manage. Ask people to bring a set number of quarts of soup, at least six, packed for travel. Plastic containers or glass jars are preferable to plastic freezer bags. Guests should label their soups to indicate whether the soup is vegetarian — chicken broth makes a soup *not* vegetarian! — dairy-free, gluten-free, or if it contains common allergens like nuts. If a soup is not suitable for freezing — because it contains pasta, for example — ask the swapper to make a note of that as well so people know to consume it in the coming week.

A weekend afternoon is a nice time to host a soup swap. As the host, you may want to provide some snacks or ask that everyone bring an appetizer or dessert to munch on during the swap. Provide a long table or countertop to display the soups. Once everyone has arrived, draw numbers from a hat to determine the order in which you select soups. Before the selection, ask each guest to stand up and describe his or her soup. Is it spicy? A treasured family recipe? Will it cure the common cold? This part can be great fun if everyone gets into the right spirit; as the host, you may have to go first to set the tone. Then guests select quarts of soup in the order indicated by the numbers they drew. Continue until all the soup is gone. What if a vegetarian ends up stuck with a soup containing meat? Allow guests to trade individual quarts with one another at the end.

Not only is a soup swap a great way to stock your freezer, it is also a fun, easy-to-host gathering for your friends and neighbors, especially during the long winter months.

Making Your
Swap Successful

AS THE ORGANIZER of a food swap, you naturally want your swap to be successful. You want your events to be well attended, with a mix of returning regulars and newcomers. You want all the participants to have fun, to feel that their swap items were desirable, and to be excited about the items they are bringing home. A successful swap is one where everyone feels like they are coming home with more than they brought. It is mathematically impossible but still somehow achievable.

Most importantly, you want your swappers to feel that they are part of a community. My heart swells with pride when I overhear swappers exchanging recipes or cooking tips, or learn that swappers have formed friendships and networked with one another outside of the swap. One of the best things a food swap can do, in my opinion, is bring together like-minded people who might not have met otherwise.

Beyond the swappers' joy and satisfaction, there are other ways to judge the success of your food swap. You want the host locations of your events to feel that hosting the swap was worthwhile, whether they judge that by sales on the day of the swap or favorable publicity. You want word to spread about your swap through blog posts, social media buzz, or stories in the media. In this section, I will talk about how to turn your swap into this kind of active, dynamic organization and your food swaps into must-attend events for food lovers in your community.

Timing

ONCE YOU HAVE DECIDED to make your food swap a recurring event, you will have to decide how often to hold swaps. Some swaps meet monthly, others every other month, and still others meet quarterly. When determining how often your food swap should meet, consider your own availability as the organizer. More events mean more work, particularly if your food swap does not have a permanent home. Especially in the early months of your swap, do not commit to more events than you can comfortably organize. I recommend meeting no more frequently than bimonthly in the beginning.

The second consideration is the level of interest in your community. If you are having trouble attracting swappers, swap less frequently. For swaps with low turnout, consider a quarterly or seasonal swap. I have heard from organizers of quarterly swaps that the participants consider each swap to be somewhat of an event and make an effort to attend. If your swap is growing rapidly and each event fills up, by all means, swap more often, assuming that you have the bandwidth to plan that many events. Even swaps that meet monthly should take a month off now and again to give everyone a break. I found that swaps during the summer and the holiday season are less well attended, so now I usually take off August and December.

You will also have to decide the date and time for ongoing swaps. Most swaps meet on the weekends, but I know of some, mostly urban swaps, that meet on weeknights and are very well attended. The day of the week and the time you choose may also depend on your host. You may need to work around the location's requirements, and if you are using the space for free, that is to be expected. In part because I am a parent, I have always held swaps on weekend afternoons — weeknights are just too busy — and have found that time to be convenient for many of my host locations as well. When your swap is young, feel free to experiment with different days and times to see which attract more participants.

Building *Community*

INEVITABLY, WHEN YOU ASK food swap organizers and attendees what they enjoy most about their swap, the answer is not the food, but rather the people. Food swaps quickly become communities: diverse groups of people brought together by a shared love of growing and cooking their own food. Regular food swap participants look forward to seeing one another at the recurring events and even form relationships outside of the swap. Newcomers are warmly welcomed into the fold. As I have said before, food swaps break down some of the barriers that separate us, such as age, geography, and dietary restrictions, and unite people around a shared passion for good food.

WHAT ABOUT THEMES?

One question that I hear frequently is: do your swaps have a theme? Some swap groups choose a theme for each event; others choose a theme for selected events. I have resisted themes because one of my favorite things about the Chicago Food Swap is the wide variety of items on offer each time. I have hesitated therefore to select a theme that would result in everyone bringing all the same kind of food, like baked goods or soups. However, themed swaps, when used judiciously, can be an effective way to promote community. A family recipe theme, for example, would encourage the swappers to share more information about their own backgrounds while still ensuring a wide variety of items.

Themed swaps can also constitute a nice gesture to some of the different segments of a swap community. People with dietary restrictions, for example, understand at the outset that their options at a given swap may be limited, but it can still be frustrating. At the Chicago Food Swap, we have a regular group of vegan swappers, and they are mostly able to find vegan items to swap for. But one time, as a courtesy to this segment of our community, I held a vegan-themed swap and encouraged — not required — all of the attendees to bring vegan items.

Many non-vegan swappers participated, considering the theme to present a fun cooking challenge, and the vegan swappers were really touched. (As it turned out, the vegan-themed swap garnered some attention nationally, and *Vegetarian Times* magazine featured the Chicago Food Swap in a March 2015 article about vegetarian swaps.) So consider holding a vegetarian, vegan, or gluten-free swap on occasion if you have participants with those dietary restrictions in your community.

For other variations, see Host a Harvest Swap (page 58), Set Up a Soup Swap (page 48), and Have a Holiday Swap (page 84).

The community aspect of the food swap is particularly important because cooking can be a solitary, even lonely, pursuit. Coming to a food swap allows a dedicated home cook to leave the kitchen for the afternoon and receive recognition for his or her hard work and expertise from an appreciative group. In my daily life, my friends and family find my passion for homemade food to be somewhat baffling. I can always find people who share my interest in DIY kitchen projects and home food preservation on the Internet. But it is even more comforting to meet such people in person and know they are present in my community.

The organizer of a food swap bears the responsibility for building this sense of community among the participants. That may sound daunting, but it's really not that difficult. At the events themselves, you can set the right tone by welcoming everyone and connecting swappers with one another. If you happen to know that two or more swappers live in the same area, have kids the same age, or share a particular interest, be sure to let them know. If you were hosting a party at your house, you would seek to introduce different guests who shared something in common. It is no different here. Of course, you don't have to do all the work by yourself: enlist some veteran swappers to seek out newcomers and make them feel welcome.

The more difficult task is taking that sense of community that forms during the events and building on it between swaps. However, fostering a sense of community outside the actual events is critical to forming a dynamic and committed group. Luckily, in the age of social media, it is relatively easy and painless to interact with the members of your food swap community and for them to interact with one another. You can also foster a sense of community by expanding your offerings beyond swaps into other food-related events.

USE SOCIAL MEDIA

SOCIAL MEDIA IS a very effective way to reach new swappers and to stay connected with existing swappers. Every swap should have its own Facebook page. People of all ages and demographics use Facebook, and the pages are easy and free to set up. A Twitter account is also helpful, but Twitter is used less widely than Facebook. An Instagram account is also fun for sharing photos during events. You may even want to have a specific hashtag for your swap.

Encourage participants to become fans of the swap Facebook page. Be sure to mention the Facebook page during your opening remarks at swaps, and you can even post signs at your food swap events with the address of the Facebook page and the event hashtag. If your swap has a dedicated website, include a prominent link to the Facebook page. You should certainly use your swap's Facebook page to announce future events and post recaps of past events, but also think of it as a place to provide interesting and engaging food-related content for your community.

Share articles and blog posts that you believe would be of interest, such as those on gardening, preserving, cooking, and nutrition. Share information about food-related events in your area, whether they be festivals, special restaurant promotions, or lectures. Share swappers' articles, blog posts, or events. I share articles that I come across about the broader food swap movement. But do not limit yourself to posting links. Ask questions. Seek advice. The goal of the page is to encourage conversation and interaction between you and the swappers, and among the swappers themselves.

If social media is not your thing, that's fine, but know that you are missing out on powerful tools to promote your event and to show appreciation to your host location. Consider recruiting someone who is more comfortable with using these social media tools to help you.

SEND A NEWSLETTER

AN EMAIL NEWSLETTER is, hands down, the best way to stay in touch with your community. Not everyone will see your social media posts no matter how active your Facebook page or Twitter feed is. Though intimidated at first, I was pleasantly surprised by how easy it was to create a newsletter. There are many websites, such as MailChimp and Mad Mimi, that allow you to create an email newsletter for free as long as you stay below a certain number of subscribers. If you use an online ticketing service such as Eventbrite for your swaps, you can even export a contact list created from past events directly to the email service. Include a place on your website or Facebook page where interested parties can sign up for your newsletter.

I use the Chicago Food Swap newsletter to announce upcoming events, both swaps and community events, to share recaps of past events — my own and those written by other swappers — and to communicate important information about how the food swap operates. When we acquired our permanent home and I began charging a small registration fee, I used the newsletter to explain the reasoning behind the changes. I make sure to limit the frequency to once or twice a month so that my subscribers do not feel spammed. Lastly, the number of email subscribers that you have can be an important way to track the growth and engagement of your community.

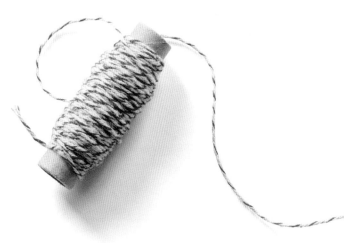

SOCIALIZING

ANOTHER WAY TO BUILD COMMUNITY is to expand your swaps to include some time for socializing. Many swap groups include time to mingle or eat as part of every swap or at least as part of a few swaps a year. Obviously such opportunities allow swappers to get better acquainted and deepen connections. On the other hand, it is difficult enough to get people to commit a few hours of their precious time to come swap; some people might be reluctant to attend a longer event or one that required them to bring a food item to share beyond their swap offerings.

You need to feel out your community's willingness to commit to a more involved event. One idea would be to hold a social gathering in lieu of a swap one month, perhaps around the holidays or during the summer, to allow swappers to get to know one another better.

If you sense that your community might not be willing to linger at the swaps themselves, you can always experiment with holding different kinds of events beyond just swaps, such as potlucks, classes, or culinary tours. Because food swap participants are likely to share common interests, it is not hard to find events that would appeal to a large swath of the community. You do not necessarily have to host all of these events yourself but rather can arrange for a group of swappers to attend an existing event. You may even find that you can access a group discount for certain events.

Opportunities to get swappers together outside the swap can be very informal. As an example, during Chicago's Restaurant Week, when many of the city's finest restaurants have

BUILDING A MEDIA KIT

Be prepared for press inquiries before they happen by creating a media kit or having background information about your swap available on your website. You can make an attractive media kit using basic word-processing software without great expense. If this seems outside of your wheelhouse, ask your swappers if any of them have experience in communications or graphic design and would be willing to help make a media kit.

Creating a media kit will save you from having to answer the same inquiries over and over, so it's well worth a few hours' investment. You will need to update it regularly, but that will only take a few minutes each time.

A media kit for your swap should include an "About" page with background information on the group, such as how the swap works, when it began, how many people attend each event, where the swappers come from, and some of the past host locations. You could also include some helpful numbers that indicate the size and strength of your community, such as how many times the swap has met, how many Facebook fans or Twitter followers the swap has, and the number of people on your mailing list. A short section about you, the founder, may also be helpful, particularly to explain why you started the swap or if your professional life relates in some way to the swap.

Including some attractive pictures from an event will make the media kit look more professional, but it is not necessary. If your swap has received press coverage in the past, be sure to include that information and links to the stories if possible. Lastly, include your contact information on each page in a heading or footer.

discounted, prix-fixe menus, I made several lunch and dinner reservations at participating restaurants and invited swappers to join me for a meal. Everyone paid their own way and the whole thing required very little effort on my part, but it was a great opportunity for swappers to deepen their relationships outside the swap. Some of the Chicago Food Swap regulars, particularly those that live near one another, have organized events themselves without any help from me.

Reaching Out
to the Press

MANY OF THE LARGER and more active food swaps in the United States, Canada, and Great Britain have, at one time, been the subject of a story in a local newspaper or digital media outlet, or on a radio or television program. The *New York Times* story about BK Swappers early in its history was crucial to kicking off the national food swap movement. Press stories are an excellent way to attract new swappers and even possible new hosts, as well as raising the profile of food swapping in general. Unless you have reason to believe that a press story might attract the unwanted attention of local officials, or you wish to keep your swap private, you should welcome press stories and even take a proactive approach in reaching out to the press.

In some cases, reporters may hear about your event and contact you for an interview or to inquire about attending a swap. Be as welcoming and helpful as you can. Offer to provide them with background information, allow them to interview you in person or over the phone, and connect them with other swappers and swap hosts who would be willing to be interviewed as well. If reporters do attend one of your events, show them around and make sure they understand how the swap works.

Think about possible story angles that might interest them: explain how swappers come from all over the metropolitan area, or point out how many different demographic groups are represented. Are there families with kids? Introduce them. Point out some of the more unusual items that people have brought. If someone at the swap wants to start a food business and is using the swap as a testing ground, be sure to bring that to the reporter's attention. Share the spotlight with the swap host as well.

You may well have to seek out reporters and bloggers and pitch your swap to them as a potential story. If you are not a public relations professional, this might seem like a daunting task. As a food blogger, I know a number of people in public relations. When I wanted to reach out to the media about the Chicago Food Swap, I asked my contacts for advice and their help in reaching the local food press. If you know someone who does public relations in your area, ask if he or she would be willing to provide some assistance in pitching your swap. It will be particularly helpful to speak to someone who understands your city or town and has local contacts.

Find *Your Focus*

WHEN CRAFTING A PRESS strategy, the first question to ask yourself is: who are the people that you want to reach with this story? Keep in mind that food swaps appeal to many different demographic groups, including foodies, gardeners, those concerned about sustainability, and modern homesteaders. What are the media outlets that reach these different groups? Plainly the basic media outlets will include the local newspapers and radio and television stations. But do not overlook digital publications, particularly those that cover local events and news. These may be the most willing takers for your story, especially in the beginning.

As you identify contacts at each media outlet, remember also that a food swap touches on many different issues, from food to gardening to environmental sustainability, and even to economic issues, particularly if you hold your swaps at local businesses. Review your local paper to find the names of the reporters who cover such stories, and email them directly. Does your public radio station have a morning or afternoon show? Identify the specific reporters who cover the relevant issues. For television coverage, which is obviously very desirable, find out who the segment producers are for local news programs. This research may take some time, but it will produce the best results. Targeted, personalized outreach is by far the most effective way to interest a reporter.

RECRUITING REPORTERS

ONCE YOU HAVE IDENTIFIED the right people, the next step is to get them the right information. Reporters these days are operating with fewer and fewer resources. You want to make it as easy as possible for them to write the piece. You cannot simply email a reporter to say that you run the local food swap and you thought it might make a good story. You have to explain what the story is. In other words, why should the reporter care?

To pique a reporter's interest, come up with possible story angles tailored to that reporter's beat. At the same time, seek to tie the food swap into larger societal trends, such as the rise of the sharing economy. For the gardening columnist, explain how food swaps offer local gardeners a new way to address the age-old problem of what to do with excess zucchini or tomatoes. Tell the business reporter how entrepreneurs are using the food swap as a testing ground for launching their food businesses, or how local stores are reaching new customers by hosting your food swap. Pinpoint swappers and hosts who would be willing to speak to the reporter, and include their contact information and all other relevant details in your pitch.

My friend Sara Fisher, cofounder of the Chicago public relations firm 2 Moms Media, offered me some good advice when I was pitching reporters about the Chicago Food Swap:

Local news outlets like to cover local stories, so emphasize how your swap is working within your community. Explain how you are partnering with local businesses or nonprofits. On that note, be sure to ask your host locations about their press contacts and whether their PR or marketing person would be willing to reach out to the press to pitch a story idea. And remember, you are not pitching yourself; you are pitching the food swap. Make the appeal of your pitch as wide as possible.

Be a food swap evangelist.

Timing your pitch is critical. Before you contact a reporter to write about your swap, finalize the next few event dates and locations so that if the reporter is interested in attending a swap, you can say when the next swaps will be. Make your pitch seasonal. During the summer, focus your pitch on how people are bringing homegrown produce to the swap. Before the holiday season, talk about how people can find unique edible gifts at the food swap. Again, make your pitch as targeted and specific as possible.

I have also learned to not let any opportunity to escape. Be a food swap evangelist. I once encountered the food reporter from the Chicago public radio station in a hotel lobby and buttonholed her to talk about the Chicago Food Swap. (Starting with a little flattery about how much you like the reporter's work never hurts.) It took several months worth of emails and follow-up, but eventually she came to a swap and did a terrific story about it that ran on the local morning news program and generated a lot of attention.

On that note, if you do end up emailing or talking with a reporter and nothing comes of it right away, don't conclude that it was a waste of time. Think of building relationships with reporters. Once they know that you are the founder of the local food swap, they may come to you when they need information about food trends or the local food scene. Be willing to be a source for articles on other subjects. Over time, the relationship could lead to a lot of helpful exposure for your swap.

Troubleshooting
Common Problems

IF YOU RUN A FOOD SWAP for any length of time, you will eventually encounter some problems. From my experience and from what other food swap organizers have told me, the most common problems seem to be (1) low attendance and (2) no-shows; that is, people who register for the swap but fail to attend. Other kinds of issues can arise, such as items going missing during a swap or people having problems with the items they brought home. Lastly, food swap organizers themselves can become burnt out from the work and stress of organizing the swap. Here are some ways to address some of these issues so that your swap can continue to grow and thrive.

VARIATION

Host a Harvest Swap

It never fails to astonish me how by the end of the summer gardeners are desperate to offload excess squash, tomatoes, or herbs from their backyards or community garden plots. In places like California, homeowners with fruit trees in their yards may feel overwhelmed with avocados or lemons and let the fruit fall to the ground. There is even a National Sneak a Zucchini onto Your Neighbor's Porch Day! (It's August 8, by the way.) An alternative to wasted harvests and rogue zucchini drops is to organize a harvest-themed swap for hardworking gardeners. Indeed, some ongoing food swaps focus entirely on excess produce.

For a robust harvest-themed swap, recruit as many gardeners as possible. Don't limit yourself to those in your immediate circle. If you are a backyard gardener, reach out to people with community garden plots. There may be a community gardening nonprofit organization in your community, such as the Peterson Garden Project in Chicago, or a local park district that you can partner with. Gardening centers and plant nurseries may be willing to host a swap and spread the word to their customers.

Well in advance of the event, contact the person who writes the gardening column in your local newspaper, as well as food and gardening bloggers in your

area, and ask them to promote it. Consider whether you want to include non-produce items such as flowers, honey from area beekeepers, eggs from backyard chickens, or foraged items in addition to more typical backyard produce.

A harvest swap unfolds much like a typical food swap. You will need name tags, swap cards, and tables or counters for participants to display their items. Swap cards may be less important with fresh produce than with prepared foods where allergies and dietary restrictions are a concern. Nevertheless, not everyone may recognize each item so swappers should complete a card for each different fruit, vegetable, or herb they bring that identifies the item and includes space for others to make trade offers. Swappers may also have questions about how the food on offer was grown, and participants should be ready to answer those questions. After an initial period of browsing, the organizer should announce when it is time to swap. As with all food swaps, trades are negotiated by the individuals themselves and they should decide the value in trade of each item.

You can organize a harvest swap once a year or several times throughout the growing season, depending on your energy and the enthusiasm of the gardeners in your area.

PDX FOOD SWAP!
Portland, Oregon

IT SEEMS FITTING THAT A CITY known for its outsized food culture was the third city in America to have its own food swap.

Bethany Rydmark, a landscape architect and eighth-generation Oregonian, had a small group of friends that met regularly to discuss books, share resources, and learn techniques for more sustainable living, including home food preservation. After Bethany spotted a few pictures on Facebook from BK Swappers in 2010, she reached out to Kate Payne to ask whether her group could model its own swap on hers. Kate readily agreed, and Bethany and a friend founded the PDX Food Swap in December 2010. As one of the pioneers of the food swap movement, Bethany has helped foster its growth, including working with Kate Payne and Emily Han to found the Food Swap Network.

After Bethany's original cofounder left Portland, Lindsay Strannigan, a Portland food writer and event planner, stepped in as a co-organizer. When Bethany spent 2012 backpacking around the world, Lindsay kept the swap going, and since Bethany's return, the two have continued to facilitate the PDX Food Swap, which has found a home in the Art Institute of Portland's culinary school kitchen.

These days, PDX Food Swap meets once a quarter. Bethany and Lindsay cap the events at 35 swappers to provide enough room for people to connect with one another and make trades. Portland's swap community includes twenty-somethings, retirees, working professionals, artists, parents (and sometimes children), professional chefs, and home cooks.

Portland's diverse DIY community means great things for the PDX Food Swap. Bethany and Lindsay frequently see innovative, experimental foods along with classic staples. Popular swap items include traditional canned goods, breads and baked goods, condiments of all sorts, plants, fresh-cut herbs, and fresh harvested produce. Beverages such as drinking vinegars, liqueurs, beers, and specialty cocktail ingredients are especially sought after.

Beverages such as drinking vinegars, liqueurs, beers, and specialty cocktail ingredients are especially sought after.

Bethany believes the future of the food swap movement lies in the motivations of swap organizers. If they can continue to build and foster a community based on sharing and celebration and resist the cultural norm of turning grass-roots ideas into money-making ventures, the Food Swap movement stands a chance to create and elevate sharing communities around the world.

Low Attendance

LOW ATTENDANCE IS a problem that plagues many food swaps, particularly those in smaller metropolitan areas. What is low attendance for a food swap? Remember that new food swaps often have very small numbers of attendees, so if you are only attracting 12 or 15 people at the beginning, don't despair. Allow time for word of mouth to spread and for your swap to grow. Also, you do not need huge numbers to have a successful swap. A group of 20 makes for a fun and engaging event.

But if your swap has been around for several months or years and you regularly have fewer than 20 people attending, it may be time to take a hard look at your operation.

Reconsider how often you hold swaps. If you are holding monthly or bimonthly swaps with low attendance, perhaps quarterly swaps would be a better fit for your community. Holding swaps less frequently makes each one more of an event, and people are more motivated to attend when they know there won't be another one for several months.

Also consider experimenting with different times and days of the week. Conduct a short, informal survey of your attendees to identify some possible times that might work better. Reconsider also your location. Is it hard to get to or far away for most of your attendees? A convenient location in an appealing neighborhood will be more attractive to potential swappers.

Examine your outreach efforts. Are you getting the word out about your swap to different constituencies? Simply using one or two methods of outreach may not be enough. If you are relying solely on Facebook or other social media channels, try an email newsletter (see page 53). Ask your host locations or other organizations that you have relationships with if they would be interested in exchanging email lists with you. Then send out a special newsletter to the new email addresses introducing

them to your swap and asking them to like your Facebook page or sign up for your newsletter.

Reach out to the local press in your area using the strategies laid out above. Contact local food or event bloggers and invite them to attend a swap in the hopes that they will write about it on their sites. (If you charge a fee, offer to waive it for these special guests.) List your swaps on as many local event calendars as you can. If you are not using a popular ticketing website such as Eventbrite for registration, try doing so. Recruit your swappers to help you. Charge each one of your regulars with bringing a friend to the next event.

Think about your events. Do they run smoothly? Is everyone having fun? Are the attendees interacting with one another and starting to form relationships? Is a sense of community developing? Are newcomers welcomed warmly? Does everyone go home feeling like they just won the foodie lottery?

The more enjoyable your events are, the more likely that the participants will rave about them to their friends. Positive word of mouth from swap participants is the single best way to attract new swappers. Consider asking some of your more frequent participants how they feel about the swaps themselves to see if there are ways in which you could improve the swapper experience.

Finally, if you are throwing terrific events and you have tried every possible form of outreach but are still unhappy with the attendance, you have two choices. One is to stop worrying. If your swappers are having fun and returning regularly, then you should consider your swap a success, even if it is small. You are enriching the lives of those people who do come, and that is a tremendous accomplishment. And perhaps, with time, the swap will grow.

The second choice is to decide that your community is not able to support a recurring food swap at this time. As I have said, food swapping is not for everyone nor is it for every community. Perhaps for your community, a food swap is an idea that is ahead of its time. You can certainly rethink the concept of the food swap to find a form that would be a better fit for your community. For some ideas, see Make It a Meal Swap (page 32), What about Themes? (page 51), Host a Harvest Swap (page 58), Set Up a Soup Swap (page 48), and Have a Holiday Swap (page 84).

Cancellations *and No-Shows*

THE OTHER MAJOR PROBLEM that seems to plague food swap organizers are last-minute cancellations and no-shows. It can be extremely frustrating to plan an event for 25 or 30 people only to have five people cancel the day before and another five people simply fail to show without any notice whatsoever. To welcome 15 people when you were expecting 25 is demoralizing. Last-minute cancellations and no-shows are even more aggravating if you had to turn away potential attendees. It used to upset me greatly to have to turn away willing participants, then have room for them at the swap after all. While emergencies do arise and sometimes people are truly not able to come, in most cases, the issue is that not everyone views their swap registration as a genuine commitment.

The truth is, there is not much you can do about people who do not take their swap registration seriously. Last-minute cancellations and no-shows will always happen. Professional event planners know this and plan accordingly. You should do the same. Thus, if you are holding a swap at a location that can accommodate 30 swappers, open registration for at least 35 spots. That may make you nervous — what if all 35 show up? — but rest assured that some folks will inevitably drop out at the last minute.

Next, be sure to communicate to your community how disruptive and rude last-minute cancellations and no-shows are — again with the exception of those due to genuine emergencies. This has worked in the past for some swap groups. Also, on your registration page, limit the number of tickets that people can register for to two. That way, people cannot reserve a large group of tickets for their friends, some of whom may well not show up.

Be sure to communicate with registered attendees in the week leading up to the swap. You do not want to inundate your community with spam, but send at least one reminder email the week before the swap. One swap organizer I know sends a personalized email to each first-time attendee who has registered to welcome them and ask if they have any questions. First-time swappers are the most likely not to show up, so this kind of personalized outreach, while time consuming, can be very effective at encouraging new participants to follow through on their registration.

You can also advertise a penalty for people who fail to cancel with a certain amount of notice. At one point, the Chicago Food Swap had a policy that if you canceled your registration with less than a week's notice, you would not be allowed to register for the next swap. I never actually enforced this policy, however, because of the administrative hassle. The threat alone may have been sufficient.

Fees and Costs

IN MY EXPERIENCE, the only truly effective method for encouraging people to treat their food swap registration as a serious commitment is to charge a registration fee.

I finally decided to institute a permanent registration fee for the Chicago Food Swap after one event where I had a very high number of no-shows. The host had gone to considerable trouble to rent extra tables because nearly 70 people had registered. So many of them failed to come, however, that the tables weren't even needed. Since that incident, I have charged $5 for every event.

Chicago Food Swap events no longer fill up as quickly as they did before I began charging a fee. But that change is more than outweighed by the reduction in the number of late cancellations and no-shows. In short, if your swap is well attended but you have a persistent problem with last-minute cancellations and no-shows, consider charging a small registration fee and see if that solves the problem. If you do decide to

charge a fee, keep the following considerations in mind.

Determine your fee policy. The registration page for Chicago Food Swap events states that the registration fee will be refunded so long as the attendee cancels with one week's notice. In truth, I often refund the fee with less notice than that. Good will is more important to me than a few dollars. On that note, it is also good practice to waive the fee when circumstances warrant. I have been known to waive the fee for a new swapper who is apprehensive about coming, for a veteran swapper who has a limited budget, and for volunteers who help me run the event. Lastly, be upfront with your host site that you are charging a fee for your event. Some offer their space for free because they believe that the food swap is a free event.

Decide what to do with the proceeds. The people in your community may wonder where their money goes. I recommend being very upfront about how the proceeds from the registration fees are used to prevent any bad feeling. Running a swap does have costs, such as printing signs and swap cards and purchasing tablecloths, pens, and other supplies. It is perfectly reasonable to use the registration fees to cover these costs. A food swap organizer should not be out of pocket for the costs of running the swap.

To Fee or Not to Fee?

Whether to charge a fee is a somewhat controversial subject among food swap organizers. Some feel that charging a fee goes against the noncommercial, grass-roots nature of food swapping and therefore find it distasteful. Others feel that charging a fee can create legal problems for the swap because it takes the event out of the private sphere and into a commercial sphere, thereby triggering the laws that regulate commercial food sales. Still others believe that charging a fee lowers attendance.

On the other hand, several food swaps, including the Chicago Food Swap, regularly charge a registration fee and still are very well attended. The argument for charging a fee is, first and foremost, that it discourages cancellations and no-shows. In my experience, having organized many swaps over the years, free swaps fill up more quickly but have a higher number of last-minute cancellations and no-shows. Fee-based swaps tend to fill up more slowly because people do not want to commit unless they know that they will be able to attend, but the people that do register treat it as a serious commitment.

COLLECTING FEES

How does one charge a registration fee? There are several ways to go about it. One is to simply collect cash at the door. This may be the easiest way, and it has the advantage of allowing the food swap organizer to keep 100 percent of the proceeds. On the other hand, collecting fees at the door does not really accomplish the primary goal of charging a fee for your food swap, which is to encourage attendees to commit to showing up.

For that, you need a system that requires participants to pay the fee when they register. A paid ticketing system, such as the one offered by Eventbrite and other popular ticketing websites, is probably the most convenient and secure. The downside is that these sites charge fees, including service fees and a payment-processing fee. These fees can add up: for every $5 registration fee that the Chicago Food Swap collects, we keep around $3.75. In my view, however, the reliability and security of the services justifies the high fees. And the truth is, most food swap organizers, myself included, do not charge fees to make money. We do it primarily as a way to prevent no-shows.

You may also need or want to use the proceeds from any registration fee to compensate your host. As an example, although Peterson Garden Project lets the Chicago Food Swap use its space for free, I always donate the lion's share of the registration fees to the organization as a gesture of gratitude and because I believe in the work that PGP does. I advertise this practice to the Chicago Food Swap community and usually present a check to someone from PGP at the swap.

I believe that donating the proceeds, after covering costs, eliminates any resentment that might arise from charging a fee. And the point was never to make money. The point was to encourage people to honor their registration.

Issues at the Swaps

OTHER PROBLEMS CAN ARISE at the swaps themselves. Most food swaps allow anyone to register for their events. Not all the participants are known to the organizer or to one another. As with any event that includes people that you do not know, attendees should exercise common sense. People should not leave their belongings unattended. Requiring registration beforehand does create some accountability, so do not permit any walk-ins. As the organizer, it is also your responsibility to keep out anyone who is not participating in the swap. The owner or manager of the location hosting the swap should assist you with this. If the location is open for business during the event, try to ensure that the swap is separated from the customers as much as possible.

It may well be necessary, however, for participants to leave their food swap items unattended while browsing. Unfortunately, there have been rare instances at food swaps where the items themselves go missing, which is extremely upsetting. Why would someone come to a sharing event like a food swap and help him- or herself to other people's homemade food? It makes no sense. The good news is that these incidents are rare. The best way to prevent them is to use a large, open space that makes it very difficult to swipe items without detection. And the more your community of swappers comes to know each other, the more they'll look out for one another.

Another problem is issues with the swap items. As the organizer, you may receive complaints from unhappy swappers about items that have spoiled or otherwise were not satisfactory. (See Legal Considerations, page 66, for dealing with liability issues, including illnesses from eating swap items.) However, you cannot be responsible for the quality of every item that is brought to the swap. Remind the dissatisfied swapper that all trades are negotiated by the participants themselves and everyone assumes the risk when making a trade. The best strategy for dealing with such issues is prevention. Constantly encourage attendees to label their items well, especially if something is perishable.

Organizer *Burnout*

LASTLY, A COMMON PROBLEM facing food swap organizers is burnout. Running a food swap can be time-consuming and full of aggravation, which is particularly painful for an activity that one does as a hobby. Sometimes the participants take your efforts for granted or, worse, complain when things do not suit them. Occasionally, in the week before a food swap, when last-minute cancellations are pouring in and people pepper me with questions that they could easily answer themselves with a quick look at my website, I want to throw my hands up and walk away. But then during the swap itself, I am once again amazed by all the creative offerings and buoyed by the warmth and joy of the swappers. As I leave the event, my frustration is forgotten, and I cannot wait to do it all again next month.

That being said, I take steps to protect my mental health, and other food swap organizers should do the same. Food swapping is supposed to be fun, remember? If running the food swap is getting to be burdensome for whatever reason, ask for help from your community. If they value what the swap brings to their lives, they should be willing to bear some of the burden of running it. Take on a partner or several.

If that does not work, take a month, or a few months, off. Perhaps doing without the food swap for a period of time will make your community appreciate it that much more. Talking to organizers of other food swaps in other areas is also helpful, whether just to vent or to seek advice on a specific issue. There are several Facebook groups that bring together food swap organizers, and many, including me, will respond to individual queries over email.

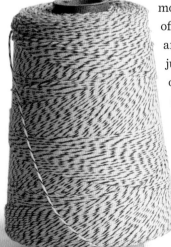

Legal Considerations

WHEN I TELL NEW PEOPLE about the Chicago Food Swap, particularly people older than the Millennial generation, one of the first things they ask is: is food swapping legal? Many of us are aware that government entities regulate the selling of food: food intended for sale typically must be prepared in a licensed kitchen by people with training in hygiene and sanitation. At the other end of the spectrum, the government does not get involved when we invite people to our homes for a meal, a church holds a potluck dinner, or neighbors exchange cookies at holiday time. Where does the food swap lie on that continuum?

In some ways, food swapping is a part of the new sharing economy that offers alternatives to traditional commercial services. On the other hand, food swapping is not in the same category as services where parties exchange money, such as ride-sharing apps or alternative lodging sites. And given the small scale on which food swapping takes place, it will not replace grocery shopping or eating in restaurants for more than one or two meals. Thus, food swapping resembles a private event, such as a cookie exchange or a potluck dinner, more than it does commercial activity. And that is a critical distinction.

State and Local *Regulations*

AS WITH MANY ACTIVITIES in the new sharing economy, most state and local laws do not have a category for a food swap. This uncertainty creates some anxiety for food swap organizers. There have been at least two food swaps — one in Minneapolis and one in California — that were shut down by local health authorities for violating regulations regarding the sale of food. Yes, those local health departments considered the exchange of homemade goods in this way to be a sale.

While most food swaps operate under the radar of local authorities or with their tacit approval, the threat of government interference and other possible legal problems worries many current and prospective food swap organizers. Health and safety regulations governing food sales are enacted at the state, county, and even city level, so there isn't a one-size-fits-all answer to whether a food swap is permitted in your community. As an example, it is important to realize that many California food swaps are thriving. The swap that was shut down was in the Lake Tahoe area and was targeted by county health officials. So the rules and viewpoint of local officials vary from county to county.

Selling food clearly triggers government regulation wherever you are located, and for that reason it is critical that food swap organizers ensure that no food sales are taking place at their events. While some states have enacted cottage food laws that permit small food businesses to operate out of home kitchens, even

those are typically limited to non-hazardous foods and may require a kitchen inspection. So again, do not permit any sales, food or otherwise, at your food-swapping events, to be safe.

Indeed, the less your food swap resembles a marketplace and the more it looks like a private party or event, the better off you will be. Just calling the swap a private event is not enough if it lacks the markers of a private event. For this reason, I strongly recommend requiring participants to register in advance. This is true even if you do not plan to charge a fee. Restaurants and marketplaces are open to the public, and you want to distinguish yourself from those types of businesses and activities. This does not mean that you need to know all the participants in the swap personally, but you should require advance registration and not permit walk-ins.

If possible, try to schedule your event for a time when your host site is closed, or if the host site is open for business during your swap, try to contain your event to a designated area and restrict admittance to registered participants. Of course, events that take place at people's homes are the most likely to be considered private events, but for the reasons I described earlier, namely safety, I still do not recommend hosting a food swap in your or someone else's home.

On-site food preparation could also trigger government scrutiny, so it may be best to require that all food swap items be prepared at home. This is usually the case anyway; most food swap host sites lack facilities for preparing food, and the participants do not have time to prepare food during the event. Sampling, naturally, is a large part of the food swap experience, so people are eating during the event. Some states and counties have enacted regulations to permit sampling during farmers' markets and other non-restaurant settings, so if your host is concerned, you may want to research whether your community has such regulations.

In general, most food swap organizers have operated under the assumption that government authorities would not trouble them if they operated their swap as a private event with no food sales, and there were no complaints. This has been mostly true with the exception of the two swaps previously mentioned.

Should a food swap organizer be proactive and affirmatively seek out government approval to put on such an event? While this may seem like a wise course of action, be forewarned that you may be more likely to trigger government intervention if you ask permission than you would if you simply start your swap and behave like you are throwing a private event. No one asks permission from the health department to host a potluck or dinner party.

Local health codes and food safety regulations most likely contain no specific provisions for food swapping; they are typically concerned with licensing and inspections for places where commercial food preparation takes place. If you go to your local health department, you could well encounter confusion about an event where the food preparation takes place in home kitchens and food is exchanged, not sold. In that case, it may be easier for the official to deny permission for an event that does not fall into a specific provision of the health code than it is for him or her to approve it.

If the health department sanctions your event and, god forbid, someone gets sick, there could be negative repercussions for that official or entity. Thus, government officials typically are quite conservative. In other words, if you do not force a local health official to rule one way or the other on your food swap, you have a greater chance of continuing to operate as a private event.

No one asks permission from the health department to host a potluck or dinner party.

SAMPLE DISCLAIMER

Here is an example of sample disclaimer language that you can adapt to your needs:

Please be aware that all the goods on display are made in home kitchens by private individuals, not professionals. We expect all swappers to maintain the highest standards of cleanliness and food safety in the preparation of their items. Nevertheless, by participating in the swap you acknowledge that the items available are not made in licensed kitchens nor inspected by any government agency. The organizers of this swap do not provide any guarantees or assurances about the safety of the swap items.

Liability **Issues**

ANOTHER CONCERN, and not an unreasonable one, is being sued by one of the participants in the food swap. This could happen if someone is injured during the event, perhaps by slipping and falling, or if someone becomes ill from eating food received at the swap.

The first category would most likely be covered by the insurance of the host site. Most businesses or other public places that hold events have insurance for accidents occurring on-site, but always ask your host explicitly about its insurance coverage. Sometimes a site's insurance may be limited — perhaps it does not cover serving alcohol on the premises, for example — so it is important to have those conversations. If you do decide to hold a food swap in your home, you may want to confirm that your homeowners' insurance would cover any such incidents.

As for food safety and food-borne illness, everyone at a food swap is there by choice and knows that the food is homemade. Nevertheless, we live in a litigious society. For that reason, many food swaps have a disclaimer on their websites or registration pages stating explicitly that the food is prepared in home kitchens, it is not subject to inspection, and the participants therefore assume any risk from eating such food. Such disclaimers are a good idea in my view. Consider also displaying signs at the event repeating the disclaimer. The more visible such reminders are, the better.

Issues around *Alcohol*

ANOTHER CATEGORY OF government regulation that a food swap organizer might encounter concerns alcohol. It is not uncommon for swappers to bring home brews and alcoholic infusions for swapping and sampling. Alcohol sales are highly regulated, and of course no one is permitted to sell alcohol to anyone under the age of 21. Again, a food swap participant is not selling alcohol, so you should not need a liquor license, but you may want to research the BYOB laws in your area for more information.

In any event, there's a whole host of reasons why you do not want to facilitate someone underage getting access to alcohol. Thus, you may want to institute protections to ensure that all swappers are either over 21, or that those who are not are accompanied by a parent or guardian. Or you can simply ban the swapping of alcoholic beverages. If you do intend to permit alcohol at your swap, confirm that your host site does not have any objection.

MEETING MONTHLY SINCE June 2011, the Boston Food Swap is one of the oldest and most consistent food swap groups in North America. Founders Lyn Huckabee, Tara Bellucci, and Susan Johnston read the 2011 *New York Times* article about BK Swappers and immediately decided to bring the food swap concept to their hometown.

Tara, a writer and photographer for the popular interior design blog *Apartment Therapy*, and Lyn, who works for the state department of energy policy, continue to run Boston Food Swap's events. Lyn is passionate about sustainability and a devoted home cook who had struggled in the past to use up her CSA share from a local farm. The food swap seemed like a logical outlet for her experiments in home food preservation. Tara, who grew up in a large Italian family of great cooks, uses her social media savvy to promote the Boston Food Swap.

Boston embraced food swapping from the beginning. *The Boston Globe* wrote a story about the first meeting of the Boston Food Swap, and the local NPR station has aired two stories about the group. The city health department has attended swaps to see how they work, not to offer objections. At the time the Boston Food Swap began, the city's mayor was working to promote local foodways, and city officials viewed the Boston Food Swap as consistent with that mission. The Boston Food Swap has since become an integral part of the city's food community.

Drawing participants from Boston and the suburbs, the Boston Food Swap brings together food lovers of all ages, from teens to senior citizens. One regular, a private school teacher, once brought her entire high school class as part of a lesson on sustainable food. The students even swapped their own items. Because Boston's famous universities attract people from all over the world, the Boston Food Swap has an international flair, and the attendees regularly see items from many global cuisines, such as the Egyptian spice mix *dukkah* and marinated Japanese vegetables on skewers.

The Boston Food Swap has become an integral part of the city's food community.

Every December, the Boston Food Swap holds a cookie swap to raise money for Cookies for Kids' Cancer, a nonprofit organization that funds pediatric cancer research, which hundreds of people attend. What an inspiration for other swap groups!

Another way to protect yourself as the organizer is to ask participants to sign a waiver absolving you or the swap from liability and agreeing not to sue in the event of food-related illness. Agreeing to a waiver can be a part of the registration process, or you can ask participants to sign a physical document when they arrive at the swap. While you may worry that this may be off-putting to the participants, if you explain that, as the organizer, you need to protect yourself and the swap, people usually understand. Emphasize that you are all in this together. In my experience, the swappers recognize how much work the organizer does to coordinate the swap and, as a result, are understanding of any special requests.

Prevention **Is the Best Cure**

THE BEST PROTECTION OF ALL, of course, is to try to prevent any problems from arising in the first place. The absence of any complaints about food-borne illness will not only protect you from liability but it also reduces the risk of government interference. To that end, encourage safe food handling as much as possible. Much of the food that participants bring to food swaps, such as baked goods, jams and jellies, or backyard produce, is considered by most regulatory schemes to be non-hazardous and thus not likely to cause food-borne illness.

However, some common swap items, such as dairy products, eggs, prepared foods, and meat products like bacon and jerky, could well make a participant sick if improperly handled. Encourage people over and over to label their swap items. Remind swappers to indicate on each swap item itself — not only the swap card, which does not go home with the swapper — if the item is perishable and should be stored in the refrigerator. (See the section on safety and spoilage prevention on page 79 for more detailed suggestions for labeling.)

Inform the swappers that if they see something that looks amiss, such as improper food handling, they should tell the organizer right away. Again, emphasize to the swap community that you are all responsible for making sure that the swap does not encounter any problems that could cause it to close or be shut down.

I've said it before that food swapping is not for everyone. If you, as the organizer, sense that a potential swapper is uncomfortable with the concept, then perhaps it is best to gently discourage that person from attending. On that note, if you receive queries from a swapper with food allergies or a serious medical condition, such as celiac disease, it is important to be honest with that person about your inability to guarantee that the food at the swap is safe for him or her. No one can guarantee that the food at the swap is safe, and every participant has to assess the potential risk for him- or herself. Many swappers find it reassuring that they can talk directly with the people who prepared the food, but even that is no guarantee of anything.

In short, it is reasonable for a food swap organizer, host, or participant to have concerns about government regulation and liability. I would hope, however, that these concerns would not be enough to prevent you from starting or participating in a food swap. A few simple precautions should be sufficient to prevent such problems from happening and allow you to sleep soundly at night.

Many swappers find it reassuring that they can talk directly with the people who prepared the food.

3

Strategies for
SUCCESSFUL
SWAPPING

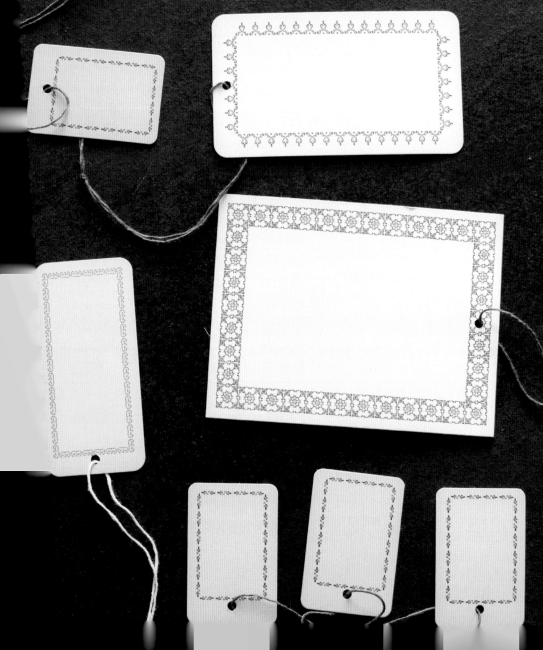

Whether you are a new or seasoned food swapper, successful swapping requires some planning and strategic thinking. Every swapper wants to bring appealing, distinctive items that are not excessively labor-intensive and for which they will receive fair value in trade. How can you ensure that your swap items are the ones that are at the top of everyone else's must-have list while still being fun and affordable to make? (See dozens of recipes that will make you the toast of any swap, starting on page 87.)

Not only do you need to create desirable swap items, you also need to be strategic about *how* you swap. The actual swapping can be a blur. If you do not have a plan going in, you could easily find yourself coming home with eight kinds of cookies or three kinds of hummus. If that doesn't bother you, then perhaps you don't need a strategy. But you may find yourself scrambling to eat everything before it goes bad.

For that reason, it is usually preferable to swap for a mix of different kinds of items; for example some baked goods, some dips and condiments, and some shelf-stable pantry items. In this chapter I present a few techniques to help you swap effectively so that you do not miss out on the best items and that you come home with a diverse array of foods that spread out the swap bounty over time.

What *to Bring*

WHEN THINKING ABOUT WHAT TO BRING to a food swap, keep in mind the following goals: be flexible and appeal to a wide group, stand out from the crowd, play to your strengths, and fill a need. You do not have to accomplish each of those goals with a single swap item. In fact, it may not be possible to do so. But you do want to ensure that your swap item accomplishes at least one of those goals, if not two or three. Here are some keys for success.

Bring more than one item. This is part of appealing to a wide group of potential swap partners. Between food allergies, dietary restrictions, and just plain personal preference, you never know what swap items will appeal to which swappers. Having at least two different swap items gives you better odds when trying to make a deal with the swapper who has the one item that you cannot live without.

As an example, say that you brought spicy cheese crackers to the swap and the item you most want to bring home is a kombucha SCOBY. But the man who brought the kombucha SCOBY is a vegan and your cheese crackers do not appeal to him. But if you had brought cheese crackers and fabulous pickled fennel (recipe on page 225), you would have had a much better chance of bringing home that kombucha starter.

In my house, we have multiple food allergies, including my daughter's allergies to peanuts and tree nuts. Out of sympathy for her, I rarely bring home items that contain nuts or peanuts, no matter how delicious they look. I am not saying that you should not bring items with common allergens like nuts or peanuts to a food swap. Quite the contrary: items with nuts are often extremely popular. However, if you *do* bring an item with gluten or nuts or dairy, consider bringing a gluten-free or vegan or nut-free item as well, just in case a person that you hope to swap with cannot or will not eat your other item.

Think small. Hand pies and cupcakes are easier to swap than regular-size pies and cakes. Many of the typical items come in small serving sizes, such as an 8-ounce jar of jam or a pint jar of pickles. Given how much work it is to make a pie and how many people a whole cake can feed, you may well be reluctant to swap that whole pie or cake for a small jar of jam or hummus. You are much more likely to find a fair trade for items in individual serving sizes.

TAP INTO YOUR INNER MARKETER

I remember one swapper named Kat who made kimchi; she had a graphic, handmade sign that read "Kat's Kickin' Kimchi" and explained what kimchi was for those who were not familiar with the fermented Korean cabbage dish. The sign drew people in and prompted potential swappers to ask questions and sample Kat's wares.

Another couple brought enormous peanut butter–banana muffins labeled with a black-and-white photo of Elvis Presley, which made everyone smile. Using fun marketing in this way elicits a response from browsing swappers and gives them a reason to strike up a conversation with you and try your samples.

If you are making an item that comes in multiples, like cookies or brownies, package them in groups of two, four or six depending on their size. Again, smaller packages allow you to be more flexible and open to more trades. You can always offer to trade two packages of your cookies or brownies if the item you want is larger, took more labor to make, or is particularly sought after. For every recipe in this book, I offer a suggestion on how to portion it for swapping. You can use these suggestions as guides when making your own recipes as well.

Make your items appealing. One way to make your swap items eye-catching, of course, is the packaging. I will talk more specifically about packaging your swap items, but beyond packaging, a creative display of your swap items is another way to draw people to your table. A little effort can go a long way.

Think printed or handmade signs, brightly colored tablecloths and runners, and enticing samples. Bring props for display, such as cake plates or baskets. If you can, raise your items or display them vertically so that they literally stand out from all the other items on the same table or counter. Many people who participate in food swaps have websites, blogs, or even food businesses. If you fall into that category, be sure to include information about your blog or business on your table display and packaging so that people can find out more about you.

If you are not particularly artistic or crafty and my description of eye-catching table displays and packaging fills you with dread, please don't be discouraged. Certainly not every swapper puts a great deal of effort into packaging and displays, and those people usually end up making great trades too. Beyond clever marketing and attractive packaging, another way to make your swap items stand out is simply to bring unusual and unique food.

Tell a Story

ITEMS WITH A STORY behind them are very appealing to other swappers. Is this your grandmother's rugelach recipe? Are these apple buns a traditional Easter food? Let other swappers know if your items reflect your ethnic heritage or family traditions. Everyone loves the opportunity to try an old family recipe or learn about a different culture's traditions. Be willing to answer questions and offer samples, particularly if the item is unusual. One of the best things about food swapping is that it introduces traditional homemade foods to a wider audience.

People also love to know where their food comes from. So if you have a story about where you got the ingredients for your swap items, whether you foraged them or bought them from a nearby farm, be sure to share that as well. My friend Dora often makes her swap items from fruits that her Jamaican in-laws send her from their farm in southwestern Florida. At a swap where Dora was offering three different confections made with mangoes from her in-laws' farm, she displayed a photograph of the farm next to her items. Everyone who passed by stopped to ask about the farm and try her mango curd and mango jelly. The idea that her father-in-law picked the mangoes Dora used to make these delicious spreads was so charming that everyone wanted to swap with her.

What is so enticing about foods made from recipes handed down for generations and mangoes grown on a family farm? It's the fact that you couldn't have bought the items in question, "not even for ready money," to quote Oscar Wilde. One of the reasons people love food swaps is that they can access foods they could never find in a store or restaurant. Some foods you can find only if you make them yourself or if someone else brings them to a food swap. Making something that other swappers can't get anywhere else will make your items wildly desirable.

SUGGEST USES FOR PANTRY ITEMS

One way to make pantry items more appealing is to offer suggestions on how to use them if it is not immediately obvious. No one needs advice on how to use homemade vanilla extract or red wine vinegar, but if you are offering an unusual spice mix such as garam masala, include a recipe card with the item or explain how it is used. Also, try to offer a sample if possible. For a spice mix or flavored salt, one way to allow potential swappers to sample the item is to bring some popcorn or a flatbread flavored with the salt or spice.

One attendee at the Chicago Food Swap, who is Sri Lankan, was swapping curry powder and brought a pot of beef curry so that people could taste a dish made with the spice mix. Needless to say, her table was very popular. You do not need to go to that extreme, but samples always help when swapping something a little unusual.

Play to Your *Strengths*

ANOTHER WAY TO ENSURE that your items are the toast of the swap is to play to your strengths. Make what you love. If you are a talented baker, by all means, bring baked goods to trade. Don't feel that you should not bring baked goods to a food swap because there are too many of them already. Have confidence that your baked goods are special and that other swappers would be lucky to bring them home. In short, do not force yourself to make something that you would not otherwise simply because you think other swappers will like it. Participating in the swap is supposed to be fun and a labor of love, not a tiresome obligation. If you make your swap items with enthusiasm, others will notice and be excited to sample your items.

Be *Practical*

LASTLY, WHEN TRYING TO DECIDE what to bring to your next food swap, consider making something practical. While everyone loves to indulge in red velvet cupcakes, homemade limoncello, and chocolate–peanut butter buck-eyes, useful items such as hummus, soups, salad dressings, mini-frittatas, breads, and yogurt are always very popular. One of the little-known secrets of food swapping is that there tend to be more sweet than savory items on offer, and as a result, savory items are always highly sought after. When newcomers ask me for advice on what to bring to their first swap, I always suggest bringing something savory as a way to guarantee that their item will be popular.

BON APPETIT!

Philly Swappers

Philadelphia PA

FOUR IS A MAGIC NUMBER for the Philly Swappers. Its four organizers work together to put on four swaps per year. Fifty to sixty people attend these quarterly swaps, which are held at different sites around Philadelphia, including an urban farm in summer, the main branch of the Philadelphia Public Library in winter, and the historic Reading Terminal Market in spring. Started in September 2011, Philly Swappers counts itself as one of the oldest and most popular food swaps in the country.

Philly Swappers has some serious foodie star power behind it. One of the organizers is fermentation expert Amanda Feifer, who blogs at *Phickle* and authored the 2015 cookbook *Ferment Your Vegetables*. Marisa McClellan, the writer behind the popular canning blog *Food in Jars* and two preserving cookbooks, is another. Indeed, many people, myself included, first heard of food swapping from reading about the Philly Swappers on Marisa's blog. The third organizer is Alexis Siemons, a tea consultant and writer who blogs at *teaspoons & petals*.

But food swaps are a great equalizer. At any swap, home cooks, professional chefs, and food writers are all on the same level. Georgia Kirkpatrick, the fourth organizer and the only one who is not a culinary professional, points out that for the Philly Swappers, food is second to the sense of community. People keep coming to the Philly Swappers because, above all, it is a fun event, and the fact that attendees get to bring home amazing food is a bonus.

> At any swap, home cooks, professional chefs, and food writers are all on the same level.

Philadelphia is a city with a vibrant local food scene, from farmers' markets to craft beer festivals. Some swappers own local food businesses; others are their customers. The organizers take special pride in seeing swappers who were inspired to start artisanal food businesses or write cookbooks because of the feedback and confidence they gained from the swap. Philly Swappers has also inspired at least four swaps in other parts of Pennsylvania and nearby New Jersey, a fact that makes Georgia Kirkpatrick proud.

Swap items that can make up all or part of a meal in the days after the swap are highly desirable because they make that swapper's life easier. I love to come home from a swap with a delicious treat that my children can eat for dessert that evening. But even more, I love to come home with items that I can eat for breakfast and lunch the next day. If I swap on Sunday for granola, yogurt, quinoa salad, and soup, then I know my week will start off full of delicious homemade foods without my having to lift a finger. I can bask in the glow of a good swap for days.

On a related note, consider bringing an item that will help the recipient to cook and bake better in the weeks and months following the swap. Examples are extracts, spice mixes, flavored salts and sugars, and infused oils and vinegars. While pantry items may not have the curb appeal of a luscious-looking fruit tart, passionate cooks are always looking for something new and exciting to enhance their dishes.

Packaging Items for Swapping

ONE OF THE WAYS COOKING for a food swap is different from cooking for your friends and family is that you have to package your swap items, transport them to the swap, and display them. In this regard, getting ready for a food swap is akin to preparing edible gifts, something many of us do for the holidays. There are several important considerations when packaging items to swap, including safety, portability, looks, and affordability. For each recipe in this book, I offer specific packaging suggestions. For now, here are some general thoughts on how to package items for food swapping.

Safety and spoilage prevention. The most important consideration when packaging any food, whether for swapping or not, is safety. Protecting the food from spoilage or contamination is the primary purpose of any food container. Use only food-grade containers with appropriate closures for all of your swap items. If using glass jars, check them for chips or cracks, especially if they have been used before. After canning items for shelf stability, check the seals of all your jars before storing or swapping them. (For more detailed information about canning, see Safe Water-Bath Canning Procedures, page 198.)

For perishable swap items, keep in mind that they could be sitting out at room temperature before, during, and after the swap. If spoilage is a concern, such as for items containing dairy, consider transporting your items to the swap in an insulated cooler with ice packs and perhaps displaying one as a sample while keeping the rest in the cooler during the event. I have seen people swap homemade ice cream this way.

Portability and protection. Not only do you have to transport your items to the swap, but once you are there, the other swappers may want to pick them up and examine them. Then, of course, your trading partners will need to bring the items home with them. Plainly, you need to package your items in such a way that they will not break, leak, be crushed, or otherwise incur any damage. Many swappers have learned this lesson the hard way. Some items, such as pickles and jam, come in sturdy packaging; namely, a glass jar. Others, such as baked goods or candies, will need to be properly packaged. Dividing your items into swap-size portions and packaging them for transport is a critical part of your preparation for the swap.

LABEL, LABEL, LABEL!

As part of the discussion of safe and effective food packaging, I would like to underscore the importance of labels. Describing an item, its ingredients, and whether it is perishable on the swap card is necessary but not sufficient. Swappers do not take the swap cards home, and hours after the swap, people can forget the name, ingredients, or flavoring of an item they traded for.

At a bare minimum, include an identifying tag or label on each individual item; indicate clearly if the item is perishable and needs to be refrigerated. (As a side note, some swappers get annoyed by labels that are stuck on reusable items, such as glass jars, but better that than no label at all.) If an item contains a common allergen like nuts and this is not obvious in the name, it is considerate to note that on the label as well.

Lastly, if you are comfortable doing so, it is a nice touch to include your name and perhaps contact information, such as an email address, on the label in the event the recipient has a question or simply wants your recipe.

Pretty *Packaging*

IF YOUR SWAP ITEMS are packaged in a safe and effective manner and labeled, you can stop there. However, many swappers enjoy decorating their items to make them more eye-catching and believe that doing so increases their value in trade. Some discerning food swap attendees have told me that they specifically seek out items that both look and taste amazing.

The possibilities for decoration are endless. I have seen people add fabric, ribbons, and twine to glass bottles and jars. Baked goods look professional, and are protected from harm, when packaged in bakery boxes or plastic clamshells or wrapped in cellophane and tied with ribbon or twine. Even items baked in disposable foil or paper pans look nicer with a ribbon and hanging tag. Candies shine in glassine treat bags and have an old-fashioned charm when individually wrapped in waxed or parchment paper. And personalized labels and tags make any item more appealing, in addition to providing important information.

If beautiful packaging is an aspect of the swap experience that interests you, you can develop your own signature look over time with certain styles of packaging materials. Just remember not to obscure the food with too much adornment.

Saving Money

IT IS VERY easy to package and decorate your food swap items beautifully if you are willing to spend a lot of money. Doing so without spending several dollars per item requires more effort but is certainly possible. Buying a lot of containers, especially glass ones, can quickly get expensive if you shop at craft or kitchen stores. Online retailers, such as Fillmore Container or Specialty Bottle, often have the best prices, but shipping can be costly.

One way to save money, although this requires some organization, is to get together with other swappers and place a large order for bottles or jars. Often the unit price goes down the more you buy, and placing one large order allows you to share the shipping costs. If this is appealing, reach out to the swap community, or ask the swap organizer to do so, to gauge interest. (See Resources, page 237.)

To save money on decorations, start by using what you have around the house, such as plain white or colored paper to make labels and decorations made with baker's twine, ribbon, rickrack, fabric, and so forth. The rustic look is popular and can be achieved with very inexpensive supplies such as brown butcher paper and burlap. Rather than buy labels or tags, many swappers create their own customized labels at home using online templates and blank label sheets, such as those sold by Avery or World Label, that are compatible with word processing programs. You can also create unique tags using a craft punch on card stock: a 2-inch circle punch fits a regular-mouth canning lid; tag-shaped punches are also useful.

Many stores that do not usually carry food and gift packaging do so around the holidays. This can be a good time of year to stock up. Obviously you won't want materials covered with reindeer and holly, but simple red-and-white striped packaging doesn't look out of place at other times of year. Better yet, many of these items will be on sale right after Christmas, and this can be a great time to score some bargains.

Recycling Containers

BECAUSE ONE OF THE THEMES of the food swap movement is sustainability, many swappers recycle or upcycle items for their food packaging. As an example, many people save and reuse glass jars, from food they bought at the store or got at a swap, to package sauces or dips. (In this vein, some swap participants bring glass jars or bottles that they do not plan to reuse to the swap for others to take home. Swap organizers should facilitate this kind of exchange.)

One swapper I know saves cardboard quart containers from the farmers' market to package small baked goods. I save and reuse ribbons from presents that my family receives. Thrift stores and yard sales are also a surprisingly good, cheap source for glass jars, bottles, cookie tins, and similar items.

In short, there are more ways to package and adorn your food swap items than I could possibly describe. Fortunately, there are many resources out there to inspire you. Cookbooks, blog posts, and articles about how to decorate homemade edible gifts are particularly helpful. And of course, there is Pinterest, source of many terrific crafty ideas. See Resources, page 237, for a list of retailers that are good sources for food containers and decoration.

Savvy Swapping

AFTER WEEKS OF PREPARATION — deciding what to make, and then making and packaging your swap items — you are finally here. Now what? With any luck, the organizer of the swap will welcome you, explain how the swap works, and direct you to a place to set up your items. After you set up your eye-catching display and exchange greetings with your tablemates, what should you do? What is the best strategy for ensuring that you come home with a basket full of homemade treats that will keep you eating happily for days and even weeks?

The first part of any food swap is devoted to browsing and sampling. Participants need a chance to see what everyone else has brought and determine what items they are most interested in. To that end, it helps to arrive on time. Not only is this more considerate to the organizer, but it also ensures that you have enough time to see all the items on display and that everyone else notices your items. Latecomers often get the least visible spots, and their items may be overlooked.

Browsing and Sampling

AS YOU WALK around the room, if you see something that you are interested in, go ahead and make an offer for it on the swap card. That is always a good first step, and it is not binding. Savvy swappers bring a pad or notecard with them and when they see something they want, they jot its location down on their "must-have" list. Otherwise it can be very hard to remember all the different items that caught your eye and where they are in the room.

Another strategy is to snap photos of the best-looking items with your smartphone. Then when the swapping begins, you have a handy list or easy-to-access photos to guide you. Identify the two or three items that you would be the most disappointed to leave without. You will want to head for those first when it is time to begin swapping.

As you consider which items to make a play for, keep in mind that you want to bring home a diverse mix of items. Look for some that are highly perishable, such as candies and baked goods; some that will last a few days or weeks in the refrigerator, such as dips or condiments; and some that are shelf-stable, such as jams, pickles, or spice mixes.

Many first-time attendees come home from the swap with piles of perishable baked goods that they struggle to finish before they go stale. Not only is this frustrating, but it prevents them from experiencing one of the best things about the swap, which is that one event can provide weeks of home-made deliciousness. Most experienced swappers look for an array of different kinds of items.

Scrambling to Swap

WHAT ABOUT THE actual process of swapping? Everyone approaches the exciting moment after the organizer announces that it is time to swap differently. Some stand by their items and field offers; others load their items into a basket or tray and head out into the fray. This is where it can be helpful to come with a friend or partner. If you swap as a team, one of you can stand by your items while the other goes out in search of those must-have trades.

Again, head for your most desired items first, or risk losing them. The actual swapping is hectic and goes quickly. Everyone feels a bit stunned afterwards. That is why it is so crucial to have a strategy to ensure that you get the items you want, and a good mix of different kinds of items.

When you return home after the swap, go through your items right away to determine what needs to be refrigerated and what can sit on a shelf. If something is highly perishable, like homemade ricotta or compound butter, be sure to eat it in the next day or two. If you have brought home a lot of baked goods, identify ones that could be frozen without harming the quality. (See Freezing and Thawing Baked Goods, page 111.)

Losing delicious homemade food to spoilage or mold is heartbreaking and defeats one of the purposes of food swapping, which is to reduce food waste. So have a plan to use your more perishable food swap items in a timely manner.

DON'T FEEL OBLIGED

Remember that you are never obligated to trade with anyone. Saying no to a trade is part of the process, and everyone should know that. Many food swap organizers reiterate this important fact at the beginning of every event. Just as you should feel free to politely decline a trade, you should also expect that others may not want to trade with you. Try not to take it personally. The other swapper may have an allergy or dietary restriction that makes a particular trade undesirable, or he or she may simply not want your item for reasons that have nothing to do with how delicious it is or how good a cook you are.

MILE HIGH SWAPPERS founder and opera singer Eve Orenstein is a busy lady. A nonprofit arts fund-raiser by day, she runs the Colorado chapter of Opera on Tap by night. When her career brought her to Boulder from Brooklyn, Eve was looking for ways to meet like-minded people. Coloradans are known for having an adventurous pioneer spirit, but that can sometimes make it hard to build community. After reading about BK Swappers, Eve thought that a food swap would be the perfect way to meet other passionate cooks and create community around local food. In that spirit, she launched the Mile High Swappers in the spring of 2011.

Mile High Swappers is unusual in that it encompasses several different groups that meet in different parts of northern Colorado, each about an hour apart. Eve runs the website and takes care of the administrative tasks while the local organizers pick the dates and locations for their events. Each town's swap has a slightly different feel, and some devotees attend more than one.

The Boulder swap leans vegetarian, as one might expect from a college town with a reputation for being eclectic and alternative. After all, this is a town that organizes an annual bicycle tour of backyard chicken coops. Because of the university, Boulder attracts new residents from all over the country, and Eve has found that many of the new participants at the Boulder events used to attend food swaps in other cities.

Mile High Swappers meets at many different kinds of locations, including Boulder's Savory Spice Shop, various community gardens, and Denver Organic Homesteaders, a collective of organic retailers. In the summer, the Boulder swap meets at local farms, all of which offer tours to attendees. The farmers even join in the swapping as well.

Each town's swap has a slightly different feel, and some devotees attend more than one.

How does Eve find time to organize the Mile High Swappers with all of her other commitments? It is hard, but she remains excited about every event. Even if she has worked all week and performed all weekend and hasn't had time to cook, she goes to the swap and always leaves rejuvenated. When she sees friendships forming among the swappers, she knows that her work has been worthwhile.

VARIATION

Have a Holiday Swap

Many people today decry the commercialism of the holidays and long for a time when the season focused on more personal, and even homemade, gifts rather than the ubiquitous bottle of wine or gift card. If you share this sentiment and your holiday gift-giving list has grown out of control, consider gathering a group of willing friends and relatives and organizing a holiday food gift swap in lieu of exchanging presents. The best part of a holiday food swap is that all the presents will soon be eaten and will not add to the clutter in your home!

Like a meal swap, a holiday food swap is a wonderful excuse to get together with friends and family. And if your extended family is already planning to gather, it will be easy to add a food gift swap to the holiday events.

To set up a holiday food swap, first decide whether every participant should give a gift to every other participant or whether you want to hold a "Secret Santa" or "White Elephant" gift exchange where each person only has to bring one gift. In the latter case, you will have to figure out a system to determine who gives a gift to whom: pick numbers at the swap or assign "Secret Santas" in advance. However you decide to organize the swap, everyone should clearly communicate their dietary restrictions and the organizer should establish guidelines — vegetarian, gluten-free, no nuts — with those restrictions in mind. Also decide whether the gifts must be edible or whether homemade lotions, face scrubs, or soaps are permitted. The most important rule, however, is that all gifts be homemade.

Emphasize to your friends and family that one does not have to be a gourmet cook to participate in a holiday food swap. Many charming food gifts do not require any skill or cooking experience. Indeed, there are several recipes in this book that almost anyone could make, any of which would constitute a thoughtful and useful gift: Examples include Rum Vanilla Extract (page 186), Infused Vodka (page 176), Raspberry Vinegar (page 184), flavored salts (page 192), infused sugars (page 194), and Preserved Lemons (page 202). Other foods suitable for gifting include homemade candy, cookies, granola, spiced nuts, jam, or pickles. Many of these gifts are also easy to make on a limited budget, which is helpful for students or younger family members.

Pretty packaging will make your homemade gifts seem special and festive. See Pretty Packaging (page 80) for plenty of ideas on how to package and decorate homemade food gifts in ways that will delight your friends and family.

Recipes for **PORTABLE,**
DISTINCTIVE & AFFORDABLE
Food Swap Items

This collection of recipes offers ideas for items to bring to a food swap as well as demonstrating the different kinds of items one might see there. For each category, I offer several examples so you can find one that appeals to you and your cooking style.

SOME OF THE RECIPES included here, such as flavored salts and infused vodka, are so easy that a novice cook could prepare them without any difficulty. Others are well within the skill range of a typical home cook, and some require specialized knowledge and equipment.

One of my favorite things about participating in a food swap is that it has inspired me to expand my repertoire in the kitchen and tackle projects that I never would have attempted otherwise. I hope this book provides that same sort of push for you. Begin with the recipes that are familiar and manageable. But as you participate in more food swaps and become more expert in do-it-yourself kitchen projects, challenge yourself.

If you have never made candy before, try making caramels. If you have never canned before, try pickling something. If you have never baked bread before, give my focaccia recipe a try. Knowing that you will be able to show off the results to your fellow food swappers will be all the motivation you need.

As I explained earlier, packaging your swap items for safe transport and for visual appeal is another important part of getting ready for a food swap. For each recipe, I note how that item is typically packaged or offer packaging suggestions. Remember to label items well as a courtesy to other swappers. If an item contains a common allergen, like nuts, and it is not immediately obvious, note that on the item's label. It is also helpful to label perishable items so that those you trade with will know to refrigerate the item when they get home.

When I come home from a food swap, the first thing I do is sort my haul into (1) food to eat over the next few days, the most perishable items; (2) food to eat over the next few weeks, including items that keep well in the refrigerator, such as dips, sauces, condiments, and drink syrups, as well as some of the hardier snack items, like granola and crackers; and (3) food that is shelf stable and will last for a month or longer, including pantry items, such as spice mixes, extracts, and vinegar, as well as jarred foods like jam and pickles. So that is how I have organized the recipes in this book. Each category has its merit, and I hope you will experiment with each one.

GIVE A LITTLE GIFT

It is worth mentioning that many of the recipes in this book, in addition to making terrific food swap items, make impressive edible gifts. I especially recommend the candies, the Ancho Chile Pecans, the Citrus Curd, the alcoholic drinks, all of the pantry items, and any of the preserved fruits and vegetables as outstanding homemade gifts for holidays or a simple thank you. Indeed, many of the recipes in this book have uses outside a food swap. The soup recipes, for example, are great for feeding a large crowd. The recipes for baked goods come in handy for bake sales. The recipes for Tomato Jam, Zucchini Relish, Applesauce with Quatre Épices, and many others, will help gardeners and pick-your-own enthusiasts deal with a glut of homegrown or hand-picked produce.

4

Quickly Consumed:
ITEMS TO MAKE
FRESH & ENJOY SOON

CANDIES & CONFECTIONS

IT IS NOT UNUSUAL to see several different kinds of homemade candy at a food swap, including caramels, truffles, toffee, and marshmallows. I have also seen taffy, maple sugar candies, lollipops, and chocolate bark — and no one seems to mind when there are several confections on offer. Many people, even experienced cooks, are intimidated by candy making, so they are very impressed by other swappers' homemade confections. If they only knew how easy some candies can be! But let's not ruin the mystique for those folks.

Candies have the advantage of being small, light, and easy to transport, especially when compared with foods in heavy glass bottles or jars. So if you are using public transportation, candies might be a good option. Just remember that you might trade for heavier items that you will have to bring home.

In making candies, it is worthwhile to seek out the freshest ingredients possible. Use European-style unsalted butter with its higher butterfat content, and try to find cream that is not ultra-pasteurized and does not contain any stabilizers. For truffles and other chocolate confections, you should use high-quality dark chocolate that contains at least 60 percent cocoa solids.

In terms of special equipment, a candy thermometer ($10 for a basic one and $20 for a fancy digital one) will make the process of candy making go much more smoothly. As always when making candy, give the project your full attention. Often you are working with very hot ingredients that could cause serious burns, and confections can go from just right to burnt in a matter of seconds.

Packaging candy is fairly straight forward. Many candies look lovely in basic glassine treat bags tied with a bit of ribbon or twine. A label or hanging tag will add to the visual appeal. You can also package candies in small bakery boxes, take-out-style boxes, metal tins, or glass jars, although these will certainly be more expensive.

Some candies need to be individually wrapped in waxed or parchment paper or foil wrappers. You can find precut candy wrappers at craft and kitchen stores, which will save you the trouble of cutting them yourself. You can also find at those stores single-size glassine treat bags for wrapping lollipops, pretzel sticks, and other larger confections. Lastly, miniature baking cups make attractive packaging for larger candies like truffles.

VANILLA RUM CARAMELS

MAKES 6 DOZEN CARAMELS

Caramels are an ideal entry into the world of homemade candy because they do not require any obscure ingredients and are relatively straightforward to make. I prefer softer, chewier caramels, so I cook the sugar syrup in the first stage only to 250°F (120°C) and go a bit heavy on the cream. Cutting the cream back to 1 cup and cooking the sugar syrup to closer to 300°F (150°C) will result in a harder candy.

You can flavor caramels in many different ways. For a more subtle flavor, infuse the cream-and-butter mixture by allowing the flavoring to steep in the warm cream for up to 30 minutes. This is a good method to try with herbs. For a bolder flavor, stir in a small amount of flavoring at the end of the process. Here I use both methods by infusing the cream with vanilla, then stirring in vanilla extract and rum at the very end. Feel free to skip the rum altogether or try a different flavoring.

1¼ cups heavy cream

5 tablespoons unsalted butter

1 vanilla bean, split in half lengthwise

Pinch of kosher salt

1½ cups sugar

¼ cup light corn syrup

¼ cup water

1 teaspoon vanilla extract

2 tablespoons rum (optional)

Flaky sea salt, for decoration and extra flavor

Packaging

Wrap the caramels in squares of parchment or waxed paper. You can buy precut candy wrappers at craft and kitchen stores or cut your own. Package the wrapped caramels — a dozen makes a nice portion for swapping or giving — in glassine treat bags and close with a twist tie or twine. Decorate with a label or hanging tag.

1. Line an 8-inch square baking pan with parchment paper and spray the paper with nonstick cooking spray.

2. Combine the cream, butter, vanilla bean, and salt in a small saucepan, and heat on low until the butter has melted. Keep this cream mixture warm until ready to use, but do not allow it to scorch.

3. In a medium saucepan, combine the sugar, corn syrup, and water, and stir until combined. Bring the mixture to a boil over medium heat, but do not stir: stirring can cause the sugar to crystallize. Keep a small glass of water nearby and, as needed, brush down any sugar crystals that form on the sides of the pot using a pastry brush dipped in water. Continue to boil the sugar syrup until it registers at least 250°F (120°C) for softer caramels and up to 300°F (150°C) for firmer ones.

4. Remove the vanilla bean from the cream mixture. Off the heat, slowly pour the cream mixture into the sugar syrup and whisk to combine. The mixture will bubble up dramatically.

5. Return the saucepan to the stove and heat over medium-high heat, again not stirring, until the mixture begins to turn golden brown and registers between 245 and 250°F (118 and 120°C). Remove from the heat and whisk in the vanilla and rum (if using). Pour the caramel into the prepared pan but do not scrape the bottom of the saucepan, which may contain burnt pieces. Sprinkle flaky sea salt over the top.

6. Allow the caramel to cool completely before cutting, at least 2 hours and preferably longer. When the caramel is firm and cool, lift the parchment paper from the pan and place on a cutting board. Using a sharp knife, cut the caramel into square or rectangular pieces. If the candies stick to your knife, spray it with a light coating of nonstick cooking spray.

PEANUT BUTTER BUCKEYES

MAKES 3 DOZEN CANDIES

The Ohio State sports teams are nicknamed the Buckeyes after the state tree, the Ohio buckeye. The buckeye tree bears an oblong nut that is dark brown except for a patch of lighter brown on top, and that is exactly what these chocolate-covered peanut butter candies are designed to resemble. I have a degree from the University of Michigan, Ohio State's hated rival, so it pains me to tell you how delicious these peanut butter buckeyes are.

A member of the Chicago Food Swap community brought these candies the first time she attended a swap, and people pounced on them. When the swapper returned the next month with different items, several people, myself included, indignantly asked where the buckeyes were. I had no choice but to create my own recipe.

12	ounces unsweetened peanut butter at room temperature
½	cup (1 stick) unsalted butter, softened
2	teaspoons vanilla extract
2	cups powdered sugar
1	teaspoon salt
8	ounces semisweet or bittersweet chocolate
1	tablespoon vegetable shortening

Packaging

Package the buckeyes in glassine treat bags and close with a twist-tie or twine. Half a dozen makes a nice amount for swapping. Decorate with a label or hanging tag.

Note: *Shortening gives melted chocolate a smoother consistency and results in more even coating. Do not substitute butter as it contains water, which will cause the chocolate to seize.*

1. Cream the peanut butter and butter in the bowl of a standing mixer until well combined, about 2 minutes at medium speed. Add the vanilla, sugar, and salt, and mix well, scraping down the sides as necessary, until all the ingredients are combined. The mixture may be crumbly.

2. Line a baking sheet with parchment paper.

3. With dampened hands, gather a small amount of the peanut butter mixture and roll it into a ball about 1 inch in diameter. Place the ball on the parchment paper and repeat with the remaining dough. Place the baking sheet in the refrigerator until the balls are firm to the touch, at least 30 minutes.

4. Melt the chocolate and shortening in a double-boiler set above simmering water, stirring occasionally. Alternatively, put them in a microwave-safe bowl and heat for 15-second intervals, stirring in between, until melted.

5. Insert a toothpick in a chilled peanut butter ball and dip it in the melted chocolate, leaving a circular patch of undipped batter at the top. Return to the parchment-lined baking sheet and repeat with the remaining balls. Smooth over the small holes left by the toothpick. Return the baking sheet to the refrigerator until the chocolate is firm.

6. Store the buckeyes in the refrigerator until ready to eat or swap.

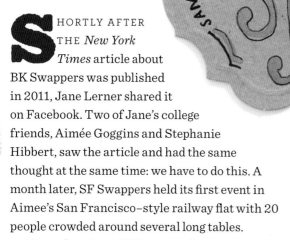

SHORTLY AFTER THE *New York Times* article about BK Swappers was published in 2011, Jane Lerner shared it on Facebook. Two of Jane's college friends, Aimée Goggins and Stephanie Hibbert, saw the article and had the same thought at the same time: we have to do this. A month later, SF Swappers held its first event in Aimee's San Francisco–style railway flat with 20 people crowded around several long tables.

Since that time, SF Swappers has met every other month, alternating between weekend afternoons and weekday evenings. Each swap begins with a potluck meal at which the swappers demonstrate their culinary prowess. Aimee and Stephanie do not control who brings what to the potluck, but it always seems to work out, and the time for socializing creates a strong sense of community among the group.

While the SF Swappers has a core group of devoted regulars, every swap has a large percentage of newcomers who come from all over the Bay Area. Because California has a year-round growing season, the offerings at the SF Swappers tend to be very seasonal and heavy on locally grown ingredients. Many participants bring homegrown produce.

While Aimee is a passionate home cook like many of the other swappers, Stephanie is a professional chef with her own catering business. But she does not find that her professional training separates her from the other participants. Indeed, one of the reasons that Stephanie was so keen to start the swap was to be able to interact with people around food without a commercial transaction being involved. Witnessing the swappers' passion for food and their sense of pride and accomplishment in their creations is inspiring. Aimee revels in the creativity demonstrated by the swappers, whether it be a surprising combination of flavors, an item she wouldn't think of making at home, or beautiful packaging.

As one of the organizers says, the swap is like a family without all the baggage.

While San Francisco is known as home to hipsters and tech millionaires, SF Swappers remains a relaxed, down-to-earth, friendly gathering. The participants make unusual and sophisticated items that would appeal to a foodie crowd, but the feeling is welcoming, inclusive, and non-competitive. As Stephanie says, the swap is like a family without all the baggage.

ENGLISH TOFFEE

MAKES 1¾ POUNDS TOFFEE

When I was growing up, my mother adored Almond Roca, the gold-foil-wrapped toffee coated in chocolate and chopped almonds that came in an elegant pink tin. Occasionally she even shared a piece with me. There was something so satisfying about the way the buttery toffee shattered in my mouth and stuck in my teeth. I loved it.

This is my version of an English toffee studded with almonds and coated in chocolate. Its popularity as a swap item leads me to believe that others love toffee as much as I do.

- 1 cup raw almonds
- 1 cup (2 sticks) butter
- 1⅓ cups sugar
- 3 tablespoons water
- 2 tablespoons light corn syrup
- 1 teaspoon vanilla extract
- ¾ cup semisweet chocolate chips

  Flaky sea salt (optional)

Packaging

Package the toffee into four 7-ounce portions. This toffee looks quite festive packaged in cellophane bags and tied with a nice ribbon. A pretty tin or box would be adorable but is certainly not necessary to make this confection a must-have item. Do note the presence of nuts on the label.

Note: *I prefer to buy whole almonds and chop them myself because it is less expensive, but if you prefer the convenience, feel free to buy slivered almonds. Also, seek out high-quality chocolate chips for this recipe, such as Callebaut.*

1. Toast the almonds in a dry skillet over medium heat until lightly browned and fragrant, about 5 minutes. Allow them to cool, then chop thoroughly and set aside.

2. Line a 9-inch square baking pan with parchment paper.

3. Melt the butter in a medium, heavy-bottomed saucepan.

4. Add the sugar, water, and corn syrup and stir to dissolve the sugar. Once the sugar is dissolved, do not stir again. (Over-stirring can cause the sugar to crystallize and make the toffee grainy.) If sugar crystals appear on the side of the saucepan, brush them down with a pastry brush dipped in water.

5. Bring the mixture to a boil over high heat and boil until the caramel reaches the hard crack stage (300°F or 150°C) on a candy thermometer), 8 to 10 minutes. You will see the mixture darken, and it will begin to smell like caramel.

6. Remove the pan from the heat, then stir in the vanilla extract and chopped almonds.

7. Pour the toffee mixture into the prepared baking pan and spread it evenly. Allow the toffee to firm up for a few minutes, but do not allow it to cool completely.

8. Pour the chocolate chips over the warm toffee. Allow the chocolate to melt from the heat of the toffee, then spread the melted chocolate to coat the toffee evenly. If desired, sprinkle the top with flaky sea salt. Allow the toffee and chocolate to cool completely.

9. Break the toffee into pieces with your hands. Store in an airtight container.

MEXICAN HOT CHOCOLATE TRUFFLES

MAKES 3 DOZEN TRUFFLES

Truffles seem like a luxurious treat, but they are actually quite easy to make and infinitely customizable by varying the flavorings used to infuse the cream at the beginning or added to the ganache at the end, or both. To finish your truffles, you can dip them in melted chocolate for a hard outer shell, roll them in a coating such as chopped nuts, or simply dust them with cocoa powder, as I do here.

These truffles were inspired by my favorite coffeehouse drink, Mexican Hot Chocolate. With a double dose of cinnamon and a pinch of cayenne, they mimic the warm spiciness of that delicious concoction.

- 1 cup heavy cream
- ½ vanilla bean, cut in half lengthwise and opened
- 1 cinnamon stick
- 1¼ pounds bittersweet or semi-sweet chocolate
- ½ teaspoon ground cinnamon
- ¼ teaspoon cayenne powder
- ¼ teaspoon espresso powder (optional; see box, below)
- Pinch of salt
- 2 tablespoons butter, softened
- Cocoa powder for dusting

1. Combine the cream, vanilla bean, and cinnamon stick in a small saucepan and bring just to a boil over medium-high heat. Remove the pan from the heat, cover, and allow the vanilla and cinnamon to steep in the cream for up to 1 hour.

2. In the meantime, finely chop the chocolate and put it in a heatproof glass bowl. Add the cinnamon, cayenne, espresso powder, and salt.

3. When the cream is infused to your liking, remove the cinnamon stick and the vanilla bean and bring the cream back up to a simmer over medium heat.

4. Pour the warm cream over the chocolate and stir until completely smooth. (If the cream was not warm enough to melt the chocolate, microwave it in 10-second bursts until the chocolate is completely melted.) Stir in the butter. Cover the bowl and refrigerate until the mixture is firm, about 2 hours.

5. Cover two baking sheets with parchment paper.

6. Using a melon baller or two teaspoons, scoop spoonfuls of ganache onto the baking sheets. You should be able to get at least 3 dozen. (If the ganache is too firm to scoop, allow it to come to room temperature and try again.) Use your hands to roll the scoops of ganache into smooth balls. Dust the truffles with a light coating of cocoa powder.

7. Store the truffles in the refrigerator until ready to serve or swap.

Packaging

You can package the truffles by the dozen in a cellophane bag, or for a fancier presentation, place each truffle in an individual paper or foil candy cup in a pretty box.

USING ESPRESSO POWDER

Espresso powder is made of coffee crystals that dissolve quickly in liquid and is different from regular instant coffee. When used in small quantities, espresso powder enhances the flavor of chocolate without adding a coffee taste. If you do not have espresso powder, feel free to omit it.

SALTED CARAMEL SAUCE

This recipe makes a French-inspired, less sweet, more buttery version of caramel sauce. A small drizzle turns ordinary ice cream or pound cake into a dessert fit for company. A pint-sized jar of salted caramel sauce, such as this recipe makes, sells for $15 at fancy grocery stores. So imagine everyone's delight when you bring this delectable confection to the food swap. Just do not tell them how inexpensive and quick it is to make.

The only tricky thing about this recipe is knowing when the sugar syrup is done. With sugar, it is a fine line between caramelized and burnt. Do not be tempted to multitask or walk away from the stove while the sugar syrup is boiling. Give the pot your full attention, and watch the changing color and smell as the sugar caramelizes.

1½	cups heavy cream
1	cup sugar
2	tablespoons corn syrup
¼	cup water
½	cup (1 stick) butter, cut into pieces
2	teaspoons vanilla extract
1½	teaspoons kosher salt

Packaging

Package the caramel sauce into four clean 4-ounce glass jars. Decorate with a label or hanging tag, and label as perishable.

Note: *The caramel will bubble up furiously when the cream is added in step 4, so select a deeper pot than you might be inclined to otherwise.*

1. Bring the cream to a boil over high heat in a small saucepan. Turn the heat down to low and keep the cream at a simmer until step 4.

2. In a large, heavy-bottomed saucepan, combine the sugar, corn syrup, and water, then turn heat to high. Stir just until the sugar is dissolved, then stop and do not stir again. Bring the mixture to a boil, occasionally brushing down the sides of the pot with a pastry brush dipped in water to dissolve any sugar crystals.

3. Continue to boil the sugar syrup over high heat without stirring until it turns a golden brown and smells like caramel, 7 to 8 minutes. Do not allow it to burn.

4. Turn down the heat to medium and slowly pour in the cream while stirring, being careful, as the mixture will bubble up.

5. Remove the pot from the heat and add the butter. Stir until the butter is melted and the mixture is completely smooth. Then stir in the vanilla extract and salt.

6. Allow the sauce to cool before pouring into glass jars. Refrigerate until ready to swap or use.

BAKED GOODS

BAKED GOODS ARE the food swap gateway drug. People who are new to a food swap or a little unsure of the concept typically bring baked goods. After all, we are all familiar with bake sales and cookie exchanges. Newcomers often think a food swap will be similar to those events and then are amazed by the diversity of the offerings.

Veteran food swappers sometimes announce at the beginning of a swap that they will bring home only healthy items this time, but inevitably I see those same people packing up cupcakes or macaroons at the end of the afternoon. Who can resist bringing home a fabulously indulgent dessert, especially if it looks beautiful, is charmingly packaged, or has a unique twist? And if you have left your children for the afternoon to attend the food swap, you had better bring home something sweet to atone for your absence.

Of course, not all the baked goods one sees at food swaps are sweet. Many swappers bring savory baked goods, such as bagels, rolls, and other small breads. Bread bakers are perfectionists, seeking that perfect recipe or technique for re-creating fabulous bakery breads at home. Those people make ideal food swappers, because perfection only comes with repeated attempts.

A few things to note about bringing baked goods: There are likely to be many choices, so make yours stand out. Because most of the attendees are relatively experienced cooks and bakers themselves, basic cookies or brownies probably won't receive a lot of attention. Unusual or hard-to-make items will. Of course, if your item is insanely delicious even though it appears simple, provide a sample and you should have plenty of offers.

Packaging also matters. First, make sure that your baked goods are well packaged for transport; if your treats arrive smashed, you will have fewer takers, and if they do not make it home to their final destination in good condition, people may be reluctant to trade with you again. But also consider the appearance — bakery boxes, pretty treat bags tied with twine or ribbon, and charming labels will make your baked goods stand out.

Lastly, think small. Bringing a whole loaf of bread or a pie to a food swap will make it hard to find a swap item that is equal in value. So think about miniature loaves, individual-size cakes, and other smaller items — you'll find plenty of ideas in this section. And when packaging multiples of cookies, cupcakes, or bars, think in small quantities. Package items by twos, fours, or sixes, not by the dozen. You can always offer to swap two or more bags for a highly desirable item.

MELTED-BUTTER BACON
CHOCOLATE CHIP COOKIES
MAKES 2 DOZEN COOKIES

Bacon! It's not just for breakfast anymore. Bakers and confectioners have started incorporating the smoky, salty goodness of bacon into all kinds of dessert recipes from chocolate bars to cupcakes. Here it makes an appearance in gooey chocolate chip cookies.

This recipe comes from MaryBeth Jirgal, a mother of four and a passionate baker. MaryBeth originally used regular chocolate chips in this recipe but changed to chopped dark chocolate at the suggestion of Katherine Duncan, the owner of Katherine Anne Confections, which hosted the Chicago Food Swap in February 2013. What an amazing opportunity for a home cook to learn from one of Chicago's finest artisan candy makers.

- 8 slices thick-cut, applewood-smoked bacon
- 1½ cups all-purpose flour
- ¾ teaspoon baking soda
- 1 teaspoon salt
- 6 tablespoons butter, melted and cooled slightly
- 2 tablespoons bacon fat
- ¾ cup packed light brown sugar
- ¼ cup sugar
- 1 extra-large egg at room temperature
- 8 ounces dark chocolate, cut into small chunks

Packaging

Because these cookies are soft and gooey, package them carefully in a sturdy cookie box or a grease-resistant cookie bag. If using a box or tin, line the bottom with waxed paper. Package 4 to 6 cookies together, depending on the size.

1. Preheat the oven to 400°F (200°C) and arrange the bacon in a single layer on a rimmed sheet pan. Cook the bacon for 15 minutes, then turn the slices and continue to cook for 5 to 10 more minutes until bacon is crisp but not overdone. Save 2 tablespoons of the rendered bacon fat for the cookie batter. Drain the bacon well on paper towels and, when cool, dice. You should have 1 cup of chopped bacon. Turn heat down to 375 °F (190°C).

2. In a small bowl, whisk together the flour, baking soda, and salt. Set aside.

3. Combine the butter, bacon fat, and both sugars into the bowl of a stand mixer and beat on medium speed until butter is incorporated, 2 to 3 minutes.

4. In a small bowl, lightly beat the egg with a fork. Add the egg to the butter mixture and beat on medium speed until creamy and light, about 4 minutes. Reduce the speed to low, add the dry ingredients, and mix until just incorporated. Mix in the chocolate chunks and chopped bacon.

5. Using a large cookie or ice cream scoop, scoop 2 tablespoons of batter onto cookie sheets, 9 cookies to a sheet. Flatten slightly.

6. Bake, one sheet at a time, until golden, 11 to 13 minutes.

7. Transfer the cookies to a rack to cool. Repeat with the rest of the batter, using cooled baking sheets.

VARIATION

These cookies can be made vegetarian by replacing the bacon fat with melted butter and replacing the diced bacon with diced dried fruit, such as cherries.

OATMEAL BREAKFAST COOKIES
WITH PEPITAS AND DRIED CRANBERRIES
MAKES ABOUT 3 DOZEN COOKIES

There are always a lot of baked goods at a food swap, but these breakfast cookies stand out because they are more than just an indulgence. With whole-wheat flour, wheat germ, oats, pumpkin seeds, and dried cranberries, these cookies are filling and nutritious, making them an ideal on-the-go breakfast or snack.

I developed this recipe to be nut- and peanut-free because many schools today ban these common allergens. I wanted these cookies to be something that a child could bring to school for a snack or in a lunchbox. If nuts are not a concern for your family, feel free to replace the pumpkin seeds with your favorite nut for added protein.

FOR THE COOKIES

- 1½ cups all-purpose flour
- 1 cup whole-wheat flour
- 2 tablespoons wheat germ
- 2 teaspoons cinnamon
- 1 teaspoon baking soda
- 1 teaspoon salt
- 1 cup butter (2 sticks), at room temperature
- 1½ cups brown sugar
- 2 large eggs at room temperature
- 1 teaspoon vanilla extract
- Zest of 1 orange
- 2 cups rolled oats
- ½ cup dried cranberries
- ½ cup green pumpkin seeds (pepitas)

FOR THE GLAZE

- 1 cup powdered sugar, sifted
- ¼ cup maple syrup
- 1 tablespoon orange juice

1. Preheat the oven to 350°F (175°C). Line three baking sheets with silicone baking liners or parchment paper.

2. In a small bowl, whisk together the flours, wheat germ, cinnamon, baking soda, and salt. Set aside.

3. In the bowl of a standing mixer, cream the butter and brown sugar until light and fluffy, about 3 minutes. Add the eggs one at a time, the vanilla extract, and the orange zest, and mix well.

4. Gradually add the flour mixture and mix thoroughly, scraping the sides of the bowl as necessary. Fold in the rolled oats, dried cranberries, and pumpkin seeds.

5. With dampened hands, scoop balls of dough the size of ping-pong balls onto the cookie sheets. You should get 9 cookies to a sheet. Flatten the balls gently with a spatula or your hand.

6. Bake 15 to 17 minutes until the edges are golden. Cool on a wire rack.

7. While the cookies are cooling, make the glaze: In a small bowl, whisk together the sifted powdered sugar, maple syrup, and orange juice. Drizzle the glaze over the cooled cookies. Allow the glaze to harden before storing the cookies.

Packaging

Package 6 cookies together in a small bakery box or treat bag for swapping.

LAVENDER SHORTBREAD

MAKES 4 DOZEN COOKIES

This elegant cookie appeals to sophisticated palates. Shortbread makes a great swap item, because it keeps for several days without going stale. The rice flour gives the shortbread a melt-in-your-mouth texture.

Be restrained when baking with lavender, or you will feel like you are eating soap. Here, dried lavender is mixed with sugar to add a subtle floral note to the dough; then the cookies are garnished with a few blossoms for visual appeal. The lavender sugar, by the way, makes a charming, easy-to-prepare swap item in its own right.

2	cups (4 sticks) butter at room temperature
¾	cup lavender sugar (see recipe, page 195)
¾	cup caster or powdered sugar
2	teaspoons vanilla extract
1	teaspoon salt
4	cups all-purpose flour
½	cup rice flour
½	cup turbinado or other coarse sugar
1	egg white
1	tablespoon dried lavender

Packaging

Package the cookies by the dozen in a cellophane bag or small box. A decorative sprig of dried lavender tied to the label is a nice touch.

1. Cream the butter, lavender sugar, and caster/powdered sugar in the bowl of a standing mixer just until combined, 1 to 2 minutes. Add the vanilla and salt.

2. Combine the all-purpose and rice flours and gradually add in batches, mixing just until combined. The dough will be stiff and crumbly.

3. Divide the dough into 2 equal pieces. Roll each piece of dough into a log approximately 12 inches long, and wrap the logs in parchment or waxed paper. Refrigerate dough overnight or for at least 2 hours.

4. To bake the cookies, preheat the oven to 350°F (175°C) and line two baking sheets with parchment paper or silicone baking liners. Spread the turbinado sugar on a piece of waxed paper. Paint the outside of each log of dough with egg white and roll in the sugar until well coated.

5. Slice the log into cookies ¼ inch thick and place them on the baking sheet, leaving ample room between them, for they will spread. (You should get a dozen to a sheet.) Poke each cookie with the tines of a fork several times to create holes. Sprinkle 5 or 6 lavender blossoms on each cookie and gently press in. (If you have trouble getting your lavender blossoms to stay on, try baking the cookies for 2 minutes before adding them.)

6. Bake the cookies for 18 to 20 minutes until the center is firm to the touch and the outside is browned. Cool on a wire rack. Store in an airtight container.

MINIATURE FRUIT PIES

MAKES 8 (5-INCH) CRUSTS FOR 4 DOUBLE-CRUSTED PIES

Not just for food swapping, miniature desserts are quite popular for entertaining as well. To bake them, invest in a set of 5-inch miniature pie plates, which often come sold in sets of four. They are useful for baking individual savory pies and quiches as well. You can also purchase a miniature pie baking sheet; Wilton sells one that has six cavities.

I make pie dough in the food processor because I find that is the best way to incorporate the butter into the flour while still leaving some small pieces of butter intact for an extra-flaky crust. You can work the butter in by hand using a pastry cutter if you prefer. I recommend an all-butter pastry for the best flavor. Using European-style butter with a higher butterfat content will make a difference. The acid in the lemon juice or vinegar acts as a tenderizer.

1   cup (2 sticks) cold butter

2½   cups all-purpose flour

1   tablespoon sugar

2   teaspoons salt

1   tablespoon lemon juice
    or red wine vinegar

½   cup ice water

1   quart fruit pie filling (such as
    Sour Cherry Pie Filling, page
    218)

1   egg (optional)

    Turbinado
    or other coarse sugar

Packaging

I suggest putting something supportive under the pies, such as cardboard, for storage and transport. Package in a bakery box and tie with a ribbon or piece of raffia.

Note: *Because the pie will be removed from the plate before swapping, you have to be sure that the bottom crust is sturdy, or else you could end up with a mess on your hands. A less risky alternative is to bake them in disposable miniature pie plates. You can find these online at restaurant supply stores.*

1. Cut the butter into small cubes and put half of them in the freezer; return the other half to the refrigerator until needed.

2. Combine the flour, sugar, and salt in the bowl of a food processor and pulse a few times to mix. Add the chilled butter from the refrigerator to the dry ingredients and process until the mixture resembles coarse meal.

3. Add the frozen butter to the food processor and pulse until the butter is in small but still visible pieces. Remove the dough and put it in a medium bowl.

4. Combine the lemon juice or vinegar and ice water, add 10 tablespoons of the mixture to the butter-flour mixture, and stir with a fork until the dough begins to come together. Pinch a bit of the dough, and if it holds together, you do not need to add more liquid. If it is still dry, add the remaining liquid, ½ tablespoon at a time.

5. Knead the dough in the bowl or on a floured board until it forms a ball. Divide the dough into 8 equal portions, each weighing about 3 ounces, and wrap each portion well in plastic wrap. Place the dough in the refrigerator to relax for at least a half hour but preferably for several hours.

6. Working with one or two balls at a time, remove the dough from the refrigerator. If chilled for more than a half hour, allow it to soften a little before rolling it out.

recipe continued on next page

7. Prior to rolling out the dough, strike it with your rolling pin to flatten; this will soften it further. Liberally dust a pastry board or mat and a rolling pin with flour.

8. Roll the dough out in a circle, rotating it and turning it frequently, adding more flour as necessary to keep it from sticking, until it is 6 inches in diameter and 1/4 inch thick. (Do not roll the dough too thin, because these miniature pies will not have a pie plate to support them and therefore need a thicker bottom crust than full-size pies do; see note.)

9. Spray the miniature pie plates with nonstick cooking spray. Place four of the dough circles in the pie plates. Lightly dust the bottom of the crust with flour. Add 1 cup pie filling to each pie.

10. Top each pie with another circle of dough — you can roll the top crusts out a bit thinner than the bottom crusts — and pinch the edges together. Seal by crimping the edges with your finger or the tines of a fork. Cut small holes or a ½-inch slit in the top crust to vent. Alternatively, you can cut half of the pie dough circles into ½-inch strips and weave a lattice top.

11. Place the pie plates in the freezer to chill for at least 20 minutes. (You can also wrap the pie plates well in plastic wrap and freeze the unbaked pies for up to a week.)

12. To bake, preheat the oven to 400°F (200°C). For a glossy finish, beat an egg with 1 tablespoon of water to make an egg wash. Brush the tops and sides of the pies with the egg wash. Sprinkle with turbinado sugar, if desired.

13. Bake at 400°F (200°C) for 15 minutes. Reduce the heat to 350°F (175°C) and bake for an additional 30 to 35 minutes until the crust is golden and the filling bubbly. Keep an eye on the pies while baking. If the crust begins to brown, cover it with a pie shield or strips of foil.

14. Set the pies in their plates on a wire rack and allow them to cool completely.

15. Carefully remove the pies from the plates when cool.

MINI BUNDT CAKES WITH CHOCOLATE GANACHE

MAKES 12 TO 14 CAKES

While this sounds like one of those recipes aimed at tricking children into eating more vegetables, chocolate zucchini cake is a real dessert. As with carrot cake, the zucchini adds moisture, a little bit of a texture, and some marginal nutritional value.

This recipe is adapted from one that food writer Kim O'Donnel posted on her *Washington Post* blog in the early 2000s. It had already been a staple in my kitchen for a dozen years when I adapted it into the more swappable mini Bundt cake size and added a ganache glaze. The cakes can be made a day or two in advance, then topped with the ganache on the day of the swap. Or if the chocolate ganache is too much trouble, just dust the tops with some powdered sugar.

FOR THE CAKES

- 3 ounces unsweetened baking chocolate
- 3 cups all-purpose flour
- 1½ teaspoons baking powder
- 1 teaspoon baking soda
- 2 teaspoons espresso powder (optional; see page 98)
- 2 teaspoons cinnamon
- 1 teaspoon salt
- 1½ cups sugar
- 4 large eggs at room temperature
- 1½ cups vegetable oil
- 2 cups grated zucchini (typically 1 large zucchini)
- 1 cup semisweet chocolate chips

FOR THE GANACHE

- 8 ounces semisweet chocolate, chopped
- ½ cup heavy cream

Note: A 6-cavity mini Bundt pan is required for this recipe. Two such pans will make the baking go even quicker. Miniature Bundt cakes also make wonderful desserts for entertaining and giving.

1. Preheat the oven to 350°F (175°C). Spray the insides of two 6-cavity mini Bundt pans with nonstick baking spray.

2. Melt the unsweetened chocolate in a small saucepan over very low heat. Set aside and allow to cool.

3. Whisk together the flour, baking powder, baking soda, espresso powder (if using), cinnamon, and salt in a medium bowl and set aside.

4. In the bowl of a standing mixer, mix the sugar and eggs together on medium speed until light and thick, about 2 minutes. Gradually add the oil while mixing on low speed. Continue to mix until the batter is thick and bright yellow, about 1½ minutes.

5. Add the melted chocolate to the batter and mix. Gradually add the flour mixture, scraping down the sides as necessary. Mix in the zucchini and chocolate chips by hand, making sure that they are thoroughly incorporated.

6. Ladle the batter into the cavities of the pans, making sure to not fill them more than two-thirds of the way full. Smooth the tops with a knife dipped in water. (It is critical that you do not overfill the cavities, or you will end up with something that looks like a muffin with a dimpled bottom, not a cake with a hole in the middle.)

7. Bake for 20 to 25 minutes, or until a tester inserted in the middle comes out clean.

Packaging

Package in bakery boxes,
2 cakes per box, for swapping.

8. Cool the cakes on a wire rack before removing them from the pan. Cool the cakes completely before glazing.

9. To make the glaze, put the chopped chocolate in a heatproof bowl. Bring the cream just to a boil and pour it over the chocolate. Allow the heat of the cream to melt the chocolate, then whisk together. Allow the ganache to cool for 5 minutes.

10. To glaze the cakes, drizzle the ganache on the top of each cake, letting some run down the sides. Alternatively, you can dip the tops of the cakes directly in the ganache, then allow it to cool.

FREEZING AND THAWING BAKED GOODS

What if you come home from a food swap and realize that you have more baked goods than you can possibly eat before they go stale? Freeze some of them for the following weeks. Some baked goods freeze better than others, so be smart about which items to eat right away and which to freeze for later. Anything without frosting or glaze will freeze better than a frosted or glazed item. Muffins and quick breads freeze especially well. Items should be completely cooled, not warm from the oven, before freezing.

To preserve the quality of your item, wrap it well before freezing to keep out air and avoid freezer burn. I suggest wrapping items twice: once in plastic wrap, so that the entire surface of the item is covered, and then a second time either in foil or a plastic freezer bag. Well-wrapped, baked goods will keep for at least 2 weeks and up to a month without losing quality. (Baked goods may be safely frozen for even longer, but the quality will begin to deteriorate.) If freezing multiple items, such as muffins, wrap them individually and combine into a freezer bag. That way you can thaw one or two at a time.

To thaw frozen baked goods, remove from the freezer but do not unwrap. Most baked goods can be thawed at room temperature, but thaw glazed or frosted items in the refrigerator.

MATCHA CUPCAKES
WITH GINGER FROSTING
MAKES 2 DOZEN CUPCAKES

The proliferation of cupcake shops, cupcake cookbooks, and cupcake competition shows would seem to indicate that Americans are powerless in the face of a good cupcake. Food swappers are no different. There is always at least one cupcake at every food swap, and it is usually a hot item. Cupcakes for a food swap should stand out in some way, whether because of an unusual flavor profile or a particularly beautiful presentation.

This recipe falls into the category of an unusual flavor profile, and the combination of matcha, or green tea powder, and ginger usually draws curious trading partners. Matcha has a slightly earthy, vegetal flavor and ginger has a bit of a kick, so this cupcake appeals to adult palates.

FOR THE CUPCAKES

- 2 cups all-purpose flour
- 1 tablespoon matcha powder
- 2 teaspoons baking powder
- 1 teaspoon ground ginger
- ½ teaspoon salt
- ½ cup (1 stick) plus 2 table-spoons butter, softened
- 1½ cups sugar
- 2 extra-large eggs (or 2 large eggs and 1 egg yolk) at room temperature
- 2 teaspoons vanilla extract
- 1¼ cups whole milk

FOR THE FROSTING

- 3 cups powdered sugar
- 1 tablespoon ground ginger
- ¾ cup heavy cream
- Candied ginger (optional)

1. Preheat the oven to 350°F (175°C) and line two cupcake pans with paper liners.

2. Whisk together the flour, matcha, baking powder, ground ginger, and salt in a small bowl and set aside.

3. In the bowl of a standing mixer, cream the butter and sugar until light and fluffy, about 3 minutes. Add the eggs one at a time, scraping down the sides after each addition. Add the vanilla extract and combine.

4. Alternate adding the dry ingredients and milk, starting and ending with the dry ingredients and scraping down the sides as necessary. Stir just until combined.

5. Divide the batter evenly among the prepared pans, filling each cavity half to two-thirds full, about 2 heaping tablespoons per cupcake.

6. Bake for 18 to 22 minutes or until a tester inserted in the middle comes out clean. Cool on a wire rack. Cool completely before frosting.

7. To make the frosting, sift the powdered sugar and ginger together in a bowl. Whisk in the heavy cream until smooth.

8. Spread icing on each cupcake with an offset spatula or pipe it with a piping bag. Garnish each cupcake with a small sliver of candied ginger, if desired.

Packaging

Package cupcakes in groups of 4 for swapping. Use a bakery box, preferably one with a cupcake insert, for easy transport.

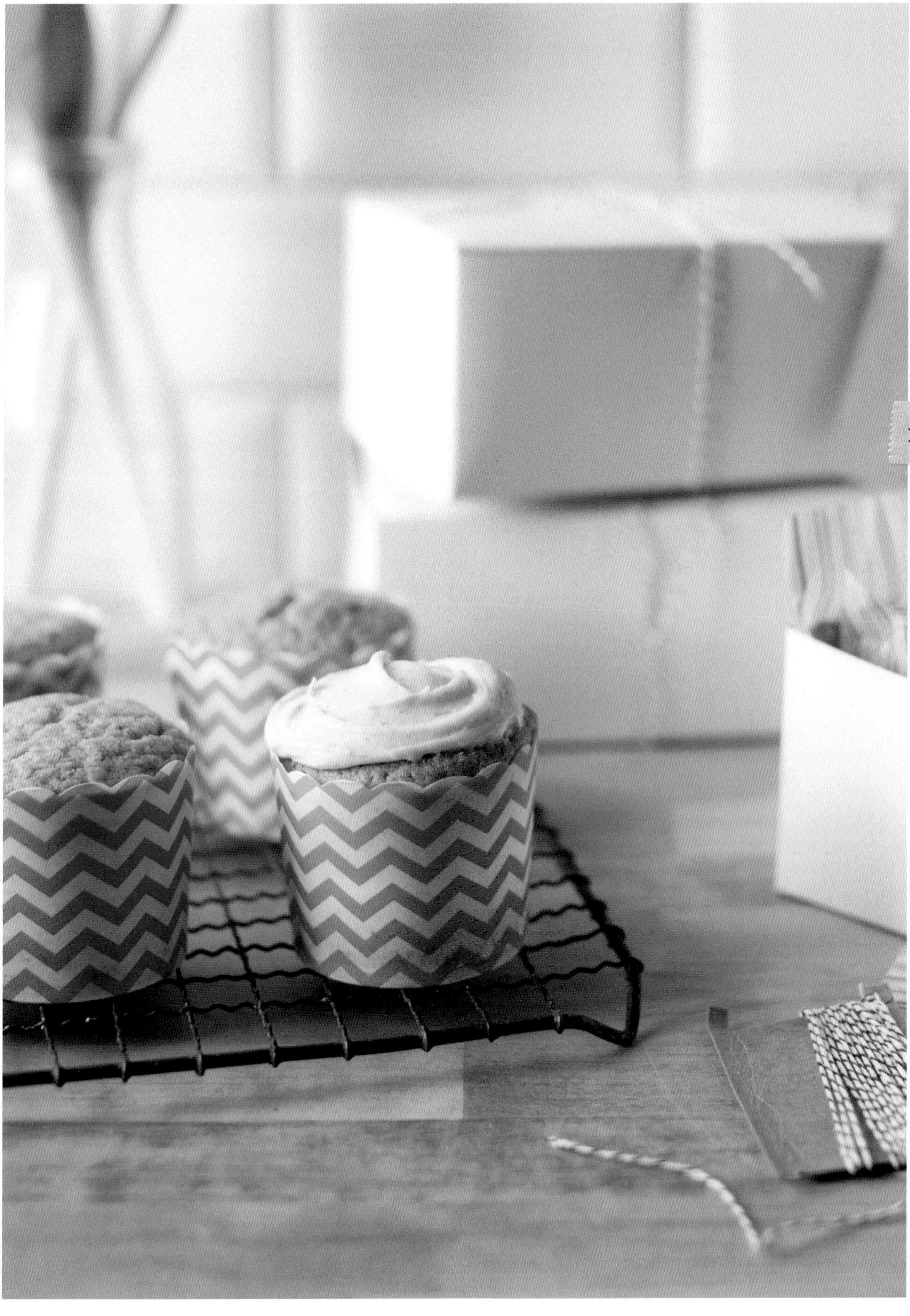

WHOOPIE PIES

MAKES 1 DOZEN WHOOPIE PIES

The same traits that made whoopie pies an old-fashioned lunchbox staple also make them an ideal swap item: small size and portability. Plus, whoopie pies are clearly having a moment right now. While I would not say that I see whoopie pies at every swap, they do appear frequently and when they do, people are thoroughly delighted.

Most whoopie pies are filled with marshmallow creme combined with a buttercream frosting. Because the zeitgeist of the food swap is homemade, I prefer to make my own marshmallow creme, which is relatively simple. To streamline this project, you can always buy the marshmallow creme. On the other hand, homemade marshmallow creme would make a fun swap item in its own right.

FOR THE CAKES

2	cups all-purpose flour
¼	cup cocoa powder
2	teaspoons espresso powder
1	teaspoon baking powder
1	teaspoon baking soda
1	teaspoon salt
½	cup (1 stick) butter at room temperature
1	cup sugar
1	large egg at room temperature
1	tablespoon vanilla extract
1	cup buttermilk

FOR THE FILLING

8	ounces marshmallow creme (see recipe, facing page)
6	tablespoons butter at room temperature
1⅓	cups powdered sugar, sifted
1	teaspoon vanilla extract
	Pinch of salt

1. Preheat the oven to 350°F (175°C). Line two baking sheets with parchment paper or, if using a whoopie pie pan, spray the pan lightly with nonstick cooking spray.

2. Sift together the flour, cocoa powder, espresso powder, baking powder, baking soda, and salt in a medium bowl. Set aside.

3. In the bowl of a standing mixer, cream the butter and sugar until well combined, about 3 minutes. Add the egg and vanilla extract, and mix until combined.

4. Alternate adding the flour mixture and the buttermilk, starting and ending with the flour mixture. Mix just until combined. The batter will be thick.

5. Spoon 2 tablespoons of batter onto the prepared baking sheets, leaving plenty of space in between each cake, and spread in a circle. Repeat with the remaining batter. You should have 24 cakes, 12 on each sheet. If using a whoopie pie pan, fill each cavity approximately two-thirds full and spread the batter to the edges.

6. Bake the cakes 10 to 12 minutes or until the top springs back when touched. Cool in pans for 5 minutes before removing to a wire rack. Cool completely before filling.

7. To make the filling, combine the marshmallow creme, butter, powdered sugar, vanilla extract, and salt in the bowl of a standing mixer, and beat until smooth.

8. Place a heaping tablespoon of filling on the bottom of one cake and top with a second cake. Do not overfill. Repeat with the remaining cakes.

Marshmallow Creme

MAKES 1 PINT (8 OUNCES) CREME

2 egg whites (about ¼ cup) at room temperature

¼ teaspoon cream of tartar

¾ cup sugar

½ cup light corn syrup

¼ cup water

1 teaspoon vanilla extract

Packaging

Package 2 whoopie pies together in a bakery box or plastic clamshell. For home consumption, I recommend wrapping pies individually in plastic wrap.

1. Combine the egg whites and cream of tartar in the bowl of a standing mixer. Beat on high speed until the eggs form soft peaks. Set aside.

2. Combine the sugar, corn syrup, and water in a medium saucepan and bring to a boil over high heat but do not stir. Heat until the mixture registers 240°F (116°C) on a candy thermometer. Remove from the heat.

3. With the mixer on low, slowly pour the sugar syrup into the egg whites. Turn the speed to high and beat until the mixture resembles marshmallow creme, about 5 minutes. Add the vanilla extract and beat for 1 minute.

4. Pour the creme into a pint jar and refrigerate until needed.

VARIATION

For a refreshing alternative, try substituting 1 teaspoon peppermint extract for the vanilla extract in the filling.

FOOD WRITERS AND RECIPE developers always have more food than they can consume themselves. That was enough motivation for Emily Han to start a food swap in her hometown after reading about the Portland food swap on the blog *Cooking Up a Story*. When Emily held the first LA Food Swap in March 2011, almost 30 people showed up.

The LA Food Swap quickly became so popular that Emily could not keep up with the demand, and she didn't want the swaps to become so large that swappers could no longer talk about the food they had brought. The solution was to encourage people to start food swaps throughout Southern California. As part of her role as a mentor to others looking to start food swaps, Emily joined forces with Kate Payne to create the Food Swap Network, an invaluable resource for the broader food swap movement.

The solution was to encourage people to start food swaps throughout Southern California.

Emily attributes the growth of the Southern California food swap scene to the area's natural abundance. In a place where people have amazing produce growing in their yards, a food swap is a fun and rewarding way to deal with the otherwise overwhelming bounty. Another explanation for the popularity of food swapping in Southern California is the geography: in an area that is so spread out, people crave a sense of community. People find community through food swaps by meeting their neighbors and others who share their passion for local, homemade food.

The offerings at the LA Food Swap reflect the cultural and ethnic diversity of the city. Emily reports that swappers regularly bring items from different global cuisines, from kimchi to chimichurri to Latin American pastries and salsa. The LA Food Swap is especially known for creative and eye-catching food packaging.

Emily did not set out to create a community with the LA Food Swap; she just thought it would be a fun way to share food. Later, she realized that many connections had formed as a result of the swap. Some of the early swappers have since started food businesses, and they support each other. And of course, there are all those Southern California food swaps that trace their roots back to the LA Food Swap.

BANANA-CHOCOLATE MUFFINS

MAKES 2 DOZEN MUFFINS

This recipe comes from swapper Genevieve Boehme, a regular at the Chicago Food Swap, where these muffins are very popular. Genevieve has adapted a favorite recipe to include whole grains and be less sweet than the typical breakfast muffin. With whole-wheat flour, wheat germ, and bananas, these muffins are practically health food. Okay, maybe not. But the whole grains do add a delightful nuttiness.

1½ cups all-purpose flour

1½ cups whole-wheat flour

1 cup sugar

2 tablespoons ground flaxseed or wheat germ

1 tablespoon baking soda

1 teaspoon salt

½ teaspoon ground nutmeg

½ teaspoon ground ginger

1 cup vegetable oil

2 large eggs, at room temperature

5 overripe bananas, mashed

6 tablespoons buttermilk

1½ cups semisweet chocolate chips

1. Preheat the oven to 375°F (190°C). Grease muffin pans or line with paper liners.

2. Combine the flours, sugar, flaxseed, baking soda, salt, nutmeg, and ginger in a medium bowl and whisk thoroughly with a fork.

3. Whisk together the oil, eggs, bananas, and buttermilk in a large bowl until well combined.

4. Add the dry mixture to the wet ingredients, and mix well with a fork until everything is well incorporated. Fold in the chocolate chips.

5. Scoop the batter into the muffin pans, filling the cups three-fourths full. (An ice cream scoop works well for this purpose.)

6. Bake for 18 to 22 minutes until muffins are golden brown and the tops spring back when touched. Cool them in the pan for about 5 minutes, then remove to a wire rack.

Packaging

Genevieve packages these muffins by four in a quart-size box, such as those you find at farmers' markets, lined with parchment paper. Cover with plastic wrap, tie with a pretty ribbon, and add a tag for an attractive presentation.

MINI CRANBERRY-ORANGE
QUICK BREADS
MAKES 3 MINIATURE LOAVES

This is a favorite item to bring to winter food swaps. I buy quarts of fresh Wisconsin cranberries in the fall and freeze them to use throughout the winter months. I love cranberries in baked goods because of the way that they retain their shape and turn bright scarlet. They are tart, however, so feel free to add a little more sugar if you prefer sweeter baked goods.

I am a nut for streusel. I like to finish my baked goods with a sweet, crumbly topping wherever possible. I make mine in the food processor because I find that it is the most effective way to break up the butter, but you can use a pastry blender if you prefer. This recipe makes much more streusel than you need, so plan to freeze the excess and save it for another use.

FOR THE TOPPING

- 1 cup all-purpose flour
- ¾ cup sugar
- ¼ cup brown sugar
- ½ teaspoon salt
- ½ cup (1 stick) cold butter cut into cubes

FOR THE QUICK BREADS

- 1¾ cups all-purpose flour
- ¾ cup sugar
- 2 teaspoons baking powder
- 1 teaspoon salt
- ½ cup vegetable oil
- 2 large eggs at room temperature
- 1 tablespoon vanilla extract
  Zest of 1 orange
- ½ cup sour cream
- 2 cups fresh or frozen cranberries

Packaging

Cut pieces of cardboard to fit the bottom of each loaf. Place the loaves on the cardboard and wrap in plastic or festive paper.

Note: To bake these miniature loaves, you can choose to invest in a set of miniature loaf pans of approximately 5 ¾ inches by 3 inches. They are typically sold in sets of three or four and cost under $20. Oven-safe paper bakeware also works.

1. To make the streusel topping, combine the flour, sugar, brown sugar, and salt in a food processor and pulse a few times to combine. Add the butter and pulse 25 to 30 times until the butter is in gravel-size pieces and the mixture resembles coarse crumbs. Put in the freezer until ready to use.

2. Preheat the oven to 350°F (175°C) and grease three miniature loaf pans.

3. To make the quick breads, combine the flour, sugar, baking powder, and salt in a small bowl and set aside.

4. In the bowl of a standing mixer, cream the oil and sugar until light and fluffy. Add the eggs one at a time, the vanilla, and the orange zest, scraping down the bowl as necessary, and mix until combined.

5. Alternate adding the dry ingredients and the sour cream, beginning and ending with the dry ingredients, and mixing each just until combined.

6. Fold in the cranberries by hand so as not to crush them.

7. Divide the batter evenly among the three prepared pans.

8. Top each pan with one-third of the streusel topping.

9. Bake until the top of each loaf is golden and a tester inserted in the middle comes out clean, 45 to 50 minutes. Cool the loaves on a wire rack before removing them from the pans.

BRINGING SAVORY BAKED GOODS TO A FOOD SWAP

As with sweets, savory baked goods are best in small sizes, such as rolls, individual flat-breads, packages of crackers, bagels, and so on. Also, stick with breads that will travel well and do not turn stale quickly. Doughs that contain some fat will result in a product with a longer shelf life.

A beautiful small loaf of bread hardly needs fancy packaging to make it stand out. For smaller items such as flatbreads, rolls, and crackers, bakery boxes or a cellophane bag tied with a nice ribbon make for easy and attractive packaging. Depending on the size, you may want to package 2, 4, or 6 small breads together.

NAAN

MAKES 1 DOZEN

When my daughter, Zoe, was in sixth grade, she volunteered me to make naan and mango lassi for her social studies project on India. I had never made either. But I was pleasantly surprised by how fun and easy making naan turned out to be. I began making it regularly for family meals, particularly Indian-inspired ones. I soon realized that, because of its small size, naan is a perfect savory baked good to swap.

Naan is best enjoyed hot and brushed with melted butter or ghee, so advise your trading partner to wrap it in foil and reheat it in a hot oven before consuming. A sprinkle of chopped cilantro is a nice touch.

1   package (2¼ teaspoons) active dry yeast

    Pinch of sugar

¾   cup warm water, between 110 and 120°F (43–49°C)

3   cups all-purpose flour

1   teaspoon honey

½   cup plain Greek yogurt, preferably full fat

2   tablespoons vegetable oil

1   teaspoon salt

Packaging

Package 3 or 4 naan together in a plastic bakery bag.

1. Combine the yeast, sugar, and water in a large bowl and allow to stand until foamy, about 10 minutes.

2. Add flour, honey, yogurt, oil, and salt to the bowl and stir together until a dough forms.

3. Turn the dough out onto a well-floured board and knead until smooth, about 5 minutes.

4. Place the dough in a well-oiled bowl and cover with plastic wrap. Put the bowl in a warm place and allow the dough to rise until doubled in size, about 1 hour.

5. Punch down the dough and turn it out onto a well-floured board. Knead a few times to expel any additional gas. Divide the dough into 2 equal halves, then divide each half into 6 equal portions.

6. Heat a 12-inch nonstick skillet over high heat until very hot. Meanwhile, using a well-floured rolling pin, roll out a portion of dough into a thin circle.

7. Place the rolled dough onto the hot skillet and cook for 1 minute. While the naan is cooking, roll out a second portion of dough.

8. Turn the naan in the skillet and cook the other side for 30 to 45 seconds. Set aside. Repeat with the remaining portions of dough.

9. Move the skillet to the side, turn the burner down to medium, and grill each naan directly over the flame for a few seconds on each side until slightly charred and puffed. To do this, you can either place the naan directly on the burner or hold it a few inches above the burner with tongs. If using an electric stove, preheat a ridged, nonstick grill pan and place the naan in the pan and grill until charred. Flip and repeat on other side.

10. Cool completely before packaging.

ZA'ATAR FLATBREAD

MAKES 16 CRACKERS

With the increasing popularity of Middle Eastern cuisine, more and more people are discovering za'atar, a traditional blend of sumac, thyme, and sesame seeds. You can make your own za'atar or buy it premade from a good spice store. Commonly eaten with pita, za'atar adds color and interest to this flatbread cracker — I've included a recipe for it on page 191. Za'atar makes an appealing swap item on its own, as well.

Flatbread is easy and fun to make and holds appeal as a savory swap item. It was swapping for a rosemary flatbread one time that opened my eyes to the tastiness of homemade crackers, and I have been making them ever since. Crackers are also a natural pairing with many of the dips that one typically sees at a food swap.

3	cups all-purpose flour
1½	teaspoons baking powder
2	teaspoons salt
¾	cup plus 1 tablespoon water
½	cup olive oil
1	large egg
4	teaspoons za'atar
	Flaky sea salt

Packaging

Package 4 pieces of flatbread together in a cellophane bag and close with a twist tie or ribbon. Flatbread will keep for several days.

1. Preheat the oven to 450°F (230°C) and line two sheet pans with parchment paper.

2. In a large bowl, whisk together the flour, baking powder, and salt. Make a well in the center of the flour, and slowly add the ¾ cup of water and the olive oil. Stir with a fork until the dough begins to come together.

3. Gather the dough and knead it against the side of the bowl until it forms a ball. Divide the dough into 4 equal parts.

4. Working with one piece at a time, keeping the unused pieces wrapped in plastic until needed, roll out the dough on a lightly floured board until very thin. Aim for a 9- by 11-inch or 10- by 12-inch rectangle, but an irregular shape is fine, too. (If the dough resists, let it rest for 5 minutes.)

5. Using a pizza cutter, cut the rolled-out dough into 4 equal pieces. Transfer the pieces to the prepared baking sheet.

6. Beat the egg with the remaining tablespoon of water to make an egg wash. Brush the pieces of dough with the egg wash. Poke all over with a fork to prevent bubbling. Sprinkle ¼ teaspoon of za'atar and a pinch of flaky sea salt on each piece of dough. Bake the flatbread until browned and crisp, 10 minutes. Cool on a wire rack.

7. Repeat with the remaining dough, using fresh parchment paper each time.

VARIATION

You can vary this recipe in countless ways by replacing the za'atar with fresh herbs, other spice blends, or flavored salt. You can also make this recipe vegan by brushing the flatbread with more olive oil in lieu of egg wash prior to baking.

FOCACCIA

MAKES 1 (2-POUND) LOAF OR ABOUT 20 (1 X 6-INCH) SLICES

Versatile and forgiving, focaccia makes an ideal bread for food swapping. The presence of oil in the dough ensures that the bread will last for a few days without going stale. And focaccia is easy to cut into small portions for swapping. Someone who swapped for soup may see focaccia on offer and instantly put together a meal in his or her head. What a nice post-swap dinner that would be!

Experiment with different toppings, including herbs, tomatoes, olives, cheese, nuts, and even dried fruit.

1   package (2¼ teaspoons) active dry yeast

1½ cups warm water, between 110 and 115˚F (43–46˚C)

4   cups bread flour

2   tablespoons olive oil plus more for the pan and brushing on the dough

2   teaspoons salt

1   teaspoon sugar

Flaky sea salt

Packaging

Package 4 or 5 slices together in a cellophane bag secured with a ribbon or twist tie for swapping.

1. Dissolve the yeast in the warm water until it blooms, about 10 minutes. (If the yeast fails to bloom, discard and start over with new yeast.)

2. Combine the flour, oil, salt, and sugar in the bowl of a standing mixer. Add the water with the yeast.

3. Beat the mixture with the paddle attachment just until the dough comes together, about 45 seconds.

4. Switch to the dough hook and knead until the dough is smooth and elastic, about 10 minutes. (You can also knead the dough by hand.)

5. Grease a bowl with oil and place the dough in the bowl, turning to coat it with oil. Cover the bowl with plastic wrap and place it in a warm spot until the dough has doubled in size, about 90 minutes.

6. Punch down the dough and knead it a few times to expel any gas. Return the dough to the bowl, cover again, and allow to rise in a warm place until doubled in size again, about 40 minutes.

7. Coat the bottom of a half-sheet pan with olive oil. Place the dough in the pan and press it with your fingertips into an 8- by 10-inch rectangle. If the dough springs back, allow it to rest for 5 minutes and try again.

8. Brush the top of the dough with olive oil and sprinkle with flaky sea salt. If adding toppings, such as chopped herbs, olives, or sliced tomatoes, do so now.

9. Preheat the oven to 450°F (230°C). Cover the focaccia loosely with a clean tea towel and allow to rise until puffy, about 25 minutes.

10. Prior to baking, poke the focaccia all over with your finger to make small indentations. Bake the focaccia for 20 to 25 minutes or until golden and crusty. Allow it to cool on a wire rack.

11. Trim the edges and cut the loaf in half. Cut each half into 1-inch slabs, approximately 10 slices per half.

DAIRY & EGGS

THE INTEREST IN GROWING AND MAKING our own foods has led to a revival in homemade dairy products. Compound butters, crème fraîche, yogurt, and cheese are all fun DIY projects that make for popular swap items. Those who have never tried to make butter or yogurt at home are amazed to see it at the swap, and those who bring it never reveal how easy it is to do.

Among the most popular items at food swaps around the country are fresh eggs. Backyard chickens have become quite trendy, and when chicken keepers bring eggs to swap, there is inevitably a line of people begging to trade with them. With their bright yellow, richly flavored yolks, fresh eggs are worth seeking out. Even more popular at the Chicago Food Swap are fresh duck eggs, which make baked goods and custards especially rich. We have one couple that comes to the swap from Indiana, and the frenzy around their duck eggs is not to be believed.

Sometimes people bring egg dishes to swap. While I do not see miniature quiches or frittatas at every event, when people bring them, they are extremely popular. As I have said before, savory foods always do well.

CULTURED BUTTER

MAKES 1 POUND BUTTER AND 2 CUPS BUTTERMILK

Homemade butter is a fun, no-cook project. In fact, this project results in three possible swap items: first, if you simply culture the cream and do not go any further, you have crème fraîche, a tangy, thick version of soured cream that is delicious spooned into soups or dolloped onto fruit desserts.

If you do make butter, you will end up with not only a pound or so of cultured butter but also 2 cups of tangy, sour buttermilk. Bring the buttermilk as its own swap item or use it in baked goods. (You can skip the step of culturing the butter and simply make sweet cream butter if you are pressed for time or if you prefer the taste, but the resulting liquid will be whey, not buttermilk.)

Homemade butter comes together very quickly in a high-speed blender or food processor. Think of those devices as butter churns on steroids. Work in batches with no more than 2 cups at a time for best results.

1 quart heavy cream, preferably not ultra-pasteurized

2 tablespoons buttermilk

1 teaspoon salt (optional)

Packaging

Butter is typically simply packaged wrapped in wax or parchment paper and labeled.

Note: *Cultured butter will last up to 1 week refrigerated, so be sure to make it shortly before your food swap and label it with the date.*

1. Pour the cream and buttermilk into a large glass bowl and whisk to combine. Cover and allow the mixture to sit in a warm place for 24 hours, until thickened and slightly sour. (At this point, what you have is crème fraîche, which will last about 2 weeks in the refrigerator.)

2. Working in batches, pour half the crème fraîche into a food processor. Add the salt — it is optional, but salt will help the butter keep longer. Process on high and keep a close watch until the butter globules begin to separate into small curds, about 1 minute. You will begin to see and hear a change in how the liquid moves in the bowl after 30 seconds.

3. Pour the mixture into a fine-mesh strainer set over a large bowl. Repeat the previous step with the rest of the cream.

4. Next, strain the butter. The goal in this step is to remove as much buttermilk from the butter as possible. Keeping the strainer over the bowl, work the butter in the strainer, stirring and pressing it with a spatula, to remove the liquid. Add an ice cube or two to the strainer to keep the butter cold. Periodically scrape up the butter that collects on the underside and return it to the strainer. Use a slotted spoon to scoop out any globules of butter that end up in the buttermilk, and return them to the strainer as well.

5. When the butter begins to take on a yellow hue and you are not able to extract any more liquid with the spatula, after about 5 minutes, gather the butter in your (clean) hands and knead it over the bowl to extract any remaining liquid.

6. When you are confident that you have extracted as much liquid from the butter as possible, divide it into 4 portions, 4 ounces each, shape each portion into a log, and wrap each log in parchment or waxed paper. Refrigerate until ready to use or swap.

COMPOUND BUTTER

EACH RECIPES MAKES 12 OUNCES (3 STICKS) OF BUTTER

Compound butter, known as hotel butter in restaurant parlance, is butter that has been combined with flavorings, such as aromatics, herbs, spices, and even sweeteners. These flavored butters are sometimes served at restaurants as an accompaniment to the bread basket. Beyond their use as a spread, compound butters are often used to flavor grilled meats, seafood, and steamed vegetables or added to sauces.

Compound butters are yet another quick, no-cook swap item. The more creative you are with your flavorings, the more takers you will have.

12 ounces (1½ sticks) unsalted butter, softened (not melted)

Honey cinnamon
3 tablespoons honey and 3 teaspoons cinnamon

Shallot and tarragon
¼ cup minced shallot and 1 tablespoon minced tarragon

Bleu cheese and walnut
4 ounces softened bleu cheese and ¼ cup finely chopped, toasted walnuts

Herb
¼ cup chopped mixed herbs such as parsley, thyme, and basil

1. Combine the butter and flavorings in the bowl of a standing mixer, and mix on medium speed for several minutes until thoroughly combined. Aromatics, nuts, and herbs should be finely minced and all ingredients at room temperature.

2. To prepare the compound butter for swapping, divide the flavored butter into 3 equal portions of approximately 4 ounces each. Shape each piece into a log using your hands or a piece of waxed paper. Cover the log in plastic wrap. Refrigerate or freeze until ready to use or swap.

Packaging

With such a simple item, presentation matters. Wrap each log in a 6-inch-wide piece of parchment paper, and twist the ends to seal. Tie each end with twine or raffia. Label the butter using a hanging tag or write directly on the parchment paper. Note on the label that the flavor fades quickly, so storing the butter in the freezer is recommended.

CREAMY RICOTTA

MAKES 3 (8-OUNCE) JARS

More of a science experiment than cooking, homemade ricotta is surprisingly easy, and the resulting creamy concoction will make you weak in the knees. I know of at least one person who made ricotta to bring to a swap, then could not bear to part with it. This recipe makes a large quantity, allowing you to keep some for your own use and to swap the rest. You will certainly be entertaining many offers.

Homemade ricotta is highly perishable, so do not make it more than one day in advance of the swap itself.

2   quarts whole milk

2   cups cream, preferably not
     ultra-pasteurized*

1¼   cups buttermilk

     Squeeze of lemon juice

Ultra-pasteurized cream contains stabilizers that can prevent the curds from developing.

Packaging

Jars make nice, sturdy packages for swapping. Be sure to indicate on the label that the ricotta requires refrigeration and should be used within a few days of the swap.

Note: *You will have quite a large quantity, 2 quarts or so, of whey left over. Whey is very nutritious and can be used in place of water in making soup, baking bread, or soaking beans or nuts or as a protein boost in smoothies. If you do not plan to use the whey, rather than discard it, bring it to the swap and see if someone there would like it.*

1. Combine the milk, cream, buttermilk, and lemon juice in a large saucepan, and heat over medium heat. Avoid stirring.

2. When the mixture has just started to boil and has reached approximately 200°F (95°C), turn the heat down to its lowest setting and continue to simmer until you see visible curds, about 2 minutes.

3. Remove the mixture from the heat and allow it to sit for at least 30 minutes and up to 1 hour to allow the curds to develop.

4. Line a fine-mesh sieve with two layers of cheesecloth and place over a large bowl. Gently ladle (do not pour) the curds into the sieve, allowing the whey to drain.

5. Fold the cheesecloth over the top of the ricotta and continue to drain the whey until the ricotta has reached your desired consistency, between 15 and 30 minutes. The longer it drains, the drier it will be.

6. Ladle the ricotta into four clean, 8-ounce jars and refrigerate until ready to use.

YOGURT

MAKES 2 PINTS (WITH SOME LEFT OVER) OR 5 (8-OUNCE) JARS

One of my favorite things to do at a food swap is seek out someone trading yogurt and someone trading granola. If I score both, I will have delicious breakfasts all week, especially once I add some of my homemade jam or lemon curd.

Making yogurt at home is easy and does not require any special equipment. You can, of course, invest in a yogurt maker if you want to make large quantities of yogurt or prefer the convenience of pushing a button and letting a machine do all the work. These machines tend to sell for between $20 and $100. Some people make yogurt in their slow-cookers with great success. If you are new to making yogurt or do not plan to do it often, try this basic method as a first step. It is very reliable.

Here we start the yogurt-making process with a small amount of store-bought yogurt. When buying yogurt for this purpose, make sure that it contains live and active cultures. These cultures will turn the milk into yogurt and give you all those healthy probiotics.

1   half-gallon whole milk

½   cup plain yogurt with
     live cultures, at room
     temperature

Packaging

For swapping purposes,
label as perishable.

1. Pour the milk into a large saucepan and heat uncovered over medium-high heat until almost boiling, 200°F (95°C) on a candy thermometer. Watch out for vigorous bubbling toward the end of the process.

2. Remove from heat and pour the milk into a large bowl. Allow it to cool to around 110°F (43°C), which is cool enough that you can leave your finger in the milk without discomfort but it still feels hot. This process usually takes about 30 minutes.

3. You want to maintain this temperature, so at this point, transfer the milk to an insulated container or wrap the bowl in towels.

4. Spoon the yogurt into a small bowl. Remove a cup of the warm milk and whisk it into the yogurt.

5. Slowly pour the yogurt-milk mixture back into the warm milk while whisking.

6. Cover the milk and place it in a warm place. You can use a warm place in your house, such as on top of a radiator, or leave it in the oven with the oven light on. The milk will not spoil due to the presence of live cultures. Maintain a warm temperature to allow the yogurt to become firm.

7. Allow the yogurt to sit for at least 4 hours or overnight.

8. Place a colander over a large bowl and line it with several layers of cheesecloth.

9. Ladle (do not pour) the yogurt into the colander and allow the whey to drain until it has reached your desired thickness. I usually strain mine for around 2 hours. (See note in Creamy Ricotta recipe about what to do with leftover whey.)

10. Ladle the yogurt into glass jars for storage or swapping. Refrigerate until needed.

TORTILLA ESPAÑOLA

MAKES 6 LARGE WEDGES

Tortilla española is a Spanish version of a frittata made with potatoes and onion. It is served all over Spain as a cold or room-temperature tapa, appetizer, or light meal. In Spain, tortilla española is viewed as on-the-go food and even sometimes stuffed between bread for a sandwich or bocadillo. Cut into thinner wedges or squares, it makes a great appetizer.

The first time someone brought wedges of tortilla española to a food swap, I was struck by what a brilliant swap item it was. Here is a savory dish, easy to transport, and meant to be served room temperature. It is tailor-made for swapping. Not surprisingly, the swapper who brought it was mobbed with offers.

1   cup extra-virgin olive oil

2   pounds waxy potatoes, such as Yukon Gold or Red Bliss, peeled and finely diced

2   yellow onions, halved and thinly sliced

12 large eggs

Salt and pepper

Packaging

Wrap cooled wedges in waxed paper and decorate with a label or hanging tag. Label as perishable.

1. Heat the olive oil in a 12-inch, nonstick skillet over medium-high heat. When the oil is hot enough that a piece of potato dropped in it sizzles, add the potatoes and stir to coat with oil. Turn the heat down to medium-low and cook the potatoes, stirring until tender, but not brown, about 10 minutes. Remove them from the skillet with a slotted spoon and drain on a plate lined with paper towels. Set aside.

2. Reheat the oil in the skillet and add the onions. Toss to coat with oil, turn the heat down to low, and cook, stirring until tender, about 10 to 12 minutes. Do not allow the onions to brown. Remove them to a second plate lined with paper towels and drain.

3. Pour out the oil from the skillet, reserving 1 tablespoon. Wipe out the skillet with a paper towel.

4. Beat the eggs in a large bowl and add the potatoes and onions. Season well with salt and pepper. Toss gently to combine.

5. Add the tablespoon of oil back to the skillet and heat over medium-high heat. Pour the egg mixture into the skillet and cook for 1 minute to allow the edges to set. Then turn the heat down to medium-low and cook until the bottom and edges of the tortilla are browned. Gently loosen the edges from the sides of the skillet with a knife or metal spatula.

6. Remove the skillet from the heat and cover it with a large flat platter. Carefully flip the tortilla onto the platter, taking care not to break it apart.

7. Return the skillet to the heat and gently slide the tortilla back in with the browned side on top. Tuck the edges under, if necessary to preserve the rounded look. Cook over medium-low heat until the bottom is browned and the tortilla is cooked through. (Test by inserting a skewer into the middle. If it comes out clean, the tortilla is done.)

8. Carefully transfer the tortilla to a platter or cutting board. Allow it to cool completely before cutting it into wedges. Store in the refrigerator until ready to eat or swap.

KALE AND ONION
MINIATURE FRITTATAS
MAKES 12 MINI FRITTATAS

I have seen many adorable miniature quiches and frittatas at the Chicago Food Swap over the years and have loved every single one. Egg-based swap items work as breakfast, lunch, or dinner food for the upcoming week, which makes them very attractive.

While quiche is wonderful, individual frittatas have the advantage of being gluten-free, which makes them appeal to a wide range of swappers. With a delicious filling of sautéed onion and kale and sharp cheddar, these muffin-sized frittatas are flavorful and nutritious.

1 tablespoon extra-virgin olive oil or butter

1 yellow onion, diced

1 bunch kale, stems removed, sliced into ribbons

2 cloves garlic, minced

⅛ teaspoon red pepper flakes

Salt and freshly ground pepper

12 large eggs

¼ cup milk, preferably whole

1 cup grated sharp cheddar cheese

Packaging

Package the frittatas in groups of 3 or 4 and decorate with a label or hanging tag. Label as perishable. Four of these mini frittatas would look adorable packed together in a bakery box and tied with a ribbon. Or see the packaging suggestion for the Banana-Chocolate Muffins on page 117.

1. Preheat the oven to 375°F (190°C) and spray a 12-cavity muffin tin with nonstick cooking spray.

2. Heat the olive oil or butter in a large, deep skillet over medium heat and add the onion. Sauté the onion over medium-low heat until softened, about 5 minutes. Add the kale and garlic, and continue to sauté until the kale is wilted, another 5 minutes. Season with the red pepper flakes, salt, and pepper and remove from the heat.

3. Divide the kale and onion mixture evenly among the cavities of the muffin tray, approximately 2 tablespoons of filling per cavity.

4. Beat together the eggs and milk in a large bowl, preferably one with a spout for pouring. Or transfer the mixture to a 4-cup measuring cup. Pour the egg mixture into the cavities with the kale and onions, dividing it evenly and filling each cavity almost to the top. Top each cavity with a heaping tablespoon of grated cheese.

5. Bake until cooked through and firm, 20 to 25 minutes.

6. Allow the frittatas to cool for 5 minutes. Remove from muffin tin by gently running a knife around the edge of each frittata. Cool completely on a rack before storing or wrapping. Store in the refrigerator until ready to eat or swap.

SUZANNE KROWIAK WAS TAKING TIME OFF from teaching dance to nurse a broken foot when she read a short article in *Eating Well* magazine about Kate Payne and BK Swappers. As a passionate canner, Suzanne loved the idea of a food swap and decided to start one in Indianapolis.

While only a dozen people came to the first swap in August 2011, a reporter from the *Indianapolis Star* was also in attendance, and her resulting story on the swap generated a lot of attention. Since that time, every Indy Food Swappers event has filled to capacity. Suzanne caps attendance at 35 swappers to maintain an intimate feel.

When its host location closed in 2012, the Indy Food Swappers were already such a valued part of Indianapolis's food community that offers to host the swap poured in. The best offer came from the Indianapolis City Market, a historic building located in the heart of downtown that is home to artisanal food producers and small eateries. Indy Food Swappers now meets every other month on the upper level of the market.

Despite its popularity, it has not always been smooth sailing for the group. An official from the county health board showed up at the second event and expressed concerns about the concept. Although the local authorities ultimately did not close her swap, Suzanne continues to worry about regulation. She takes pains to emphasize that the swap is a private, ticketed event, not a commercial marketplace.

Suzanne relishes the strong sense of community among the Indy Food Swappers and admires how home cooks use the swap as motivation to try new things in the kitchen. Because Suzanne was at the forefront of the food swap movement and has created such a dynamic swap, she serves as a mentor to those looking to start new swaps in other cities, particularly in other parts of Indiana. Her goal is for the Indy Food Swappers to remain a vital part of the local food renaissance in Indianapolis. Since starting the swap, Suzanne has become a certified master food preserver, just another way she shares her passion for local, seasonal, and homemade food.

Suzanne relishes the strong sense of community among the Indy Food Swappers and admires how home cooks use the swap as motivation to try new things in the kitchen.

SOUPS

WHILE THE VARIETY AND INGREDIENTS change with the seasons — chili and creamy vegetable soups in winter, and cold soups or gazpacho in summer — soup's popularity as a swap item remains constant. Everyone loves to bring home something for dinner that night or lunch the next day.

Soups are easy and relatively inexpensive to prepare in large quantities, making them an ideal item to bring to a swap. Alternatively, you can make an especially large batch of soup, serve some to your family for dinner, and swap the rest. However, not all recipes work equally well, as soups made for swapping will by necessity sit for several hours, if not several days, before being eaten. Avoid soups containing ingredients such as tortillas, dumplings, rice, or pasta that will absorb liquid if the soup is not consumed right away. Soups that improve with age are, of course, ideal.

I often make vegetarian or vegan soups, to appeal to as many swappers as possible. Remember to label your soups with care, because it can be hard to look at the jar and identify all of the ingredients. For example, a vegetable soup containing chicken broth is not vegetarian, and the label should indicate as much.

Soup is almost always swapped in pint-size glass jars, although plastic containers are sometimes used. Many swappers make an extra effort with the packaging and add a pretty jar topper, ribbon or twine, a label, or a hanging tag. If you want to offer samples of your soup, and it is best served warm, I suggest bringing some in an insulated thermos: many swap locations will not have facilities for reheating it.

BUTTERNUT SQUASH
& APPLE SOUP
MAKES 4 PINTS

My version of butternut squash soup is made with apples for sweetness and lots of warm spices. If I were serving this soup at my home, I would add a half cup of cream at the end of the cooking. I do not call for cream here, to make this appealing to as many people as possible, but you can suggest that the recipient add a splash of cream before serving.

8   cups peeled and cubed butternut squash (from 2 medium-size squash)

¼   cup extra-virgin olive oil

    Salt and freshly ground pepper

1   large yellow onion, diced

3   apples, peeled. quartered, and chopped

1   2-inch piece fresh ginger, peeled and minced

3   cloves garlic, minced

⅛   teaspoon each ground cloves, ground allspice, and ground nutmeg

    Pinch of red pepper flakes

4   cups chicken or vegetable broth

½   cup apple cider (optional)

1. Preheat the oven to 425°F (220°C). Toss the squash with 2 tablespoons of the olive oil and salt and pepper, and arrange in a single layer on a baking sheet. Roast the squash for 20 minutes or until soft.

2. Meanwhile, heat the remaining 2 tablespoons of olive oil in a large stockpot over medium heat. Add the onion and sauté until translucent, about 5 minutes.

3. Add the apples, ginger, and garlic, and stir to combine. Sauté until tender but not browned, lowering the heat as necessary, about 10 minutes. Add the cloves, allspice, nutmeg, and red pepper flakes, and continue to sauté a few more minutes until fragrant.

4. Add the roasted squash and the broth and cider (if using), and stir to combine.

5. Bring the soup to a boil, then reduce the heat and simmer until the vegetables are very soft, about 10 minutes.

6. Purée the soup until smooth using an immersion blender, or by transferring it to a food processor or high-speed blender. Store in the refrigerator until ready to eat or swap.

Packaging

Pour the soup into clean glass pint jars and decorate with a label or hanging tag. Label as perishable.

PATTY'S CARROT SOUP

MAKES 4 PINTS

This recipe comes from Patty Heinze, a frequent participant in Chicago Food Swap events and a member of the Culinary Historians of Chicago. The soup boasts an intense carrot flavor that makes it a favorite with adults and even children. And the bright orange color looks stunning in a glass jar.

Use the best carrots you can find, such as heirloom varieties from the farmers' market or, at the very least, bunches with the tops still attached in the grocery store. When made with maple syrup or sugar and vegetable broth, this soup is vegan and therefore appeals to a wide variety of swappers.

134

2 tablespoons extra-virgin olive oil

2½ pounds sliced carrots (about 20 to 24 carrots or three bunches of carrots with tops attached)

1 large yellow onion, diced

8 garlic cloves, minced

8 whole cloves

1 cinnamon stick

5 cardamom pods

4 cups chicken or vegetable broth

2 tablespoons lemon juice

1½ teaspoons sugar, maple syrup, or honey

1½ teaspoons salt

1 teaspoon white pepper

Note: *While not common in American kitchens, white pepper is often used for aesthetic reasons in light-colored dishes, such as white sauces and mashed potatoes. You should be able to find white pepper at most grocery stores. It is a useful item to have on hand.*

1. In a large stockpot, heat the olive oil over medium heat. Add the carrots, onion, and garlic, and sauté until the vegetables are slightly softened, 5 to 10 minutes.

2. Combine the cloves, cinnamon, and cardamom in a spice bag or a square of cheesecloth and add to the pot. Add the broth and cover. Simmer the mixture until carrots are very soft, about 30 minutes, stirring occasionally.

3. Remove the spice bag and purée the soup until smooth using an immersion blender, or transfer the soup, working in batches if necessary, to a food processor or high-speed blender. If using a blender or food processor, return the soup to the pot.

4. Add the lemon juice, sweetener, salt, and pepper, and stir to combine. Simmer until heated through, adding more broth if needed to achieve a smooth consistency. Store in the refrigerator until ready to eat or swap.

Packaging

Pour the soup into clean glass pint jars and decorate with a label or hanging tag. Label as perishable and refrigerate until the swap. Patty suggests garnishing the soup with a dollop of plain yogurt or sour cream, a drizzle of cream or crème fraîche, chopped fresh herbs, or even a bit of diced bacon. You may want to pass along these ideas to your trading partners.

RED LENTIL SOUP

MAKES 6 PINTS

I use berbere, an Ethiopian spice blend, in this soup because I love its gentle heat and the mix of warm spices with the lentils. You can find berbere at good grocery stores, spice stores, or online. If you cannot find berbere, I suggest seasoning the soup with an additional half-teaspoon of cumin, a half-teaspoon of coriander and a pinch each of cayenne and cinnamon.

When I make this soup for my family, I add some chopped dark leafy greens, such as spinach, chard, or kale, at the very end for additional nutrition and interest. I don't always do so when swapping the soup, because the greens are better when cooked just until wilted and served right away. But you could suggest to your trading partner that they add some greens before serving.

¼ cup extra-virgin olive oil

2 medium yellow onions, diced

4 carrots, peeled and diced

4 cloves garlic, minced

3-inch piece fresh ginger, peeled and minced

1 teaspoon Ethiopian berbere

½ teaspoon ground cumin

1 teaspoon salt

¼ teaspoon freshly ground black pepper

3 cups red lentils, rinsed and examined for pebbles

10 cups water or vegetable or chicken broth

2 bay leaves

Juice of 2 lemons

Note: *Because lentils are such an excellent source of protein, I suggest making this soup vegetarian under the assumption that vegetarian and vegan swappers would like it.*

1. Heat the olive oil over medium heat in a large Dutch oven or stockpot. Add the onion, carrots, garlic, and ginger, and sauté over medium-low heat until softened, about 15 minutes.

2. Add the berbere, cumin, salt, and pepper, and sauté until fragrant, 3 to 5 minutes. Add the red lentils and stir to combine. Pour the water or broth over the lentils and add the bay leaves. Raise the heat, cover, and bring to a boil, then reduce the heat and simmer gently, covered, until the lentils are tender, 45 minutes to 1 hour.

3. Remove the bay leaves and discard. Add the juice from the lemons and stir to combine.

4. If you prefer a smoother texture, you can partially purée the soup using an immersion blender, but do not lose all the chunkiness from the lentils. Store in the refrigerator until ready to eat or swap.

Packaging

Ladle the soup into clean glass pint jars and decorate with a label or hanging tag. Label as perishable.

POTATO, FENNEL
& LEEK SOUP
MAKES 5 PINTS

Potato-leek soup is a French bistro classic. Here I make this classic a bit more exciting, but no less French, with the addition of fennel, an anise-flavored bulb, and a splash of licorice-flavored liqueur. All three of these vegetables — fennel, leeks, and potatoes — are in season at the same time; namely, late fall, exactly when a creamy soup like this would be most welcome.

I think this soup is much improved by the addition of cream, so I include it, even though it means that vegan food swappers will not trade for it. You can at least keep vegetarians as possible trading partners if you use vegetable broth in lieu of chicken broth. Or go ahead and use chicken broth, and let the chips fall where they may.

¼   cup extra-virgin olive oil

2   leeks, washed, trimmed, and sliced

2   bulbs fennel, stems and ends trimmed and woody core removed, cut into thin slices

¼   teaspoon red pepper flakes

Salt and pepper

2   pounds waxy potatoes, peeled and cut into 2-inch pieces

6   cups broth, chicken or vegetable

¼   cup anise-flavored liqueur such as Ricard Pastis or ouzo (optional)

½   cup heavy cream

Juice of ½ lemon

1. Heat the olive oil over medium heat in a large Dutch oven or stock-pot. Add the leeks and fennel, and sauté over low heat until softened but not browned, about 15 minutes. Add the red pepper flakes and season well with salt and pepper.

2. Add the potatoes to the pot, stir to combine, and cover with broth and the liqueur, if using. Cover the pot, turn the heat to high, and bring the soup to a boil. Turn the heat down to low and simmer until the potatoes are tender, about 20 minutes.

3. Purée the soup until smooth using an immersion blender, or transfer the soup, working in batches if necessary, to a food processor or high-speed blender. If using a blender or food processor, return the soup to the pot.

4. Add the cream and lemon juice and stir to combine. Season well with salt and pepper. Store in the refrigerator until ready to eat or swap.

Packaging

Pour the soup into clean glass pint jars and decorate with a label or hanging tag. Label as perishable.

A TYPICAL DC AFTER-WORK event features name-dropping, networking, and jockeying for position. The DC Food Swap aims to be the opposite of all that. In a town not especially known for creativity, organizer Elizabeth Kruman wants the DC Food Swap to be an event for people to share what they are making in their kitchens without pressure or competition. The whole thing is not very "DC," and that is just what Liz, an attorney, likes about it.

The DC Food Swap was started in 2012 by cook and artist Jess Schreibstein of the *Witchin' in the Kitchen* blog. A feature in the *Huffington Post* early in its life brought a lot of attention, and in a city full of journalists, press coverage was practically inevitable. When Jess moved to Baltimore, Liz, who had attended the swaps from the beginning, took over running the group. For Liz, the DC Food Swap is a creative outlet. Running the group has allowed Liz to connect with the local food blogging community, and she was even asked to judge jams and jellies at the DC State Fair.

With its quarterly meetings capped at 35 attendees, the DC Food Swap fills up every time with a waiting list. But Liz prefers to keep the events small to encourage more interaction among the swappers. Maintaining the friendly, low-key feeling is important so the swap does not become just another place to network. The DC Food Swap is not the place to market your artisanal food business, says Liz. And if DC residents want more opportunities to swap food, they can cross the Potomac and join the Alexandria Food Swap in northern Virginia.

Maintaining the friendly, low-key feeling is important so the swap does not become just another place to network.

From its inception, the DC Food Swap has enjoyed being part of a national movement. In 2013, more than 70 members of the DC Food Swap participated in a "snail mail" food swap with swappers from Brooklyn and Portland, Oregon.

CHORIZO, KALE &
WHITE BEAN SOUP
MAKES 6 PINTS

I had to include at least one soup containing meat for the carnivores out there. Any smoked sausage, such as kielbasa, will work, so feel free to select your favorite variety. The green kale and the orange carrots make this soup look especially attractive in a glass jar.

2	tablespoons extra-virgin olive oil
1	yellow onion, diced
4	cloves garlic, minced
3	carrots, peeled and diced
2	ribs celery, chopped
½	teaspoon dried oregano
½	teaspoon ground cumin
½	teaspoon ground coriander
	Pinch red pepper flakes
	Salt and pepper
9	ounces chorizo or other smoked sausage links, sliced (about 4 links)
8	cups chicken broth
1	Parmesan rind (optional; see box, below)
2	(14-ounce) cans cannellini beans, drained and rinsed
5	cups finely sliced kale
2	tablespoons red wine vinegar

Note: *To cut costs, you can replace the canned beans with dried, but soak them overnight and add them when you add the broth because they will need to cook for longer than canned beans do.*

1. Heat the olive oil in a large stockpot over medium heat. Add the onion and garlic, and sauté until softened, about 5 minutes.

2. Add the carrots and celery, and sauté until tender, about 10 minutes. Season with oregano, cumin, coriander, red pepper flakes, and salt and pepper to taste. Continue to sauté a few more minutes until fragrant.

3. Add the sliced sausage and stir to combine. Cover with the chicken broth and add the Parmesan rind (if using). Bring the soup to a boil, then turn down the heat and simmer until the sausage is cooked through.

4. Add the beans and kale, and simmer until the kale is tender, about 20 minutes.

5. Add the red wine vinegar at the very end for brightness. Taste and adjust seasonings as necessary. Store in the refrigerator until ready to eat or swap.

Packaging

Pour the soup into clean glass pint jars and decorate with a label or hanging tag. Label as perishable.

PARMESAN RINDS

When I finish a piece of Parmigiano-Reggiano cheese, I wrap the rind in plastic and freeze it. I use the rinds I have saved to flavor soup and risotto all winter long. You can even make a broth from the rinds if you have enough of them. I have seen containers of Parmesan rinds sold in stores, so in a pinch use those. But it is more fun to save your own. Just remove it from the soup or risotto before serving.

COLD PEA SOUP
WITH MINT
MAKES 5 PINTS

A few years ago, my husband and I visited Paris in May and ate some amazing dishes featuring spring produce, including a memorable cold pea soup. I attempt to re-create that soup every spring when fresh peas appear at my local farmers' market. One year, a Chicago Food Swap regular, Liz Arthur, brought a cold pea soup to a spring swap, and I was delighted to know that someone else shares my affection for this elegant dish.

Fresh peas are in season for such a short time and they are truly sublime. But you can make a decent version of this soup with frozen peas, which will save you the trouble of having to shell them.

4   tablespoons butter

2   yellow onions, diced

6   cups (approximately 2 pounds) fresh or frozen peas

4   cups chicken broth

1   cup buttermilk

½   cup loosely packed mint leaves (about ½ ounce)

½   teaspoon salt

1. Melt the butter in a large Dutch oven or stockpot over medium heat. Add the onions and sweat them over medium-low heat until softened but not browned, approximately 5 minutes.

2. Add the peas and stir to combine. Add the chicken broth and bring the mixture to a boil. Reduce the heat and simmer until the peas are tender, 2 to 3 minutes. Remove from the heat. Allow to cool slightly.

3. Transfer the soup to a high-speed blender and add the buttermilk, mint, and salt, and purée until smooth. Alternatively, add the buttermilk and mint to the pot with the soup and purée using an immersion blender.

4. Chill the soup for several hours until cold. Taste and adjust the seasonings. Store in the refrigerator until ready to eat or swap.

Packaging

For swapping, pour the soup into clean glass pint jars and decorate with a label or hanging tag. Suggest serving the soup garnished with a dollop of sour cream or plain Greek yogurt. Label as perishable.

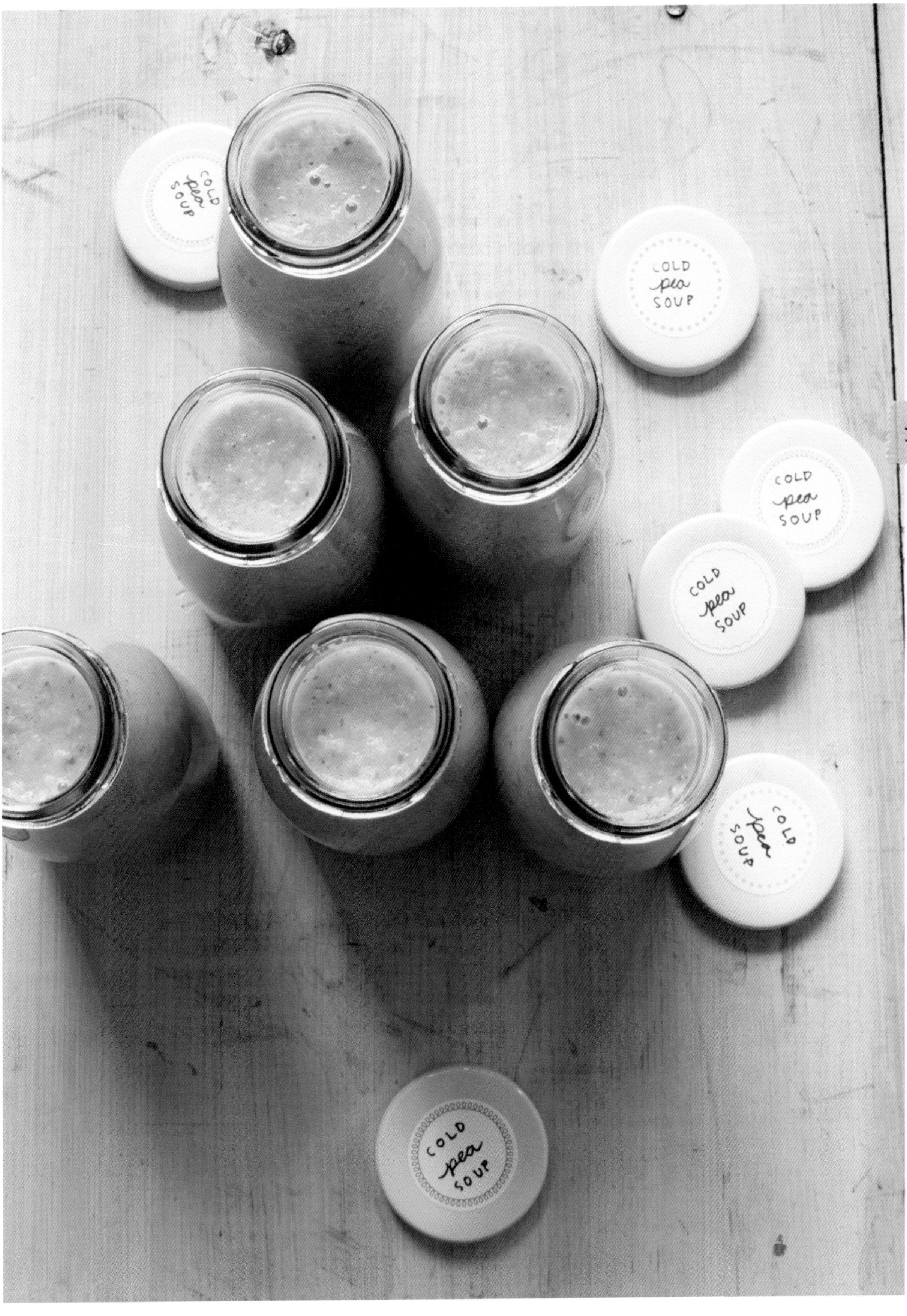
COLD
pea
SOUP

5

Sip & Savor

FOODS WITH LONGER SHELF LIFE

DIPS, SAUCES & CONDIMENTS

PESTO AND HUMMUS are food swap staples, and you may see several different kinds of each at the same swap. Their popularity never seems to diminish, however. Other kinds of dips and spreads are also extremely popular and, depending on the recipe, can serve as easy-to-make, last-minute swap items.

Many typical dips and spreads are vegetarian, even vegan, and gluten-free, so they appeal to a wide range of swappers. It is also fun to see different global cuisines represented in the array of dips and spreads on offer, from Mexican salsa to Indian raita to Middle Eastern hummus. When paired with bread or soup from other swappers, a tasty dip can complete a food-swap-based meal.

Sauces and condiments are where the DIY kitchen movement and the food swap movement truly come together. It is thrilling to see people bring homemade mustard, ketchup, hot sauce, and more to the food swap and witness the astounded reactions of the other swappers. If you have never tried your hand at these types of projects, I hope these recipes will inspire you. Once you have made your own ketchup and mustard, your backyard barbecue will never be the same.

TURNIP GREENS PESTO

MAKES 12 OUNCES OR 3 (4-OUNCE) JARS

When I spend top dollar on local farmers' market produce, I want to get as much value for my money as possible. This pesto recipe came about as a way to use up the greens that are attached to the tiny Hakurei turnips I buy in late spring and early summer. There is no cheese in this version, so it's a perfect item for vegan swappers. The lemon juice adds brightness and fixes the vibrant green color.

Turnip greens, like other greens, are incredibly nutritious. They are an excellent source of vitamins A, C, and K, folate, calcium, and lutein. Be sure to wash your turnip greens well in several changes of cold water and remove the leaves from the woody stems. They are also delicious sautéed with garlic as a side dish or cooked in a frittata.

5 tablespoons pine nuts

4 cups well-packed, coarsely chopped baby turnip greens

3 cloves garlic, peeled

1 tablespoon freshly squeezed lemon juice

¼ teaspoon salt

¼ teaspoon freshly ground black pepper

½ cup extra-virgin olive oil

1. Lightly toast the pine nuts in a dry skillet over medium heat until they are slightly browned and fragrant. Watch the pine nuts carefully so that they do not burn.

2. Combine the toasted pine nuts, turnip greens, garlic, lemon juice, salt, and pepper in the bowl of a food processor. Pulse several times to combine. With the motor running, add the olive oil in a slow, steady stream until the mixture resembles a thick paste.

3. Store the pesto in the refrigerator until needed.

Packaging

Pack the pesto into small clean glass jars and decorate with a label or hanging tag. Label as perishable.

VARIATION

For a different pesto recipe also featuring a spring farmers' market crop, replace the turnip greens with 4 cups of arugula, omit the ground pepper, and add ¼ cup finely grated Parmesan cheese.

CHOOSING THE CORRECT CONTAINER FOR YOUR DIP OR SPREAD

When swapping a dip, spread, or dressing, people typically rely on glass bottles and jars as safe and convenient packaging. The question is then, what size jar? Is a pint or a half-pint appropriate? Perhaps a 4-ounce jar or 5-ounce glass bottle? The appropriate container for your dip or spread depends, in part, on how the item is consumed and in part on your generosity. A smaller container is appropriate for items that are used sparingly, such as hot sauce or mustard, or are particularly rich or expensive to prepare, such as citrus curd. Dips and spreads that are used to feed a crowd, such as hummus or salsa, might be most appreciated in a larger container, such as a pint jar.

For guidance, consider how the item is sold in stores. Remember that while choosing a smaller jar will result in more items to swap, you will be paying more in packaging costs. That being said, when in doubt, opt for the smaller container; you can always offer two jars of your dip or spread in exchange for a particularly desirable swap item.

ROASTED GARLIC HUMMUS

MAKES 3 PINTS (WITH SOME LEFT OVER)

Every food swap that I have ever attended has had at least one person swapping hummus. More often, there are two or three different kinds on offer. And why not? Hummus is delicious, and healthy, and, being both vegan and gluten-free, it appeals to many different swappers. And you can vary it in so many ways.

I once worked near a Middle Eastern restaurant that served the most garlicky hummus I have ever tasted. After eating it, my coworkers and I had garlic oozing out of our pores for the rest of the afternoon. Our spouses could always tell — and were not especially thrilled — when we had eaten lunch there. Scarred from that experience, I created this hummus recipe with mellow, roasted garlic.

When making a large quantity of hummus for swapping, you will save quite a bit of money by using dried chickpeas in lieu of canned. The trade-off is that you have to soak and cook the beans yourself. Many cooks also find the flavor of dried chickpeas and other beans superior to canned.

16 ounces dried chickpeas

2 heads garlic

1 cup extra-virgin olive oil, plus more for drizzling

Salt and freshly ground black pepper

1 cup freshly squeezed lemon juice (from 4 or 5 lemons)

1 cup tahini (sesame paste)

3 teaspoons salt

2 teaspoons ground cumin

Packaging

Pack the hummus into clean glass pint jars and decorate with a label or hanging tag. Label as perishable and note the presence of tahini, as sesame seeds are a common allergen.

1. Put the chickpeas in a bowl, cover with several inches of water, and soak for at least 6 hours or overnight.

2. Drain the chickpeas and discard the soaking water. Put the chickpeas in a medium saucepan and cover with several inches of water. Bring to a boil, turn down the heat, and simmer, partially covered, until the chickpeas are tender, 1 to 1½ hours.

3. Meanwhile, roast the garlic: Preheat the oven to 350°F (175°C). Cut off the tops of the heads of garlic, exposing the cloves, but do not peel. Place both heads in a small baking dish, drizzle with olive oil, season with salt and pepper, and cover the dish with foil. Roast in the oven until soft, about 1 hour. Let cool.

4. Drain the chickpeas, reserving the cooking water, and allow to cool.

5. Squeeze the cloves of garlic out of the heads and discard the papery skin and husks.

6. Working in batches, combine the chickpeas, garlic, 2 cups of the reserved cooking water, lemon juice, tahini, salt, and cumin in the bowl of a food processor. Process until smooth. While processing, slowly pour in the olive oil in a steady stream. If the hummus is too thick or dry, add more of the reserved cooking water. Taste and adjust seasonings.

7. Combine the batches into one large bowl and stir well to distribute the seasoning evenly prior to packing into jars.

8. Store in the refrigerator until needed.

PORT CITY SWAPPERS

SUPPORTING AND DEVELOPING their local foodway is a top priority for Port City Swappers organizers, and life partners, Maria Ortado and Chris Dean. By day, Chris works at a two-hundred-year-old family farm that has produced herbs for local chefs and customers since 1986. In their spare time, Chris and Maria manage a small community garden that sits on a vacant lot. Oh, and they also help out at the farmers' market booth belonging to the only certified organic produce farmer in the area.

Port City Swappers was started in 2012, and Chris and Maria participated from the beginning. When the original founder moved away, they were the logical candidates to take over running the swap. Despite their other commitments, Chris and Maria didn't want to see the swap die. The community building and skill sharing that come out of Port City Swappers were too important to them.

Gardening and hunting are common pastimes in the area, which leads to lots of homegrown produce and wild game at the swap. Raccoon jerky, anyone?

Meeting monthly, Port City Swappers is unusual in that it does not require participants to register in advance. Anyone is welcome to attend. Chris and Maria send an email reminder of the date and time each month and post on the swap's Facebook page, but they do not have a formal registration process. Not surprisingly, attendance varies widely from month to month, but no one seems to mind.

Wilmington is a historic area in the southeastern corner of North Carolina, near the Cape Fear River and the beach. Gardening and hunting are common pastimes in the area, which leads to lots of homegrown produce and wild game at the swap. Raccoon jerky, anyone? Because the art of home food preservation has continued to thrive in the South, preserves and pickles are also popular food swap items. In short, Port City Swappers are a knowledgeable and self-reliant bunch. For them, a food swap is just another way to eat locally and feed their community.

SWEET & SPICY PEACH
BARBECUE SAUCE
MAKES 3 PINTS

I live near the abundant peach orchards of Michigan, so from July to September I try to preserve them in as many ways as possible, including this distinctive barbecue sauce. A fruit-based barbecue sauce, such as this one, works well with poultry or fish.

Most recipes that call for peeled peaches instruct you to blanch the peaches in boiling water for 30 seconds, then remove them to an ice-water bath. I have found, however, that this method does not always make the skins easy to remove, and it requires dirtying an extra pot. After making many batches of peach jam and peach salsa, I invested in a soft-skin peeler with a serrated blade. This small gadget saves me a lot of work.

6 cups peeled, sliced yellow peaches

2 cups finely chopped yellow onion

1 tablespoon minced garlic

1 cup lightly packed brown sugar

1 cup distilled white vinegar

2 chipotle peppers in adobo

¾ teaspoon cinnamon

2 teaspoons salt

Packaging

For swapping, decorate each jar with a label or hanging tag. Unless processed for shelf stability, label the sauce as perishable.

Note: *Chipotle chiles in adobo are small chile peppers that have been smoke-dried and then canned in a tangy vinegar-based tomato sauce. They have a spicy, smoky flavor that you may recognize from Mexican cuisine.*

1. Put the peaches, onion, garlic, brown sugar, vinegar, chipotle peppers, cinnamon, and salt in a large deep stockpot and bring to a boil over high heat. Reduce the heat to medium and gently boil the sauce, stirring frequently, until the peaches have begun to break down and the onions are soft, 10 to 15 minutes.

2. Remove the sauce from the heat and purée until smooth using an immersion blender or by transferring it in batches to your food processor.

3. Return the puréed sauce to the pot and bring back to a boil. Reduce the heat and simmer until thickened, 20 to 30 minutes. (The sauce will splatter quite a bit at this point, so use caution.) The sauce is ready when it mounds up on a spoon or plate and is no longer watery.

4. Transfer the sauce to clean, warm jars and store in the refrigerator until needed.

CANNING FOR SHELF STABILITY

This sauce can be processed for shelf stability in a water-bath canner. To do so, prepare a boiling-water bath and heat three pint jars. (See Safe Water-Bath Canning Procedures, page 198.)

Ladle the sauce into clean, warm jars, leaving ½ inch headspace at the top of the jar. Bubble the jars and wipe the rims with a damp cloth. Place the lids on the jars and screw on the rings just until you feel resistance.

Process the jars in the boiling-water bath for 15 minutes. Allow the jars to cool in the water for 5 minutes before removing to a towel to cool completely. Store in a cool, dark place for up to 1 year.

TUSCAN WHITE BEAN
& ROSEMARY DIP
MAKES 4 CUPS OR 2 (8-OUNCE) JARS

This no-cook white bean dip is the perfect item to make when you sign up for a food swap at the last minute. It is also a great choice for a beginner cook. This recipe comes from Genevieve Boehme, a veteran of the Chicago Food Swap. She reports that the first time she brought it to a swap, it flew off the table, and made her wish that she had brought more jars.

To make this item in larger quantities, consider using dried beans, which require more forethought than canned but are less expensive. Just follow the instructions on the package for soaking and cooking the beans.

2 (15-ounce) cans cannellini beans (or other white bean), drained and rinsed well

2 cloves garlic, roughly chopped

2–4 tablespoons fresh lemon juice

2 tablespoons extra-virgin olive oil

1 tablespoon finely chopped fresh rosemary

1 teaspoon kosher salt

Freshly ground black pepper

1. Place the beans and garlic in a food processor and process until finely chopped. Add the lemon juice to taste, olive oil, and rosemary. Process until very smooth. If the mixture is too thick, add more oil, or water, a teaspoon at a time, until it reaches the desired consistency. Season with salt and pepper to taste.

2. Refrigerate for several hours before serving, to allow flavors to develop. It may seem bland initially, but the flavor will intensify over time. If still a little bland after a few hours, stir in more lemon juice.

VARIATION

This recipe can be adapted by substituting different herbs for the rosemary or by adding sun-dried tomatoes, roasted peppers, or pitted chopped olives.

Packaging

Pack the dip into clean 8-ounce glass jars and decorate with a label or hanging tag. Label as perishable.

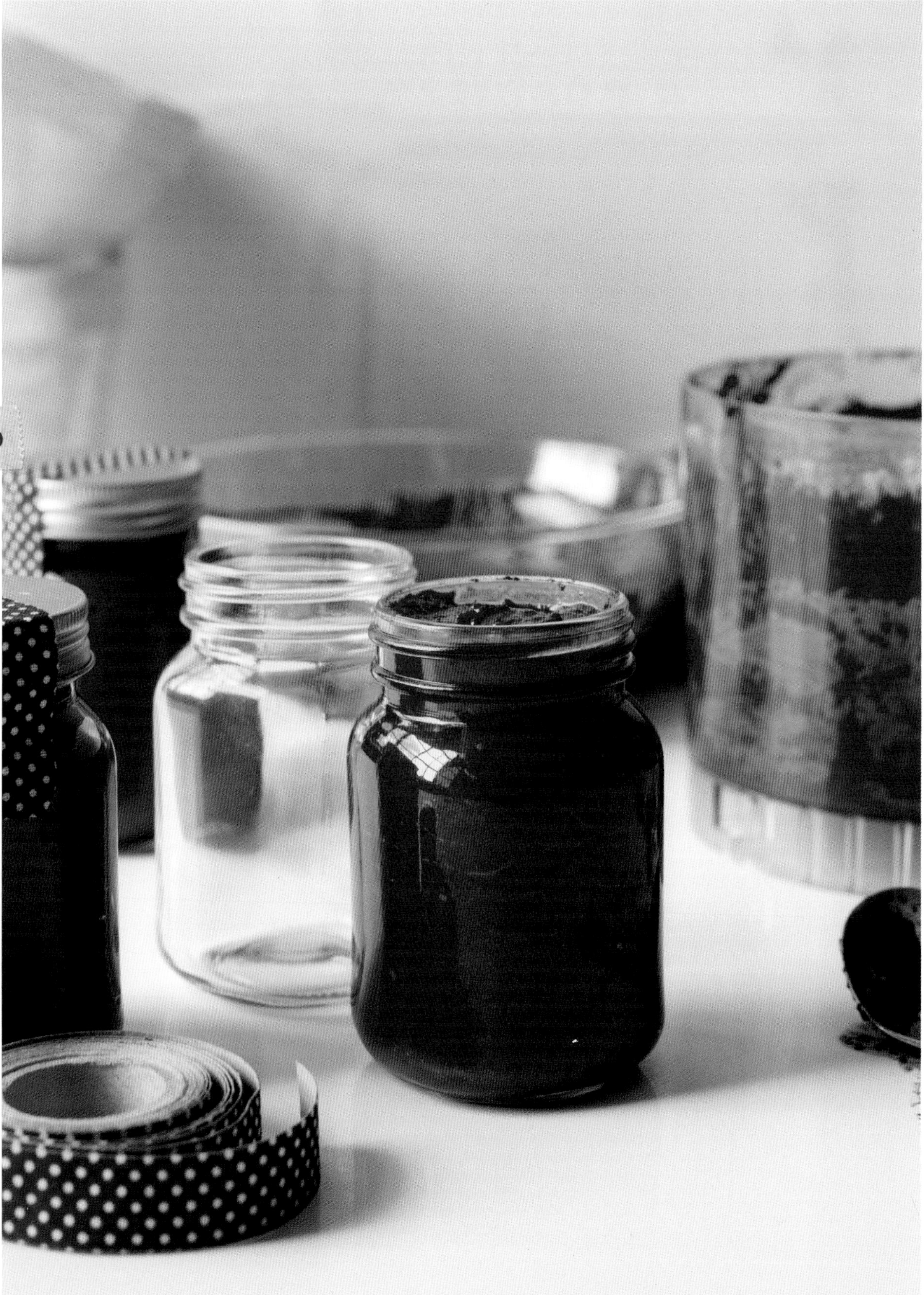

BEET-TAHINI DIP

MAKES 4 (8-OUNCE) JARS

This recipe comes from Laura Gladfelter, a member of the Chicago Food Swap community, who regularly brings this dip to swap. It is always quite popular, perhaps because of its unique color.

The taste of the dip is winning as well. The beets provide sweetness and earthiness, the yogurt and lemon add tanginess, and the garlic gives the whole thing a little bite. Make it the day before you intend to serve or swap to allow the flavors to develop.

Ground sumac is a Middle Eastern spice made from ground sumac berries; it is the main ingredient in the spice mix za'atar (see page 121). It adds an additional note of tartness to this dip. You should be able to find sumac online, in most spice stores, or in Middle Eastern grocery stores.

2 pounds beets

1 cup Greek yogurt

4 cloves garlic

½ cup tahini (sesame paste)

¼ cup freshly squeezed lemon juice

1 teaspoon ground sumac

Salt

Freshly ground black pepper

1. Preheat the oven to 375°F (190°C).

2. Wash the beets well and trim the ends off. If your beets are especially large, cut them into halves or quarters. Wrap the beets in foil and roast in the oven until tender, 1 to 1½ hours. When cool enough to handle, slip the outer skins off the beets and roughly chop.

3. Combine the beets, yogurt, garlic, tahini, lemon juice, and sumac in a food processor, and purée until smooth. Season well with salt and pepper.

4. Store in the refrigerator until needed.

Packaging

For swapping, pack the dip into clean glass jars and decorate with a label or hanging tag. The dip will last for several weeks in the refrigerator. Remember that tahini sauce contains sesame seeds, a common allergen, so be sure to include a warning to that effect.

INDIAN

YOGURT MINT DRESSING

MAKES 4 (8-OUNCE) JARS

This creamy yogurt-based dressing takes its inspiration from Indian raita. Like raita, this dressing can be used to cool the mouth after eating spicy foods, such as biryani. However, it also works well as a dip for vegetables, a dressing for salad, or an accompaniment to lamb dishes, such as kebabs or burgers. To entice possible trading partners, offer a sample with some raw vegetables for dipping and include serving suggestions.

It is easy to get your hands on a large quantity of mint in summer months, especially if you have some in your own garden or you frequent farmers' markets. Off-season, I prefer to buy fresh mint at ethnic grocery stores, where it is sold in large bunches and is usually less expensive than the small containers of fresh herbs found at Whole Foods and other chains.

2½   cups roughly chopped, loosely packed mint leaves

2   cups roughly chopped, loosely packed cilantro leaves

2   jalapeño peppers, seeded and roughly chopped

2   cups plain Greek yogurt

¼   cup freshly squeezed lemon juice

2   cloves garlic, peeled

1   (4-inch) piece fresh ginger, peeled and roughly chopped

2   tablespoons vegetable oil

½   teaspoon salt

1. Combine the mint, cilantro, jalapeño peppers, yogurt, lemon juice, garlic, and ginger in the bowl of a food processor or high-speed mixer. Pulse several times to combine. With the motor running, slowly pour in the oil. Continue processing until creamy, scraping down the sides as necessary. Add the salt and stir to combine.

2. Allow the dressing to sit for several hours in the refrigerator to develop the flavors. Taste and adjust the seasonings if necessary.

Packaging

For swapping, pour the raita into clean 8-ounce glass jars and decorate with a label or hanging tag. Label as perishable.

MIXED-PEPPER HOT SAUCE

MAKES 20 OUNCES OR 4 (5-OUNCE) BOTTLES

Makers of homemade hot sauce tend to be, shall we say, enthusiastic. They name their creations, print up customized labels, and jealously guard their secret recipes. I am not a hot sauce enthusiast myself, so my version does not have a catchy name nor have I ever designed a customized label featuring flames and devil horns. But you may well see such creations at the food swap. If you want to go that route yourself, godspeed.

This is a fairly basic pepper-salt-vinegar hot sauce. I prefer a mix of peppers, with the majority being milder jalapeños and only a few of the hotter varieties, such as serrano and habanero, because I am a wimp. Change the ratio as you see fit. When working with such a large quantity of hot chiles, gloves are a must, and a mask would not hurt either.

1	pound mixed hot chile peppers, such as jalapeño, habanero, serrano, or cherry bombs, stemmed and seeded
2	tablespoons salt
2	cloves garlic
2	teaspoons sugar
1½	cups distilled white vinegar

1. Combine the chile peppers, salt, garlic, and sugar in a food processor and purée. Add the vinegar to the mixture and stir well to combine.

2. Pour the sauce into a quart-size mason jar or another container with a lid. Cover loosely and allow to sit in a cool dark place for at least 1 day and up to 1 week. (The longer it sits, the deeper the flavor.)

3. When the taste is to your liking, strain the sauce through a fine-mesh sieve, stirring and pressing down on the solids to extract as much liquid as possible. Discard the solids.

4. Carefully pour the liquid into clean glass bottles and refrigerate until ready to use or swap.

Packaging

Because hot sauce is used sparingly, a small bottle of 4 or 5 ounces is a perfectly acceptable size for swapping. Hot sauce is typically swapped in glass bottles with screw-top caps. Customized labels are up to you.

Hot sauce will last for months in the refrigerator, but be sure to label as perishable so that your trading partners do not assume it is shelf stable.

ROASTED TOMATO KETCHUP

MAKES 6 (8-OUNCE) JARS

My friend and cofounder of the Chicago Food Swap, Vanessa Druckman, brought an ancho chile–infused tomato ketchup to a swap a few years ago, and everyone was astonished by its rich, umami-laden taste. Since that time, homemade ketchups have become quite trendy. For anyone who spurns high-fructose corn syrup and other ingredients commonly found in processed foods, making your own ketchup is practically a necessity.

Homemade ketchup requires an enormous amount of tomatoes, and it is time-consuming. On the plus side, the flavor is amazing, and of course you can customize the ketchup to your family's tastes, adding a little more brown sugar if you like your ketchup sweet or being generous with the cayenne pepper if you prefer heat. To make this ketchup, I roast the tomatoes, rather than boil them, which intensifies their flavor.

10   pounds Roma or plum tomatoes, halved

1   teaspoon celery seed

1   teaspoon whole allspice berries

1   teaspoon black peppercorns

1   teaspoon brown mustard seeds

1   teaspoon whole cloves

1   cinnamon stick, broken in half

2   cups apple cider vinegar

2   tablespoons extra-virgin olive oil

2½   cups diced yellow onion

1   cup diced bell pepper

1   cup brown sugar

1   teaspoon pickling salt

     Pinch cayenne pepper

Packaging

Decorate each jar with a label or hanging tag. Unless processed for shelf stability, label the sauce as perishable.

1. Preheat the oven to 400°F (200°C). Arrange the tomato halves in single layers on three or four baking sheets. Roast the tomatoes in the preheated oven about 45 minutes, in batches if necessary, until soft and pulpy.

2. While the tomatoes are roasting, combine the celery seeds, allspice berries, peppercorns, mustard seeds, cloves, and cinnamon stick in a spice bag or cheesecloth tied at the top. Combine the spice bag and the apple cider vinegar in a small saucepan. Bring the mixture to a boil, then remove from the heat. Allow the spices to steep in the vinegar for at least 30 minutes and up to 1 hour.

3. Heat the olive oil in a large sauté pan and sauté the onions and peppers over medium heat until very soft, about 20 minutes. Purée the onion mixture in the food processor until smooth.

4. Once the tomatoes are roasted, remove them from the oven. Place a fine-mesh sieve over a large stockpot and add the tomatoes and any liquid that has accumulated, working in batches as necessary. Press down on the tomatoes with a spatula or wooden spoon to force the juice and pulp through the sieve, leaving behind the seeds and skins. You can also use a food mill, if you prefer. Discard the solids.

5. To the tomato liquid in the pot, add the seasoned vinegar, the onion purée, the brown sugar, the salt, and the cayenne pepper. Bring the mixture to a boil over high heat. Turn the heat down to medium and continue to boil until the ketchup is thick and spreadable, and will mound up on a spoon. This can take anywhere from 1 hour to 90 minutes, depending on the size of your pot, and how well you sieved your tomatoes.

6. When the ketchup has thickened, ladle it into warm 8-ounce jars. I find that the wide-mouth jars work best for ketchup. Store in the refrigerator until ready to swap.

Roasted Tomato Ketchup

Blueberry-Port Mustard

VARIATION

The ketchup can be processed for shelf stability in a water-bath canner. To do so, prepare a boiling-water bath and heat six 8-ounce jars.
(See Safe Water-Bath Canning Procedures, page 196.)

Ladle the ketchup into clean, warm jars, leaving ¼ inch headspace
at the top of the jar. Bubble the jars and wipe the rims with a damp
cloth. Place the lids on the jars and screw on the rings just until you
feel resistance.

Process the jars in the boiling-water bath for 10 minutes. Allow
the jars to cool in the water for 5 minutes before removing to a towel
to cool completely. Store in a cool, dark place for up to 1 year.

BLUEBERRY-PORT MUSTARD

MAKES 5 (4-OUNCE) JARS

Over the years, I have seen people bring a dizzying array of homemade mustards to the Chicago Food Swap. The flavorings for these sweet, spicy, and tangy condiments have included beer, wine, herbs, spices, fruits, and even vegetables. What I have learned from seeing and tasting all these mustards is that homemade mustard is surprisingly easy to make, and it presents a versatile canvas on which to express your creativity.

This mustard recipe is slightly more involved than the Beer-Caraway Mustard on page 157 and combines fruit and spirits for a unique flavor profile. I like this sweet, sharp mustard on grilled meats, such as duck or pork.

FOODS WITH LONGER SHELF LIFE

156

1   cup sherry vinegar

1   cup mustard seeds (try a mix of brown and yellow)

2¾   cups blueberries

½   cup port wine

¾   cup sugar

¼   cup dry mustard

     Pinch of salt

     Pinch of ground cloves

1. Bring the vinegar to a boil in a small saucepan over high heat. Add the mustard seeds, remove the pan from the heat, and cover. Allow the mustard seeds to marinate in the vinegar until most of the liquid has been absorbed, about 2 hours.

2. Pour the marinated mustard seeds and any remaining liquid into the bowl of a food processor. Pulse until creamy but leave some of the grainy texture. Add the blueberries and port wine, and process until blended.

3. Pour the blueberry mustard mixture into a large saucepan and bring to a boil over high heat, stirring frequently. Reduce the heat to medium. Whisk in the sugar, dry mustard, salt, and cloves.

4. Boil the mixture gently until thickened, about 15 minutes.

5. Transfer the mustard to clean, warm 4-ounce jars and store in the refrigerator until ready to use or swap.

VARIATION

This mustard can be processed for shelf stability in a water-bath canner. To do so, prepare a boiling-water bath and heat five 4-ounce jars. (See Safe Water-Bath Canning Procedures, page 198.)

Ladle the mustard into the jars, leaving ¼ inch headspace. Bubble the jars and wipe the rims with a damp cloth. Place the lids on the jars and screw on the rings just until you feel resistance.

Process the jars in the boiling-water bath for 10 minutes. Allow the jars to cool in the water for 5 minutes before removing to a towel to cool completely. Check the seals and store in a cool, dark place for up to 1 year.

BEER-CARAWAY MUSTARD

MAKES 4 (4-OUNCE) JARS

This is my version of a ballpark mustard — just the thing to spread on grilled sausages or a ham sandwich. It is very simple to make and therefore is a perfect starter mustard. The mix of brown and yellow mustard seeds makes for an attractive presentation and has just the right amount of heat. This recipe makes a small quantity good for home use or for swapping in small jars.

One note about making your own mustard: it needs time to cure before it is ready to use. If you taste your mustard while it is cooking or right after, it will seem terribly bitter. After a week or two, the bitterness will fade and the flavor of the mustard will come through. If swapping a recently made mustard, be certain to note the date that you made it and suggest a recommended date for opening the jar.

½ cup yellow mustard seeds

½ cup brown mustard seeds

1 cup beer

1 tablespoon caraway seeds

¼ cup brown sugar

Pinch of salt

Packaging

Transfer the mustard into clean 4-ounce glass jars. Refrigerate and allow to cure for 1 week. Label as perishable.

Note: *This mustard is not cooked and therefore should not be canned for shelf stability. Store it in the refrigerator and treat it as perishable.*

1. Soak the yellow and brown mustard seeds in the beer until almost all of the liquid has been absorbed, about 2 hours.

2. Toast the caraway seeds in a dry skillet over medium heat until fragrant, about 3 minutes.

3. Combine the mustard seeds, caraway seeds, brown sugar, and salt in the bowl of a food processor and pulse until well combined and creamy but still grainy. If the mixture is too dry, you can add more beer or some dashes of red or white wine vinegar until you achieve a creamy texture.

CITRUS CURD

MAKES 3 (4-OUNCE) JARS

My family travels to southwest Florida every December to escape the Chicago winter. One of my favorite activities there is shopping at the weekly farmers' market. Among the fresh fruits and vegetables, unimaginable anywhere else at that time of year, I find all kinds of unusual varieties of citrus, from smoky Rangpur limes to glossy Meyer lemons.

If you cannot get to Florida, most good grocery stores offer a wide variety of citrus fruits in winter months. These colorful and flavorful varieties of citrus are wonderful for baking and preserving. One of my favorite uses is citrus curd. A silky concoction of eggs, butter, sugar, and juice, citrus curd is heaven on pound cake, swirled into yogurt, or as a dip for strawberries. Try it with Meyer lemons or Key limes.

158

FOODS WITH LONGER SHELF LIFE

6	egg yolks
1	cup sugar
⅔	cup freshly squeezed lemon or lime juice
2	teaspoons zest from the juiced lemons or limes
½	cup (1 stick) unsalted butter cut into cubes

Packaging

Decorate each jar with a label or hanging tag. Label the jars as perishable.

1. Whisk together the egg yolks and sugar in a medium saucepan until well combined. Add the citrus juice and zest, and stir over medium heat using a wooden spoon.

2. Do not allow the curd to boil, or the egg yolks will scramble. Continue to stir and heat the curd over medium-low heat until it thickens enough to coat the back of a spoon, about 170°F (75°C), around 10 minutes. Keep an eye on the heat and lower it as necessary to heat the curd without boiling it.

3. When the curd has thickened, remove the pan from the heat. Stir in the butter until it melts.

4. Strain the curd through a fine-mesh sieve into a bowl. (Do not be tempted to skip this step. It removes any pieces of cooked egg, which would detract from the desired silken texture.)

5. Pour the curd into clean 4-ounce jars and refrigerate until ready to use or swap.

SAVE THOSE EXTRA EGG WHITES

When making citrus curd, don't discard those leftover egg whites! There are so many ways to use them. The classic "egg whites only" recipe is meringue. Meringue kisses are a tasty, low-calorie treat and you can also make a meringue topping for a pie or bar cookies. Other light desserts, such as angel food cake, also call for egg whites only. For a savory preparation, scramble egg whites with low-fat cheese for a healthy and filling breakfast. In a pinch, egg whites can be frozen. One clever way to do this is to freeze individual egg whites in compartments of an ice cube tray.

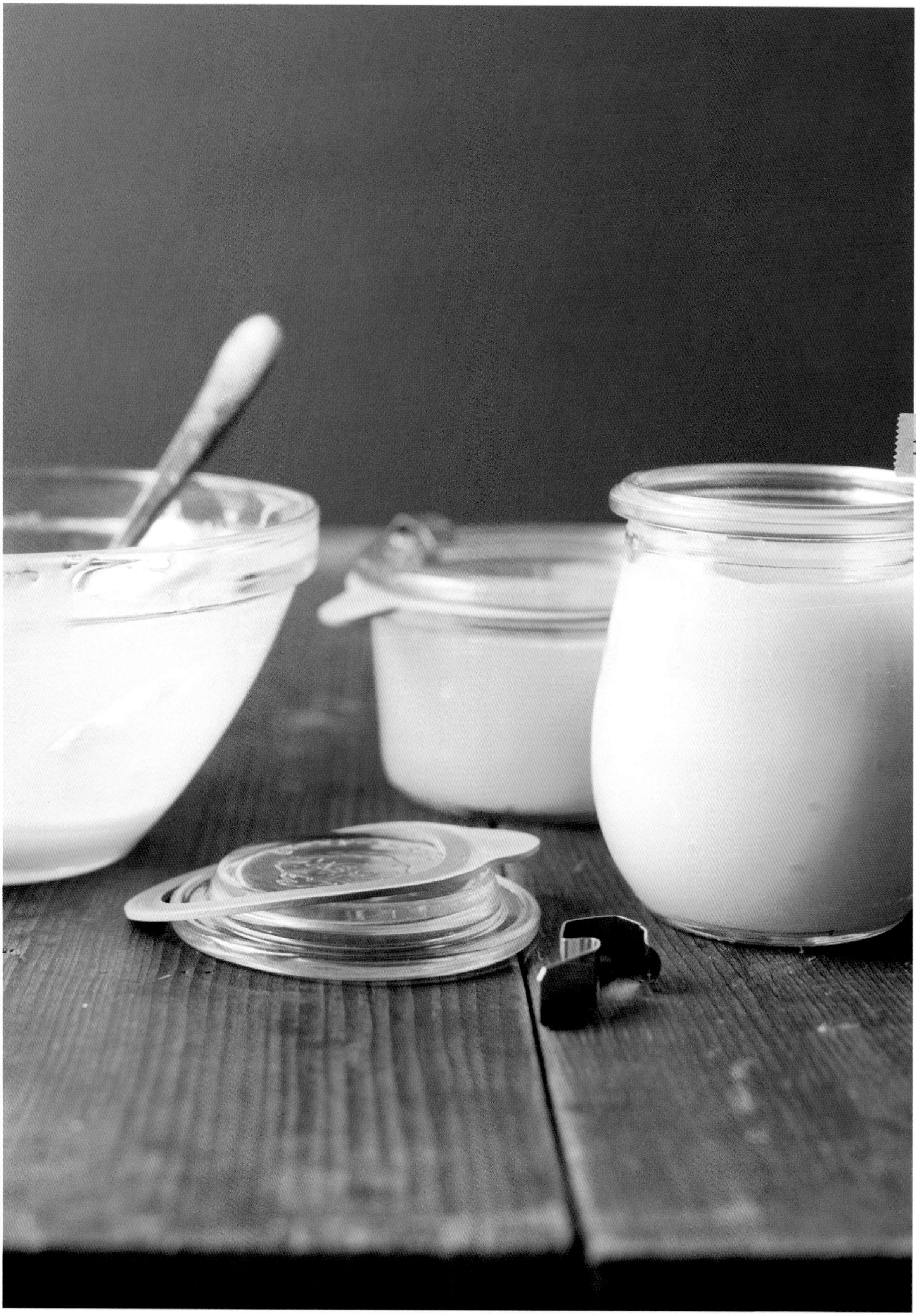

GRANOLA & NUTS

GRANOLA, NUTS, AND OTHER SAVORY snack foods are common sights at a food swap. These kinds of food are easy to make in large batches, portable, and have a decent shelf life, making them ideal for bringing to the swap. Granola is especially popular because it is such a healthy and convenient breakfast food. And it pairs well with other common swap items, such as yogurt and fruit preserves.

Buying nuts in bulk is useful to save money on these otherwise expensive ingredients, but be aware that nuts can turn rancid quite quickly because of their high fat content. Store nuts, like whole-grain flours, in the freezer for the longest shelf life.

Because peanuts and tree nuts are a common, and serious, allergen, it is extremely important to label your swap items containing nuts and peanuts clearly. Be prepared for people to decline to trade with you if you bring items with these common allergens. Some people with allergic family members do not even bring items containing nuts or peanuts into their houses.

CHERRY-ALMOND GRANOLA

MAKES 3 PINTS

Cherry and almond is a natural pairing. I think of this granola as a healthier version of cherry pie, or, with the addition of cacao nibs, Black Forest cake. I selected agave syrup to sweeten this granola because I did not want the strong flavors of honey or maple syrup to overshadow the cherry and almonds. You could also use cane syrup for the same effect.

Because it does not contain egg white or honey, which many granola recipes do, this recipe is vegan, which may make it especially desirable to some swappers.

3	cups old-fashioned rolled oats
2	cups sliced raw almonds
1	cup dried cherries, chopped
¼	cup cacao nibs
1	teaspoon salt
½	teaspoon cinnamon
¼	teaspoon ground cloves
½	cup vegetable oil
½	cup agave syrup
2	teaspoons vanilla extract

1. Preheat oven to 350°F (175°C) and line a half-sheet pan with parchment paper.

2. In a large bowl, combine the rolled oats, almonds, dried cherries, and cacao nibs. Sprinkle the salt, cinnamon, and ground cloves over the mixture and toss to combine, making sure that the spices are evenly distributed.

3. Pour the oil, agave syrup, and vanilla over the oats mixture and stir with a spatula to coat the dry ingredients evenly. Spread the granola mixture into the prepared pan and flatten into an even layer.

4. Toast the granola in the oven until brown and fragrant, 25 to 30 minutes, stirring three to four times to ensure even browning.

5. Upon removing the granola from the oven, push it toward the center of the baking sheet. This will help it form clusters.

6. Cool the granola completely before packing into jars or bags.

Packaging

Granola can be swapped in pint jars or, for a cheaper and lighter option, try clear cellophane bags secured with twist ties. Many swappers decorate their bags with ribbon and hanging tags.

PISTACHIO-HONEY
GRANOLA BARS
MAKES 1 DOZEN BARS

My son, Jamie, has been obsessed with Greek mythology for years. This granola bar was inspired by Greek flavors and what I imagine the gods on Olympus might eat: pistachios, apricots, honey, and, of course, olive oil.

The trick with granola bars is getting them to hold together. Do not skip the step of pressing down firmly on the pan of granola before baking, and wait until the bars are fully cool — you can even refrigerate them — before cutting to increase the chances of ending up with granola bars, not just granola. If your spatula sticks to the granola, place a sheet of parchment on top of the granola and press on that.

This recipe is not vegan because it includes honey, but it is dairy-free and can be made gluten-free if you take care to use gluten-free oats. Feel free to vary the nuts, fruits, and even the sweetener to customize these bars to your taste.

2½	cups old-fashioned rolled oats
1	cup roasted pistachio nuts, preferably unsalted, chopped
½	cup dried apricots, chopped
1	teaspoon ground ginger
1	teaspoon vanilla extract
½	teaspoon salt (omit if using salted pistachios)
⅓	cup honey
¼	cup extra-virgin olive oil
¼	cup brown sugar

Packaging

The bars are sticky, so wrap them individually in waxed or parchment paper and tie with twine or ribbon. Four bars make a nice portion for swapping.

1. Preheat the oven to 350°F (175°C). Cover a half sheet pan with parchment paper and spread the oats in the pan. Toast the oats for 10 minutes, stirring halfway through. Remove the oats and turn down the heat to 300°F (150°C).

2. Spray an 8-inch square baking pan with nonstick cooking spray or line it with parchment paper.

3. Combine toasted oats, pistachios, apricots, ginger, vanilla, and salt in a large bowl and toss to combine.

4. In a small saucepan, combine the honey, olive oil, and brown sugar and heat over medium heat, stirring to dissolve the sugar.

5. Pour the wet ingredients over the oat mixture and stir with a spatula to coat the dry ingredients evenly.

6. Pour the mixture into the prepared pan and, using the bottom of a metal spatula, firmly press down on the mixture until it is noticeably denser and more compact, about 1 minute.

7. Bake the granola at 300°F (150°C) for 15 minutes. Cool completely before cutting into bars.

ROASTED CASHEW BUTTER

MAKES 1 PINT

When I was writing this book, *Saturday Night Live* ran a parody commercial for a Vitamix in which the defensive owner insisted that her appliance was worth its hefty price tag because it could make nut butter. It is true that a Vitamix, or other high-speed blender, can make nut butter in a matter of minutes, but a food processor will do the job just as well given a little more time.

Homemade nut butters have a fresh, delicious taste with no mystery ingredients that you do not want. They make a terrific, healthy food swap item for carnivores and vegans alike. Nuts are an expensive ingredient, but you can save a few pennies by buying raw nuts in bulk and roasting them yourself. For nut butters, no need to buy whole nuts, which are usually more expensive; pieces are just fine.

2   teaspoons kosher salt, divided in half

16   ounces raw cashew pieces

¼   cup vegetable oil

2   tablespoons honey

Packaging

Pack the cashew butter into four 4-ounce jars or three 5-ounce jars. (Because nuts are an expensive ingredient, it is perfectly acceptable to swap nut butter in small quantities.) Label as perishable.

1. Dissolve 1 teaspoon salt in 3 cups of warm water. Soak the cashews in the water for 2 to 3 hours (see note). Drain and rinse, and shake off the excess water.

2. Preheat the oven to 325°F (165°C). Line a baking sheet with parchment paper.

3. Roast the cashews in the oven until toasted and fragrant, about 25 minutes. Allow them to cool completely.

4. Combine the cashews, 2 tablespoons of the oil, the remaining teaspoon of salt, and the honey in a high-speed blender or food processor. Process until a coarse paste forms. Add the remaining tablespoons of oil one at a time while the motor is running.

   If using a high-speed blender, use the tamper to press the nuts down into the blades.

   If using a food processor, scrape the sides down with a spatula.

5. Continue processing until you have achieved a smooth paste, 3 to 5 minutes in a high-speed blender and up to four times longer in a conventional food processor. It will be drier and not as creamy as peanut butter but should be smooth and spreadable. Cashew butter will last for several weeks in the refrigerator.

Note: Many people recommend soaking nuts for health benefits because nuts contain high amounts of phytic acid. Phytic acid binds to minerals in our digestive tract and prevents our bodies from fully digesting nuts and other foods, but its effects can be neutralized by a soak in salt water. I am not in a position to speak to these health benefits, but I do believe that soaking cashews improves their flavor. Feel free to skip that step if you are pressed for time. Roasting the cashews, however, is well worth the extra 20 minutes.

Mid-Mitten HOMEMADE

Lansing Michigan

IN 2012, REELING FROM A DIVORCE and the loss of her mother, Mid-Mitten Homemade founder Danielle Welke bought a house and moved to the charming but small town of Mason, Michigan. Within four days of moving in, she started the Mid-Michigan Food Club as a way to connect with other food lovers in central Michigan. A year later, her club was over three hundred members strong and, with the help of two other organizers, regularly put on multiple events per month, including meet-ups at local restaurants, potluck dinners, wine tastings, and tours of local farms and urban gardens.

Because of the food club, Danielle knew that her corner of central Michigan was full of great cooks. Living alone, Danielle constantly ended up with too much food when she cooked, part of what inspired her to start a food swap in early 2014. After putting together so many different kinds of events for the Mid-Michigan Food Club, hosting a food swap was, well, a piece of cake. Mid-Mitten Homemade hosts monthly swaps, which Danielle deliberately keeps small due to space constraints.

Mid-Mitten Homemade is a tight community, but it always welcomes new people. Michigan State University is located in Lansing, so the events regularly draw students and transplants to the area. Michigan is also home to a large refugee population from countries like Cuba, Iraq, and Burma. Danielle volunteers with a group teaching English to refugees and has encouraged these populations to share their food traditions with their new neighbors.

Michigan has seen more than its share of hard times. There is a large population of unemployed or underemployed people, and Danielle's area has its share of poverty and food deserts, despite the fact that it is surrounded by fruit orchards and farms.

Danielle expanded Mid-Mitten Homemade to offer casual cooking classes in addition to food swaps after she noticed that her part of Michigan had no hands-on cooking classes.

Danielle expanded Mid-Mitten Homemade to offer casual cooking classes in addition to food swaps after she noticed that her part of Michigan had no hands-on cooking classes where people could learn both the basics of cooking at home and more advanced skills like canning. Danielle hopes to use these events as another way to integrate the refugee community and as an antidote to the food deserts in her community.

CHOCOLATE-HAZELNUT SPREAD

MAKES 1 PINT

The famous, store-bought version of chocolate-hazelnut spread is known for its legions of devoted fans. Others have learned that the homemade version is even tastier. Different versions of this versatile spread appear regularly at the food swap. I like this version because it is vegan, gluten-free, and not overly sweet. Also, by making chocolate-hazelnut spread at home in a food processor or high-speed blender, you retain more of the hazelnut's texture.

Hazelnuts are an expensive ingredient, so look for them in the bulk section of your grocery store or order online. Removing their skins is a tedious but necessary task or else the spread will be overly bitter. To save yourself some trouble, you can seek out hazelnuts with the skins already removed.

16 ounces raw hazelnuts

1¼ cups powdered sugar

⅓ cup unsweetened cocoa powder

½ teaspoon salt

Pinch of espresso powder (optional)

1 vanilla bean or 1 teaspoon vanilla bean paste

3 tablespoons nut or vegetable oil

1. Toast the hazelnuts in a 375°F (190°C) oven for 10 to 12 minutes, until fragrant and the skins rub off easily. Remove as much of the skins as possible by shaking the nuts in a large, covered bowl or by rubbing them with a clean tea towel.

2. Add the hazelnuts to your food processor or high-speed blender and process until they become creamy. (This could take several minutes. The hazelnuts will start off powdery and eventually begin to break down and release their oils, forming a creamy paste.)

3. Add the powdered sugar, cocoa powder, salt, and espresso powder, if using. Cut the vanilla bean in half lengthwise and scrape the insides into the blender or food processor, or use vanilla bean paste.

4. Gradually add the oil with the motor running, scraping down the sides as necessary, and process until the mixture is a smooth spread. The finished product should be glossy and creamy.

5. Transfer the spread to a clean pint jar and refrigerate until needed.

Packaging

Package the spread into four 4-ounce glass jars. (Hazelnuts are expensive, so a 4-ounce portion is appropriate for swapping.) Label as perishable and note the presence of nuts.

Cho
Hazelnut
Spread

chocolate
Hazelnut
Spread

ANCHO CHILE PECANS

MAKES 4 PINTS

The recipe for these irresistible sweet and spicy pecans comes from Paddy Meehan, a member of the Chicago Food Swap community and the former culinary director at the Bloomingdale's Home and Furniture Store in downtown Chicago. While some people mistakenly think that food swapping is for 20-something hipsters, many food swaps count senior citizens and retirees, like Paddy, among their members. Bringing together people of different ages and from different walks of life who all share a love of food is one of the best things about food swapping.

Ancho chiles, which are simply the dried form of poblanos, are earthy and sweet but not too hot. They add a nice kick to the buttery pecans. In addition to being delicious eaten out of hand, these spiced pecans would make a great addition to a salad or a topping for ice cream.

4	dried ancho chiles
2	cups sugar
2	cups water
4	cups pecan halves
1	teaspoon chili powder
2	teaspoons salt
½	cup molasses

Packaging

Pack the pecans into pint-sized mason jars or cellophane treat bags for swapping. This recipe also makes an outstanding edible gift.

1. Preheat the oven to 250°F (120°C) and line a baking sheet with parchment paper.

2. Combine the chiles, sugar, and water in a medium saucepan and bring to a boil over high heat. Add the pecan halves and stir to coat. Return the mixture to a boil, then reduce the heat to medium-low and simmer for 10 minutes.

3. Remove the pecans from the syrup with a slotted spoon and arrange them on the parchment-lined baking sheet in a single layer. Discard the syrup and chiles.

4. Toast the pecans for 45 minutes. Remove the pecans from the oven and transfer to a heatproof bowl. Add the chili powder, salt, and molasses and toss to coat.

5. Return the pecans to the baking sheet and toast an additional 45 minutes until crisp.

6. Allow the pecans to cool fully. When cool, break up any large clusters that have formed.

DRINKS
Syrups & Infusions

DRINK SYRUPS ARE ALWAYS POPULAR with swappers because they are unusual and will last for weeks in the refrigerator. These syrups can be used to create home-made sodas or flavor cocktails. With the popularity of at-home sparkling water makers, homemade sodas have become very trendy and there are entire cookbooks dedicated to the subject.

Typical drink syrup flavors include ginger, mint, root beer, cola, celery, and berry or other fruits. But there is no limit to what your imagination can dream up. Drink syrups can be inexpensive to make in large quantities, particularly in the summer when herbs are plentiful, and make for an easy, last-minute swap item.

SOUR CHERRY SYRUP

MAKES 3 PINTS

My friend Aaron has an extremely productive sour cherry tree in his front yard in Connecticut. Every year in late June or early July, I get the same email from him: "Any ideas for what to do with a bumper crop of sour cherries?" One of my favorite uses for sour cherries is this drink syrup. Sour cherry syrup is a traditional Persian delicacy that, when mixed with cold water and ice, makes a refreshing, special-occasion drink. Sour cherry syrup can also be mixed with sparkling wine for a delicious and stunning apéritif.

Because pitted sour cherries freeze like a dream, I often have a stash in my freezer. I make this syrup in the dead of winter, and it delights the other swappers.

2½ pounds pitted sour cherries (about 2 quarts of cherries)

3 cups water

1-inch piece fresh ginger, peeled

3 cups sugar

2 limes

Packaging

For swapping, decorate each jar with a label or hanging tag. Note that syrup will last for several months but should be refrigerated.

1. Purée the cherries in a food processor or high-speed blender. Strain the purée through a fine-mesh strainer. Discard the solids.

2. Combine the cherry liquid, water, ginger, and sugar in a large saucepan.

3. Using a vegetable peeler, peel the zest from the limes in long strips. Add the strips of lime zest to the saucepan. Juice the limes and add the juice to the saucepan as well.

4. Bring the mixture to a boil over high heat, stirring to dissolve the sugar. Skim off any foam that accumulates.

5. Turn the heat down to low and simmer the syrup until thickened, about 30 minutes. (You want the syrup to remain thin enough to dissolve easily into other liquids; it will thicken more as it cools.)

6. Strain the syrup again, discarding the ginger and lime zest, and pour into three clean, warm pint jars. Refrigerate until needed.

VANILLA SYRUP

MAKES 2½ CUPS OR 3 (8-OUNCE) JARS

At one of the very first Chicago Food Swap events, my daughter, Zoe, who was eight years old at the time, insisted that I swap for an enormous bottle of vanilla syrup. I could not imagine what she was planning to use it for. By the time Zoe was 11, she was regularly ordering vanilla soy lattes at the local coffee house, so clearly her interest in that vanilla syrup was prescient.

Vanilla syrup is divine in coffee drinks, but it is equally wonderful mixed with sparkling water for a homemade cream soda. We also like to pour it on pancakes and waffles, which was how we used up that first bottle of vanilla syrup. And as with all drink syrups, vanilla syrup comes in handy for your home bar.

- 2 cups water
- 2 cups sugar
- 2 vanilla beans, split down the middle lengthwise
- 1 tablespoon pure vanilla extract

1. Combine the water, sugar, and vanilla beans in a medium saucepan and bring to a boil over high heat. Stir to dissolve the sugar.

2. Boil the syrup hard for 2 minutes, then remove from the heat and allow the vanilla beans to steep for 30 minutes.

3. Pour in the vanilla extract and stir to combine.

Packaging

Pour into three 8-ounce jars and include a half of a vanilla bean in each jar. Decorate each jar with a label or hanging tag. Note that syrup will last for several months in the refrigerator.

SOUTHERN CALIFORNIA HAS THE LARGEST number of different food swap groups of any metropolitan area in America. On any given weekend, you can find a food swap in Huntington Beach, Culver City, Long Beach, Encinitas, or elsewhere. One of the most popular food swap groups in this area is the Central OC Food Swap, located near Santa Ana.

Central OC Food Swap founder Sarah Whittenberg-Hawe has been cooking since her mother returned to work when she was seven years old. By day, she works for a nonprofit doing marketing and communications. By night, she blogs about food and food policy, studies to become a master food preserver, and cares for her husband and son. Health and wellness are important issues in Sarah's family: her husband is the recipient of a kidney and pancreas transplant.

Sarah started the OC Food Swap in 2013. She contacted local food organizations, like Slow Food Orange County and the Harvest Club Orange County, to see if there was enough interest to sustain a food swap close to her. These groups were very interested and offered up a location: a shared office that houses several nonprofit organizations serving Orange County. Volunteers from the different organizations help Sarah set up and break down the swap and staff a table during the event with information about the organizations. Mutually beneficial arrangements that promote community engagement are at the heart of many a successful food swap.

Because it is Southern California, backyard produce and citrus are especially popular swap items. Many swappers also make items with their homegrown produce, from jams and pickles to candied citrus peel. Sarah loves that the food swap allows her and the other attendees to complement one another's skills and diversify the array of homemade and homegrown foods to which they have access.

The food swap provides access to inexpensive, fresh local produce for some who could not otherwise afford it.

While Orange County is known for its wealth, Sarah points out that not every part of the area is affluent. The zip code where the Central OC Food Swap takes place is actually considered a food desert. The food swap provides access to inexpensive, fresh local produce for some who could not otherwise afford it, because these swappers can use their time and effort in preparing inexpensive, homemade food as currency.

GINGER SYRUP

MAKES 2 PINTS OR 4 (8-OUNCE) JARS

Spicy ginger syrup is one of my favorite swap items, and I always make a point to look for it. I simply mix it in sparkling water and garnish with a spritz of lime for a homemade version of ginger ale. Those more ambitious could find myriad uses for ginger syrup in cocktails such as a Dark and Stormy or a Moscow Mule.

You can reserve the ginger and use it in cooking and baking or to make another swap item, such as candied ginger. If that is your intention, take the time to peel the ginger before using it in the syrup. If you have no plans for the ginger slices beyond this syrup, there is no need to peel it.

8   ounces fresh ginger, sliced or chopped (about 2 pieces)

4   cups water

2   cups sugar

10   whole cloves

1. Combine the ginger, water, sugar, and cloves in a medium saucepan and bring to a boil over high heat, stirring to dissolve the sugar.

2. Reduce the heat and simmer, partially covered, for 1 hour. The syrup should have a strong, spicy ginger flavor.

3. Strain the syrup through a cheesecloth and pour into four 8-ounce jars. Store in the refrigerator.

Packaging

Decorate each jar with a label or hanging tag, noting that syrup will last for several months but should be refrigerated. For fun, consider including a recipe for your favorite ginger-based cocktail.

175

INFUSED VODKA

MAKES 1 PINT OR 2 (8-OUNCE) BOTTLES

Infused vodka is a particularly easy and fun swap item that allows for a lot of creativity on the part of the maker. Do not waste expensive, artisanal vodka on this project. I use a mid-priced vodka like Stoli, Svedka, Seagram's or Finlandia. Trader Joe's is a surprising source for affordable, clean-tasting vodka.

You can also infuse other kinds of light spirits, like rum or gin, if you find the right flavor combinations. Try rum with a tropical fruit like pineapple and gin with cucumber. Infusing spirits with stronger flavors, like brandy, is trickier, but you can find good combinations such as plum, cherry, or pear.

2–3 cups chopped or crushed fruit or vegetables

Optional additional flavorings such as citrus peel, ginger, or herbs

2 cups 80-proof vodka

1. Place the chopped or crushed fruit or vegetables and any optional flavorings you are using in a clean, quart-size mason jar. Cover with at least 2 cups vodka or more if there is room. Allow the mixture to steep in the refrigerator for several days, shaking it several times a day.

2. When the infusion is ready, after 3 days for stronger flavors and up to a week for milder ones, strain out the flavorings using a fine-mesh strainer lined with cheesecloth. Squeeze the fruit in the cheesecloth to extract as much liquid as possible.

Packaging

Pour the infused vodka, which may or may not have a bright color depending on the flavoring, into pretty, clean glass bottles for swapping. Label the bottles or decorate with a hanging tag.

IDEAS FOR INFUSED VODKAS

Cranberry & lime: Pop the cranberries with your finger so that they release their juices before steeping in the vodka. Combine with several long strips of lime peel. Steep for 2 or 3 days.
Cucumber: Peel the cucumbers and allow to steep for 3 days.
Hot pepper: Cut in half and only allow to steep for a day or two.
Persimmon: Chop 6 Fuyu persimmons and combine with a cinnamon stick and 2 cups vodka. Allow to steep for 1 week.

MIDLANDS FOOD SWAPPERS

Columbia, SC

WHEN MICHELLE RICHARDS, a pastor's wife and mother of four home-schooled children, saw pictures of a food swap in Savannah, Georgia, on a friend's Instagram feed, she immediately went to the Food Swap Network to learn more. Michelle approached her friend Melissa Smith, an avid gardener, cook, and part-time hog farmer, about bringing the food swap concept to central South Carolina. The Midlands Food Swappers held their first event in May 2012 at Melissa's house with six people in attendance. By the third swap, the group had swelled to 25.

These days, Midlands Food Swappers meets every other month at Michelle's husband's church and attendance is capped at 30, the number that Michelle and Melissa feel is perfect for the space and for the kind of experience that they want to foster. The friends rely on word of mouth from other swappers to bring in new people. As swappers leave, Melissa and Michelle hand out cards with the date of the next swap for them to give to friends.

Four times a year, the Midlands Food Swappers put on a craft and food swap to which people bring handmade items beyond edibles such as cloth napkins, jewelry, and pottery.

While Columbia is the biggest city in the state, the area around it is quite rural. The swap items at the Midlands Food Swappers reflect the area's tradition for farming, preserving, and hunting. Michelle's family are fishermen, and she brings fresh fish, while Melissa brings pork products from her farm. Many swappers bring homegrown produce, flowers, and eggs. Jams, jellies, and preserves are always present, as are baked goods and traditional Southern favorites like pimento cheese spread. Melissa gets particularly excited when someone brings an old-fashioned food, like pickled watermelon rind, that you cannot find in stores.

Four times a year, the Midlands Food Swappers put on a craft and food swap to which people bring handmade items beyond edibles such as cloth napkins, jewelry, and pottery. These events tend to draw a different crowd from the food-only swaps and are quite popular.

Michelle and Melissa's favorite thing about Midlands Food Swappers is the people they have met who share their love of making and growing food and the strong sense of community among the regulars. To promote the community feel, they hold an annual potluck dinner in May in honor of the swap's anniversary so the participants can get to know one another better.

MINT SYRUP

MAKES THREE 8-OUNCE JARS

Gardeners find mint to be a pest. Left unchecked, it will take over like a weed. If you find yourself with an overabundance of mint in your garden, bring bunches of it to your food swap and some poor home cook who lacks gardening ability, like me, will be happy to take it off your hands to make tabbouleh or flavor Indian dishes.

Alternatively, you can make large batches of this mint syrup and trade with budding mixologists who will find it just the thing for making mojitos. Kids and teetotalers might like it mixed into lemonade or iced tea. Mint syrup is also delightful in hot drinks or as a glaze for a cake or tropical fruit.

2 cups sugar

2 cups water

1½ ounces fresh mint sprigs (about 2 cups loosely packed mint leaves)

Packaging

Pack the syrup into bottles or clean 8-ounce glass jars and decorate with a label or hanging tag. Note that syrup will last for several months but should be refrigerated.

1. Combine the sugar and water in a small saucepan and bring to a boil, stirring at first to dissolve the sugar.

2. Roughly chop the mint sprigs, including the stems, and place them in the bottom of a heatproof bowl.

3. Pour the hot sugar syrup over the mint leaves, and immediately cover the bowl with plastic wrap. Allow the mint to steep in the hot syrup for 30 minutes.

4. Strain the syrup through several layers of cheesecloth, squeezing the mint to extract as much liquid as possible, and pour into glass jars. Discard the mint.

5. Store the syrup in the refrigerator until ready to use or swap.

DAMSON PLUM GIN

MAKES 36 OUNCES OR 3 (12-OUNCE) BOTTLES

Damson plums are an ancient variety of plum, characterized by blue-black skin and yellow flesh. They have earned the nickname "damn Damsons" for their puny size and their mouth-puckering flavor. Still popular in Britain, Damson plums had fallen into obscurity in America but are making a slow comeback. Look for them at a farmers' market in early fall. I love them for their wonderful, winelike flavor.

In England, Damsons, and their cousins, sloes, are mixed with gin and sugar, then aged for months to create a striking purple liqueur. Americans tend to have heard of sloe gin, but not Damson gin. That strikes me as backwards, because as difficult as it is to find Damson plums in this country, it is even harder to find sloes. Nevertheless, alcoholic infusions are always popular at food swaps, and this Damson gin is no exception. The color alone makes it irresistible, and the taste is sweet and plummy enough to sip all on its own.

1	quart Damson plums
2½	cups gin
1½	cup sugar
	Juice of 1 lemon

Packaging

Pour the gin into pretty, clean glass bottles for swapping. You should be able to get four 8-ounce bottles with some left over, or three 12-ounce bottles. Label the bottles or decorate with a hanging tag.

1. Prick the Damsons all over with a fork or sharp knife. Divide them equally between two glass quart jars.

2. In a small saucepan, combine the gin, sugar, and lemon juice and heat over low heat, stirring, just until the sugar is dissolved.

3. Divide the liquid equally between the two jars and cover. Shake to blend.

4. Shake the jars daily for the first week, then once a week.

5. Store the jars in a dark, cool place for 10 to 12 weeks. Once you have achieved the desired taste, strain to remove the solids and decant into glass bottles.

BRINGING LIQUOR TO A FOOD SWAP

If you want to be the belle of the food swap ball, bring hooch. Alcoholic drinks are always among the hottest items at any swap. While spirits and liqueurs can be expensive to make and package, especially if you use glass bottles, they are a terrific option for people who are less experienced in the kitchen because they do not require any cooking.

If you are planning to bring something alcoholic to a food swap, check with the organizer first to ensure that the host site permits alcohol and, if so, whether sampling is permitted. For the sake of the continued existence of your food swap group, do not under any circumstances trade an alcoholic item with someone who is underage.

Because alcohol is expensive, it is perfectly acceptable to swap spirits in small amounts. Six or eight ounces is considered a generous portion.

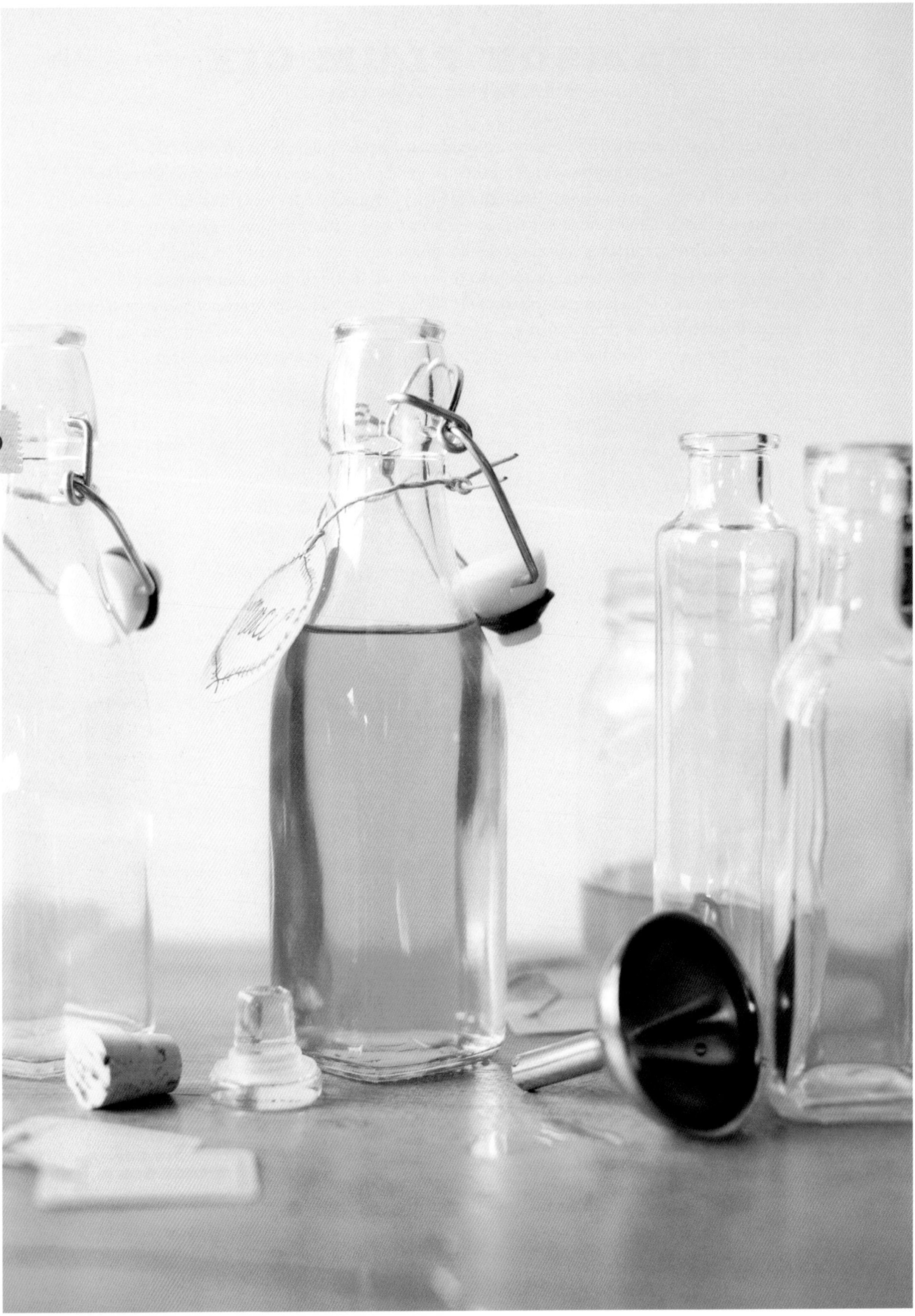

LIMONCELLO

MAKES ABOUT 3 (12-OUNCE) BOTTLES

Limoncello is a classic Italian after-dinner drink of lemon-infused vodka mixed with sugar syrup. Everyone seems to agree that Meyer lemons make the best limoncello. Larger and sweeter than a typical lemon, Meyer lemons have smooth skin and a delicious, slightly floral fragrance. Anything you can do with a lemon, you can do better with a Meyer lemon: cook with them, bake with them, clean your house with them, or better yet, tipple with them.

During the winter months, you can easily find Meyer lemons in most grocery stores that have a large produce section. And while they are more expensive than ordinary lemons, they are not outrageous. You can, of course, make limoncello with regular lemons. Whatever kind of lemon you use, do try to find organic ones, because you are using the outer rind where any pesticides or waxes would be found.

6 large lemons, preferably Meyer lemons

3 cups vodka, preferably 100-proof

2 cups sugar

2 cups water

Packaging

Pour the limoncello into attractive glass bottles. A 12- or 8-ounce size usually works well. In a pinch, you can simply use mason jars. Label the bottles or decorate with a hanging tag. Advise your trading partners to store their limoncello in the freezer, as it should be served chilled.

1. Using a vegetable peeler, remove the outer rind from the lemons in long strips. If you peel too deeply and end up with white pith on the underside of the rind, scrape it off with a knife.

2. Place the peels in a quart-size mason jar and cover with the vodka.

3. Store the jar in a cool, dark place for 2 to 4 weeks. The longer the peels steep, the more pronounced the lemon flavor will be.

4. Once you have achieved the desired flavor, strain the vodka and discard the lemon peels. You should have about 2 ½ cups of liquid.

5. In a small saucepan, make a simple syrup by combining the sugar and water and heating over high heat, stirring to dissolve the sugar. Continue stirring until the sugar is completely dissolved, about 5 minutes. Remove from the heat. Allow the simple syrup to cool to room temperature.

6. Combine 2 cups of the simple syrup with the vodka and stir to combine. Taste and add more simple syrup, or just plain water, as desired. (More simple syrup will make for a sweeter finished product, while adding water will make the limoncello smoother and milder.)

6

Future Pleasures:

SEASONINGS, PRESERVES & OTHER PANTRY ITEMS

VINEGARS & EXTRACTS

FLAVORED VINEGARS AND EXTRACTS appeal to the passionate cook or baker, so these items deserve your attention. Months after the swap is over, you could still be baking with that extract and making vinaigrette with that fruit-flavored vinegar. For these recipes, it is worthwhile to invest in attractive packaging, such as cute glass bottles, so that your item is not overlooked. Providing serving suggestions or recipes, if the item's use is not immediately obvious, is another way to reassure hesitant trading partners.

RASPBERRY VINEGAR

MAKES 3 PINTS OR 4 (12-OUNCE) BOTTLES

When people tell me they cannot attend a food swap because they do not know how to cook, I tell them that there are plenty of desirable things that they could make that do not require any cooking ability at all. Flavored vinegar is a prime example of such an item. Anyone can make it; the only skill required is the ability to plan ahead, because the vinegar has to sit for several weeks.

Feel free to experiment with different berries and vinegars, and to add herbs and other seasonings to your flavored vinegars. Invest in attractive glass bottles if you really want your flavored vinegars to stand out and be a hot swap item.

2   pints raspberries

2   cups white wine vinegar

2   cups apple cider vinegar

Packaging

Pour the vinegar into clean glass jars or bottles and label. Consider using glass bottles with a swing-top or a screw-top cap. You may also want to include dripper inserts, which are usually sold separately.

1. Crush the raspberries with a potato masher in a large nonreactive bowl until broken down. Add the vinegars and stir to combine. Cover the bowl tightly with plastic wrap and store in a cool, dark place for 4 weeks.

2. Check the vinegar weekly and stir.

3. After 4 weeks, strain the vinegar through a fine-mesh metal strainer lined with several layers of cheesecloth and discard the solids.

SEASONINGS, PRESERVES & OTHER PANTRY ITEMS

raspberry
vinegar

RUM VANILLA EXTRACT

MAKES 4 (4-OUNCE) BOTTLES

Here is another food swap item that does not require any cooking or kitchen skills. Indeed, homemade vanilla extract requires nothing more than five minutes of work and several weeks of patience, but it is always a highly sought-after item at food swaps.

I like to use rum as the base of my vanilla extract because it is sweet, but you could use vodka or bourbon if that is more to your taste. Packaging is critical to make homemade vanilla extract a must-have swap item. Source cute glass bottles online at one of the websites listed in the Resources section (page 237) or a craft store. The Internet is also a good source for reasonably priced vanilla beans, which cost a pretty penny in spice stores.

8   vanilla beans (look for Madagascar vanilla beans for the best flavor)

16   ounces light rum, such as white or silver

1. Cut the vanilla beans in half, then split the halves down the middle lengthwise. Place the vanilla beans in a clean, dry pint jar. Cover the beans with rum, filling the jar to the top and making sure the beans are completely submerged.

2. Cover the jar and store it in a dark place for at least 4 weeks. (Label the jars with the date you made the extract.)

Packaging

Place one or two of the vanilla bean halves in each bottle and, using a small funnel, carefully pour the extract over the beans. Decorate each bottle with a label or hanging tag. If you have not planned far enough ahead and want to swap this vanilla extract before 4 weeks have passed, simply note on the bottle the date the extract was made and the date it will be ready to use and advise your trading partner accordingly. Homemade vanilla extract also makes a charming gift.

SPICE MIXES

SPICE MIXES LACK THE SEX APPEAL of a cupcake or the wow factor of a truffle and are undervalued by most attendees. But you can tell who at the food swap is a serious cook by whether they are interested in that homemade chili or curry powder. Spice mixes will last for weeks, if not months, in your pantry, and they add flavor and interest to your cooking. I particularly like how spice mixes lend authenticity to my efforts to cook different world cuisines, from Indian to Middle Eastern.

It can be hard to offer samples of spice mixes. I find that dusting some of the mix on top of popcorn works well as a way to show off the mix's flavor. Do not be dismayed if only a few swappers appreciate the value of a homemade garam masala or baharat. Those people are worth seeking out.

To make my homemade spice mixes, I use a small electric coffee grinder that I reserve for that purpose. Do not grind coffee and spices in the same machine; you will find that your coffee tastes spicy and your spice mixes taste like nothing so much as coffee.

The most economical source for whole spices is ethnic markets or the Internet. Indian markets are a good source for cumin seeds, cardamom pods, cinnamon sticks, black peppercorns, and more. For dried chiles, try a Latin grocery store or order them online.

To package your spice mixes, you can order plastic or glass spice jars in small sizes, such as 1 or 2 ounces, through Amazon, Specialty Bottle, or any of the other websites listed in the Resources section (page 237). Spice mixes also look nice packaged in small metal tins with clear lids. It is very helpful to include suggestions for how to use your spice mix or even attach a card with a recipe or two.

garam masala

GARAM MASALA

MAKES 1 CUP OR 4 (2-OUNCE) JARS

Garam masala is a northern Indian spice mix the exact make up of which varies from region to region. The name means "warm spice mix," but that does not mean that the mix is particularly spicy. Rather, "warm" here references the Ayurvedic belief that these ingredients raise the temperature of the body.

Typical ingredients in garam masala include cardamom pods, whole cloves, cinnamon, cumin seeds, coriander seeds, and black peppercorns. I include nutmeg and fennel in mine. The spices are first toasted to bring out their flavor , then ground into a powder. Garam masala is typically added to a dish toward the end of cooking because it can taste bitter if cooked too long. Enjoy garam masala in all your favorite South Asian foods, but do not limit its use to that. Garam masala is finding its way into all kinds of dishes, including baked goods.

2   cinnamon sticks, broken into pieces

1   star anise

½   cup cumin seeds

½   cup coriander seeds

2   tablespoons green cardamom pods

2   tablespoons black peppercorns

4   teaspoons whole cloves

2   dried Indian chiles

2   teaspoons fennel seeds

½   whole nutmeg, grated

1. Combine the cinnamon sticks, star anise, cumin, coriander, cardamom, peppercorns, cloves, chiles, and fennel in a dry skillet and toast over medium heat until fragrant, about 3 minutes.

2. Working in batches, grind the spices to a powder in an electric coffee grinder. Transfer the powder to a glass bowl and mix in the grated nutmeg. Stir with a fork to ensure that the spices are evenly combined.

Packaging

Divide the mixture evenly among the spice jars for swapping. Store in a cool, dark place.

CHILI POWDER

MAKES 3 OUNCES

Homemade chili powder is well worth the effort. Store-bought varieties tend to be stale, bitter, and one-dimensional. By making your own, you not only know that it is fresh and full of flavor, but you can adjust the taste to your preference: do you like it spicy? More garlicky? Heavier on the cumin? It is up to you.

I like to mix several different kinds of dried chiles in my chili powder. Earthy, sweet ancho chiles are the base. Guajillos are spicier, with a bright, fruity flavor. Chipotles add smokiness, and chiles de árbol bring the heat. Toasting the chiles not only brings out their flavor but makes them crisp and dry, which is better for grinding into powder. Be careful, as always, when working with chile peppers, and be prepared to sneeze a lot.

9   dried ancho chiles

3   dried guajillo chiles

3   chipotle chiles

3   chiles de árbol

2   tablespoons cumin seeds

2   tablespoons garlic granules or garlic powder

1   tablespoon Mexican oregano

1   teaspoon smoked paprika

Packaging

Divide the powder into 3 (1-ounce) spice jars or tins for swapping. Add a label.

1. Preheat the oven to 350°F (175°C) and line a baking sheet with foil.

2. Arrange the chiles on the foil and roast in the oven for 7 to 10 minutes, or until fragrant, dry, and crisp to the touch.

3. Toast the cumin seeds in a dry skillet over medium heat until lightly browned and fragrant, about 3 minutes. Stir or shake the seeds while toasting to ensure even browning. Allow both the cumin seeds and chiles to cool before proceeding.

4. Open the chiles and remove the stems and seeds. (I find that scissors work better than a knife for opening dried chiles.) Working in batches, grind the chiles, cumin seeds, garlic granules, and oregano to a fine powder. As you finish each batch, pour the resulting powder into a large bowl. Add the paprika and whisk together to combine and evenly distribute the ingredients.

Note: *I once had the opportunity to interview Rick Bayless, the Chicago chef famous for his Mexican restaurants, cookbooks, and PBS show. I asked him to name one ingredient that home cooks could keep in their pantries to make more authentic Mexican food, and his answer was dried chiles. I find it easiest to order large quantities of dried chiles online. They will keep well in an airtight container stored in a cool, dark place. For the best flavor, look for chiles that are glossy and still pliable.*

ZA'ATAR SPICE

¼   cup dried thyme leaves

¼   cup sesame seeds, lightly toasted

2   tablespoons ground sumac

1   teaspoon kosher salt

Combine all ingredients in a small bowl and blend thoroughly with a fork. Package the mixture into 1-ounce portions for swapping; this recipe makes 3 ounces.

QUARTRE ÉPICES

4   tablespoons finely ground white pepper

4   tablespoons cinnamon

4   tablespoons ground ginger

4   tablespoons ground cloves

Combine all ingredients in a small bowl and blend thoroughly with a fork. Divide the mixture into 2-ounce portions for an easy swap item; this recipe makes 8 ounces.

FLAVORED SALTS

FLAVORED SALTS ARE ANOTHER terrific no-cook, last-minute food swap item. Indeed, some of these variations are so quick to make, you could literally prepare them five minutes before you leave for the swap. Yet swappers enjoy trading for them because flavored salt is such a useful and sophisticated ingredient to have in the kitchen to finish a dish.

Over the years, I have seen a tremendous variety of flavored salts, from saffron to Sriracha; be creative. Use a coarse salt, such as kosher (cheapest option) or a flaky sea salt (best flavor), for these recipes. Package flavored salts in spice bottles, small tins; or, if you are feeling generous, 4-ounce mason jars.

ALL COMBINATIONS MAKE 1 TO 1¼ CUPS

HERB SALT

1   cup salt

¼   cup sturdy fresh herbs, such as rosemary, sage, or thyme

Process the salt and herbs in a food processor or blender until well combined. Use one herb or a mixture. You can double or even triple the recipe for swapping.

SEAWEED SALT

Packed with umami, dried seaweed adds a startling depth of flavor to salt. While it is pricey to buy, seaweed salt is easy to make yourself. Look for dried kelp, dulse, or nori at a health food store.

⅓   cup seaweed

1   cup salt

Dice the seaweed fine and then chop in the food processor. Stir into the salt. Start with a 3:1 salt-to-seaweed ratio, but you can increase it to a 2:1 ratio if you prefer a stronger taste.

CITRUS SALT

If you ever have to juice a lot of citrus for a recipe, begin by zesting the fruits for a batch of citrus salt. Lemon salt is an obvious choice, but experiment with lime or orange as well.

2 to 3   tablespoons zest

1   cup salt

Spread the zest in an even layer on a parchment-lined baking sheet and bake in a 200°F (95°C) oven until crisp, 30 to 45 minutes. (You can also air-dry it by letting the mixture sit out overnight.)

Crumble the dried zest with your fingers and combine with salt — no need to use the food processor.

CHIPOTLE SALT

3   dried chipotle chiles

1   cup salt

Finely dice the chiles and remove as many of the seeds as possible.

Combine the diced chiles with the salt in the bowl of a food processor. Process until well combined. (Be careful of the fumes.)

INFUSED SUGARS

LIKE FLAVORED SALT, infused sugar is an easy, last-minute swap item that almost anyone can prepare, regardless of cooking experience. Flavored sugars add an extra level of flavor to baked goods and are wonderful for sweetening beverages such as lemonade or iced tea. Experiment with herbs, spices, citrus zest, and more.

ALL COMBINATIONS MAKE 1 PINT

CITRUS SUGAR

Zest of 2 lemons (or other citrus fruits, such as orange or lime)

2   cups sugar

Dry the zest by spreading it out in a even layer on a parchment-lined baking sheet and baking in a 200°F (95°C) oven until crisp, 30 to 45 minutes. (You can also air-dry it by letting the mixture sit out overnight.)

Crumble the zest with your fingers and combine with the sugar.

SPICED SUGAR

2   cups sugar

2   teaspoons ground cardamom

2   teaspoons cinnamon

2   teaspoons ground ginger

1   teaspoon nutmeg, preferably freshly grated

Combine the sugar, cardamom, cinnamon, ginger, and nutmeg in a medium bowl and whisk to combine.

LAVENDER SUGAR

2   cups sugar

2½   teaspoons dried lavender

Combine the sugar and lavender buds in a food processor and pulse until the lavender is in tiny pieces.

MINT SUGAR

2   tablespoons dried spearmint

2   cups sugar

Crush the dried spearmint with your fingers or a mortar and pestle until powdery. Combine with the sugar.

COFFEE SUGAR

2   cups sugar

1   tablespoon espresso powder (see page 98)

Combine the sugar and espresso powder in a medium bowl and whisk together.

ART STUDENT MANDY ANDREE grew up around soda and potato chips, but when she moved out on her own, she became more interested in nutrition and healthy eating. She first heard about a food swap in California while doing some research online. She expected to find one in Atlanta, but when she didn't, she launched the Atlanta Food Swap in May 2013.

At the time, Mandy worked at the Goat Farm, a historic landmark and former goat farm that had been divided up into artists' studios. Already home to an underground supper club, the Goat Farm was happy to host the Atlanta Food Swap and was able to leverage its network to spread the word about the swap.

Attendees tend to be passionate about health and nutrition, like Mandy herself, and the offerings reflect that. The Atlanta Food Swap participants bring more pickles and ferments than candies and baked goods. Many swappers are gluten-free and vegetarian or even vegan. With Atlanta's mild climate and long growing season, homegrown produce, herbs, and even fresh flowers are popular swap items. Perhaps because of the number of male chefs in town, the Atlanta Food Swap has been more successful than most at attracting large numbers of male swappers.

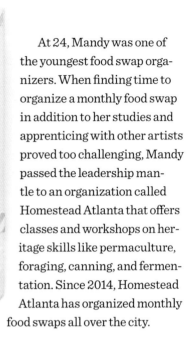

At 24, Mandy was one of the youngest food swap organizers. When finding time to organize a monthly food swap in addition to her studies and apprenticing with other artists proved too challenging, Mandy passed the leadership mantle to an organization called Homestead Atlanta that offers classes and workshops on heritage skills like permaculture, foraging, canning, and fermentation. Since 2014, Homestead Atlanta has organized monthly food swaps all over the city.

The Atlanta Food Swap participants bring more pickles and ferments than candies and baked goods. Many swappers are gluten-free and vegetarian or even vegan.

Mandy's hope is for the food swap movement to spread all over the country and for swaps to become more local, rather than have people drive from far away to attend one large, centralized swap. For Mandy, the best thing a food swap can do is to allow people to get to know their neighbors and to take time to share a meal with others in their community.

PRESERVED FRUITS

BEAUTIFUL JAMS AND JELLIES (and marmalades, conserves, and fruit butters) are among the most popular items at any food swap. Preserves made from scratch are so much tastier than commercial varieties that those swappers who have not yet embraced the home food-preservation trend actively seek out others' homemade spreads. And handcrafted preserves come in unusual and unique flavors. While jams and jellies are the most common form of preserved fruit, you can also make wonderful fruit sauces, pie fillings, and even savory fruit preserves such as chutneys and salsas to swap or give. In this section, I give you at least one recipe for every category of preserved fruits.

When making jams, jellies, and marmalades, the biggest worry is achieving a spreadable, gelled consistency. For recipes that do not call for added pectin, you need to cook the preserve to the gelling point of 220°F (105°C). A candy thermometer is useful for this process.

There are also many old-fashioned ways to test whether your preserve has gelled, and despite owning a candy thermometer, I sometimes rely on those methods as well. One method I like is the freezer test: Place a saucer in the freezer when you begin cooking your preserve. When you think the preserve is done, place a small dab on the chilled saucer and return it to the freezer for 1 minute. Remove the saucer and push the jam or jelly with your finger. If it wrinkles and appears to be set, the preserve is ready.

SAFE WATER-BATH CANNING PROCEDURES

Canning has experienced a resurgence in the past decade, although in some parts of the country, namely the South, it never really went away. Many home cooks enjoy preserving — whether they put up a few jars once a year or spend every summer weekend slaving over a hot stove — and you will find beautiful jams, jellies, relishes, chutneys, salsas, and pickles at every food swap in the country.

Yet many home cooks, even experienced ones, still find water-bath canning to be intimidating. Let me reassure you that it is not difficult or scary, but it is important to adhere to safe canning procedures and to follow tested recipes. There are many wonderful preserving cookbooks that will teach you the basics, such as the Put 'em Up series by Sherri Brooks Vinton and *Food in Jars* by Philadelphia food swap organizer Marisa McClellan. If you prefer to learn from a live person, look for canning classes and workshops in your area.

To save you from pulling another cookbook off the shelf, however, here are the basics of water-bath canning. First, remember that water-bath canning is a very safe method of home food preservation for high-acid foods. (Low-acid foods can only be safely canned in a pressure canner.) Use this method for foods that are naturally high in acidity or by introducing acid into the preserve in the form of lemon juice or vinegar. Because water-bath canning is only safe for foods of a certain pH level, below pH 4.6 to be precise, it is important to follow tested recipes and to maintain the ratios used in those recipes.

In water-bath canning, boiling water is used to process the filled jars to create a vacuum seal that makes the jars shelf stable without refrigeration. For this reason, it is critical to use the correct equipment: a large pot outfitted with a rack that will allow boiling water to circulate around the jars, and glass canning jars with lids that seal. Other pieces of equipment, such as a widemouthed funnel and a jar lifter, are helpful but not necessary. You can find large canning pots with racks at some big-box stores or online. You can also use any large, deep pot outfitted with a rack of some sort so that the jars are not sitting directly on the bottom of the pot.

widemouthed **FUNNEL**

large canning **POT**

glass canning **JAR**

RACK

JAR *lifter*

Ball

Ball

Use only glass canning jars that are either new or in excellent used condition without any cracks or nicks, and lids that are intended for home canning. These come in one-part or two-part varieties and are made of metal or sometimes plastic, such as the reusable Tattler lids. You can find canning jars and lids in grocery stores with good canning sections, hardware stores, or kitchen stores. You can also order jars online, but because of their weight, shipping tends to be expensive. (See Resources, page 237.)

The glass jars do not need to be sterilized prior to filling so long as the final product will be processed in the boiling-water bath for 10 minutes or more. However, you do need to begin with jars that are clean and warm. If you ladle hot jam or brine into a cold or room-temperature jar, it could crack.

When I begin a preserving project, my first task is to fill my canning pot with water and to place my empty jars in the pot. I then bring that water to a boil. That way I know my jars will be warm when I need them.

Stick to the Recipe

It is important to follow tested recipes and to maintain the ratios specified in those recipes. This is in order to ensure that your preserve has the correct pH level for safe canning. It is also important, especially when making jams and jellies, to use the amount of sugar called for in the recipe. Sugar acts as a preservative, and it also is critical for achieving the right consistency. You can make low-sugar jams or jams with alternative sweeteners, but you will need to use low-sugar pectins and follow tested recipes using those products.

1/2 INCH

1/4 INCH

3/4 INCH

Strawberry Jam

Dilly Beans

Apple Sauce

When the food to be preserved is ready, I remove a jar from the water, empty it, and fill it with the preserve, taking care to leave room at the top. This extra room is known as headspace, and every canning recipe specifies how much to leave, from ¼ inch in jam recipes to as much as ¾ or a full inch in other types of preserves. Failing to leave sufficient headspace can cause the food in your jars to bubble out and prevent the lid from sealing.

The amount of headspace specified in a recipe is a floor as well as a ceiling: Do not leave less headspace than called for, but do not leave more either. That would allow too much oxygen to remain in the jar and prevent a vacuum seal or cause discoloration. A jar that is only partially filled cannot be safely processed; store it in the refrigerator instead.

After the jar is filled to the height specified, run a thin plastic utensil around the inside of the jar to release air bubbles. This is known as bubbling the jars. Failing to do this could prevent your jars from sealing. Lastly, clean off the rim of the jar with a damp cloth, as residue left on the rim could also prevent the lid from sealing. Place the lid on the jar and tighten it just until you feel resistance. Closing it too tightly could prevent any air inside from escaping, which would interfere with the seal.

The jar then goes back into the boiling water. Make sure the water covers the top of the jar by at least two inches. The jar should remain in the boiling-water bath, covered with water, for the time specified in the recipe, anywhere from 10 minutes for most jams to 45 minutes for some tomato recipes. This is known as processing the jars. (People at high altitudes may need to adjust processing time.)

After the jars have been processed in the boiling-water bath for the requisite amount of time, allow them to remain in the water with the heat off for a few minutes to cool slightly before removing them to a towel placed on the counter. (The towel absorbs the water from the jars and also insulates

2 INCHES

them from the cold countertop, which could cause the jars to crack.) The jars should cool for several hours. You may hear a ping as the jars seal, but do not be dismayed if you do not: the jars may still seal without the noise.

Once the jars are cool, check the seals by eyeballing them to ensure that the button in the middle is concave. You can also check the seals by gently trying to pry off the lid with your fingernails. It should not come off if the seal is good.

What If Your Jars Don't Seal?

Remember that the food inside unsealed jars is still good, so do not discard it. A failure to seal simply means that the food is not shelf stable; those jars can be safely stored in the refrigerator. The failure to seal could be the result of residue on the rim, overfilling the jars, or simply a bad lid or two.

Sealed jars can be stored without refrigeration for up to 1 year. Put them in a cool, dark place for the best quality. Once you've opened them, store jars in the refrigerator.

A QUICK WORD ON PECTIN

Pectin is a naturally occurring substance that causes food to gel to a spreadable consistency. Some fruits (such as apples and Damson plums) are naturally high in pectin, while others (such as strawberries) are not. When making jams and jellies, you can achieve a good gel by relying on the pectin in the fruit itself, or you can add powdered or liquid pectin. Some canners love adding pectin and others abhor it. I have no such strong feelings. Sometimes I add pectin to my preserves and sometimes I do not.

There are multiple kinds of pectin on the market, but I tend to use the basic powdered kind, which is cheapest. Pomona's Universal Pectin, which some canners prefer, calls for a slightly different procedure from most commercial pectin. Be sure to follow the instructions for the kind of pectin you buy. You can find pectin in grocery stores with a good canning section or online.

PRESERVED LEMONS

MAKES 3 (8-OUNCE) JARS WITH 3–4 PRESERVED LEMONS

A staple of Middle Eastern cooking, preserved lemons add a unique pickled tanginess to dishes. You can find preserved lemons in stores, but the homemade kind is so much more flavorful. I find this project to be easier with small lemons, such as those sold in bags at the grocery stores. I especially like to make preserved lemons during the winter months when citrus is in season and you can find lots of different varieties.

Once your lemons are ready, you can package two or three in an 8-ounce jar for swapping or gifting. They make for a beautiful presentation, especially if you add a bit of rosemary or a chile to the jar. A small amount of preserved lemon adds a lot of flavor to a dish, so three whole preserved lemons will actually last quite a while.

1	48-ounce box kosher salt
10–12	small lemons, preferably organic
2	sprigs rosemary
3	dried red chiles

Packaging

For swapping, place 3 to 4 lemons and a chile in each of three clean 8-ounce glass jars. If desired, garnish with a fresh sprig of rosemary. Cover the lemons with brine. Repeat with the remaining lemons and discard any leftover brine. Lemons will last for months in the refrigerator.

1. Sterilize a quart-size glass jar: pour in boiling water to fill and allow the water to sit for a few minutes. Drain the jar and allow it to air-dry.

2. Cover the bottom of the jar with a thin layer of kosher salt, about 3 tablespoons.

3. Cut a deep X into the top of each lemon, taking care not to cut all the way through the fruit.

4. Add a teaspoon of kosher salt to the middle of the first lemon and drop it in the bottom of the jar. Repeat with two other lemons and place them in the jar, mashing them with the end of a wooden spoon to release the juices and to form a relatively even layer of lemons at the bottom of the jar. Fill in the spaces between the lemons with salt.

5. Repeat with three more lemons to form a second layer. Repeat with the remaining lemons until the jar is full. Slide the sprigs of rosemary along the sides of the jar and add the chiles.

6. If the lemons are not submerged in juice at this point, squeeze one or more additional lemons and add the juice to the jar until the lemons are submerged. You can also add a little water if needed. Cover with a layer of salt and seal. Mark the date.

7. Store the jar in a cool place for at least 4 weeks, shaking several times a week to distribute the salt and juice. The lemons are ready to use when the rinds have softened. Prior to using, rinse off the excess salt. Typically only the rind is used and the pulp is discarded.

STRAWBERRY-RHUBARB JAM
WITH JALAPEÑO
MAKES 8 OR 9 (8-OUNCE) JARS

Sometimes all you need for a great swap item is a new twist on an old favorite. Strawberry-rhubarb jam may be a classic spring preserve, but the addition of the jalapeño here will pique the interest of potential trading partners, especially once they try this sweet-spicy confection.

I like this recipe because the heat from the jalapeño is subtle and in no way precludes using this jam as you would any other strawberry-rhubarb jam. You taste the sweetness first, although the addition of lemon zest and juice prevents it from being too sweet, and only afterwards do you feel a slight tingle on your tongue from the jalapeño.

To get 4 cups of crushed berries, I recommend buying 2 quarts of whole berries. You should have some berries left over.

6 cups trimmed and sliced rhubarb

4 cups crushed strawberries

1 jalapeño pepper, seeded and minced

1 teaspoon butter (optional, to reduce foaming)

¼ cup bottled lemon juice

Zest of 1 lemon

¼ cup regular powdered pectin

5 cups sugar

Note: *When a preserving recipe calls for bottled lemon juice, do not substitute freshly squeezed lemon juice. The acidity of lemons can vary, making bottled lemon juice a safer choice in those recipes.*

1. Prepare a boiling-water-bath canner and heat nine 8-ounce jars. (See Safe Water-Bath Canning Procedures, page 198.)

2. Combine the rhubarb, strawberries, jalapeño pepper, butter (if using), lemon juice, and lemon zest in a large Dutch oven or stockpot. (The wider the pot, the faster the fruit will come to a boil.) Sprinkle the powdered pectin over the fruit and stir to combine. Bring the fruit to a vigorous boil over high heat, stirring constantly to prevent scorching.

3. When the fruit is at a rapid boil that cannot be stirred down, add the sugar all at once and stir to combine. Bring the mixture back to a rapid boil over high heat, stirring constantly.

4. Boil the jam hard for 2 minutes, then remove from the heat. Skim off any foam that has accumulated.

5. Ladle the jam into clean, warm jars, leaving ¼ inch headspace at the top of the jar. Bubble the jars and wipe the rims with a damp cloth. Place the lids on the jars, and screw on the rings just until you feel resistance.

6. Process the jars in the boiling-water bath for 10 minutes. Allow them to cool in the water for 5 minutes before removing to a towel to cool completely.

7. Check the seals and store in a cool, dark place for up to 1 year.

BLACK RASPBERRY JAM

WITH MINT

MAKES 4 OR 5 (8-OUNCE) JARS

Don't confuse black raspberries with their larger, shinier cousins, blackberries. Black raspberries are the same size and shape as regular raspberries, with the familiar hollow core, but instead of being bright red, they are purplish black with a white bloom. Native to North America, black raspberries, also known as blackcaps, are prized for their sweet, mild flavor and deep color.

Depending on where you live, black raspberries may be hard to find. I see them a few times a year at my farmers' market, where they sell for the same price as red raspberries. Black raspberry jam stands out from all the other jams on offer, and other swappers go crazy for it. But keep at least one jar of this jam for yourself! You can substitute red raspberries if you cannot source black raspberries.

4   pints black raspberries
(about 2½ pounds)

3   cups sugar

3   tablespoons freshly squeezed
lemon juice

2   sprigs fresh mint

1. Prepare a boiling-water-bath canner and heat five 8-ounce jars. (See Safe Water-Bath Canning Procedures, page 198.) Place a saucer in the freezer.

2. Put the raspberries in a large deep saucepan or preserving pan, and crush with a potato masher or fork. Add the sugar and lemon juice, and stir to combine. Place the mint sprigs in the fruit mixture. Bring to a boil over high heat, stirring frequently to prevent scorching.

3. Reduce the heat to medium, but keep the raspberries at a rapid boil, stirring frequently until the jam begins to set, 15 to 20 minutes. Be careful; the jam will splatter.

4. When the jam appears thick and comes off a spoon in a sheet rather than in thin droplets, remove the saucer from the freezer and place a dollop of jam on it. Return the saucer to the freezer for 1 minute. Remove the saucer and push the dollop of jam with your finger. If it wrinkles, then the jam is set.

5. Remove the jam from the heat and remove and discard the mint sprigs. Ladle the jam into the clean, warm jars, leaving ¼ inch headspace. Bubble the jars and wipe the rims with a damp cloth. Place the lids on the jars and screw on the rings just until you feel resistance.

6. Process the jars in the boiling-water bath for 10 minutes. Allow the jars to cool in the water for 5 minutes before removing to a towel to cool completely.

7. Store in a cool, dark place for up to 1 year.

DAMSON PLUM JAM

MAKES 5 TO 6 (8-OUNCE) JARS

Damson plum jam may be my favorite preserve. It tastes like a fruity merlot and boasts a stunning magenta color. Damsons are naturally rich in pectin, which makes the jam thick and smooth, especially if you strain out the skins. Damsons contain so much pectin, in fact, that you can actually make a fruit paste with them, similar to quince paste, which the Brits call Damson cheese because it is firm enough to be sliced like cheese.

Depending on where you live, you may have trouble finding Damson plums, but ask around at your farmers' market. There is one vendor at the Oak Park Farmers' Market, where I shop, who used to bring Damson plums in September for me and a few old ladies. Last year when I asked Brad Baser, the farmer, if he was going to bring my Damsons soon, he told me that all the other customers who requested them had died! So I got the whole crop, and I had plenty of Damson plum jam to eat and swap. Sometimes it helps to be old-fashioned.

3   quarts Damson plums
    (about 4 pounds)

1   cup water

4   cups sugar

½   vanilla bean

1. Prepare a boiling-water-bath canner and heat six 8-ounce jars. (See Safe Water-Bath Canning Procedures, page 198.) Place a saucer in the freezer.

2. Place the plums in a large saucepan with the cup of water and bring to a boil. Turn down the heat and simmer the plums, covered, for 15 minutes or until they have split open.

3. Remove the cover and simmer for an additional 8 to 10 minutes or until the plums have broken down and you see pits floating to the top.

4. Strain the plum mixture through a sieve into a large bowl, stirring with a spatula or wooden spoon to force through as much of the flesh as possible and leaving behind the skins and pits. (This is somewhat tedious, but less so than it would be to pit all the Damsons raw.)

5. Measure the plum purée. You should have around 6 cups. (If you have less, then decrease the amount of sugar in the next step, maintaining the 3:2 ratio of fruit to sugar.)

6. Return the purée to the large saucepan and add the sugar. Split the vanilla bean lengthwise down the middle, scrape out the flesh, and add it to the plums. Then add the vanilla bean. Stir to combine and to dissolve the sugar.

7. Bring the mixture to a boil over high heat, stirring frequently. Turn the heat down to medium-high and continue to boil the mixture until it begins to thicken, about 10 minutes.

8. Because of their high pectin content, Damsons gel rather quickly, and you do not want to overcook them. The jam will still look liquid even when it is ready. Test for doneness after 10 minutes by placing a spoonful of jam on the chilled saucer. Return the saucer to the freezer for 1 minute. Then push the jam with your finger. If it wrinkles, the jam is ready. Remove the vanilla bean and discard.

9. Ladle the jam into the clean, warm jars, leaving ¼ inch headspace. Bubble the jars and wipe the rims with a damp cloth. Place the lids on the jars and screw on the rings just until you feel resistance.

10. Process the jars in the boiling-water bath for 10 minutes. Allow the jars to cool in the water for 5 minutes before removing to a towel to cool completely.

11. Store in a cool, dark place for up to 1 year.

Apple
Jelly

Damson
Plum
Jam

Blood Orange
Marmalade

APPLE JELLY

MAKES 4 TO 5 (8-OUNCE) JARS

Apple jelly is an exceptionally beautiful, old-fashioned preserve. When prepared correctly, it is perfectly translucent in a maidenly shade of pale pink and has a delicate, sweet apple flavor. I think of apple jelly as quite French because my friend and Chicago Food Swap cofounder Vanessa Druckman, who is French, makes a delicious gelée de pommes. But then again, another friend, who grew up in Indiana, waxes nostalgic about her grandmother's apple jelly which she used to eat on Nilla wafers.

This project is a bit fussy because you have to start by making apple juice, but you can split the work over two days. The result, an eye-catching swap item, is well worth the trouble.

5 pounds apples, quartered, stems and bottom ends removed

5 cups water

3¾ cups sugar

2 tablespoons bottled lemon juice

1. Place the apple quarters and the water in a large saucepan and bring to a boil. Reduce the heat and boil gently, with the pot partially covered, until the apples are tender enough to crush with a wooden spoon, about 20 to 30 minutes. Do not overcook, because that will affect how the jelly gels.

2. Line a colander with several layers of damp cheesecloth and place it over a tall stockpot. Ladle the apple mixture into the colander and allow the juice to drain into the pot undisturbed for at least 2 hours. (Do not press on the apples or squeeze the cheesecloth, because that will result in a cloudy jelly.) You should end up with 5 cups of juice. Discard the remaining apple pulp.

3. To make the jelly, prepare a boiling-water-bath canner and heat five 8-ounce jars. (See Safe Water-Bath Canning Procedures, page 198.) If planning to use the freezer test to determine when the jelly is set (see page 197), place a saucer in the freezer to chill.

4. Combine the apple juice, sugar, and lemon juice in a large, deep saucepan and bring the mixture to a boil over high heat, stirring to dissolve the sugar. (This jelly will bubble up substantially, so select a larger pot than you think you need.) Reduce the heat to medium-high and boil the mixture, stirring frequently, until it reaches 220°F (105°C) on a candy thermometer, about 20 minutes. (Or test for doneness using the freezer test.) Skim off any foam that has accumulated for the clearest jelly.

5. Ladle the jelly into the clean, warm jars, leaving ¼ inch headspace. Bubble the jars and wipe the rims with a damp cloth. Place the lids on the jars and screw on the rings just until you feel resistance.

6. Process the jars in the boiling-water bath for 10 minutes. Allow the jars to cool in the water for 5 minutes before removing to a towel to cool completely.

7. Store in a cool, dark place for up to 1 year.

BLOOD ORANGE MARMALADE
WITH CAMPARI
MAKES 4 TO 5 (8-OUNCE) JARS

This recipe comes from Beth Dixon, the cofounder of the RVA Swappers in Richmond, Virginia, and an experienced craft bartender. Beth incorporates the apéritif Campari into her marmalade, then uses the marmalade in a unique cocktail. For swapping purposes, attach the cocktail recipe to the jar of marmalade using a decorative tag. Your trading partners will love it.

Named for the deep, red color of their flesh, blood oranges are usually smaller than navel oranges and have a dimpled peel. Blood oranges are prized not only for their color but also for their sweet, fruity flavor. They are often showcased in salads, and their juice is used in cocktails and sauces. You should be able to find blood oranges in most good grocery stores during the winter months.

6 blood oranges

1 cup whole cranberries, fresh or frozen

4½ cups sugar

3¾ cup water

½ cup bottled lemon juice

1½ cups Campari

1. Using a sharp vegetable peeler, peel the zest from the outside of the oranges in long strips, avoiding the white pith. Peel the oranges and discard the rinds. Break the oranges into segments.

2. Combine the orange zest and segments, cranberries, sugar, and water in a large saucepan and bring to a boil, stirring to dissolve the sugar.

3. Reduce the heat and simmer the mixture, covered, until zest and cranberries are tender, 20 to 30 minutes. Remove from the heat.

4. Strain out the solids and allow to cool. When cool enough to handle, reserve the zest and discard the rest of the solids. Slice the zest into thin strips and return them to the pot with the syrup.

5. Add the lemon juice to the pot with the zest and syrup, and return to a boil. Lower the heat and simmer, uncovered, stirring frequently to prevent scorching, until the syrup has thickened and the zest softened, about 30 minutes.

6. Meanwhile, prepare a boiling-water-bath canner and heat five 8-ounce jars. (See Safe Water-Bath Canning Procedures, page 198.) If planning to use the freezer test to determine when the marmalade is set (see page 197), place a saucer in the freezer to chill.

7. After the syrup has simmered for 30 minutes, add the Campari. Raise the heat to high and return the syrup to a boil. Reduce the heat to medium-high and boil the mixture hard, stirring frequently, until it reaches 220°F (105°C) on a candy thermometer. (Or test for doneness using the freezer test.)

8. Ladle the marmalade, dividing the zest evenly, into the clean, warm jars, leaving ¼ inch headspace. Bubble the jars and wipe the rims with a damp cloth. Place the lids on the jars and screw on the rings just until you feel resistance.

9. Process the jars in the boiling-water bath for 10 minutes. Allow the jars to cool in the water for 5 minutes before removing to a towel to cool completely.

10. Store in a cool, dark place for up to 1 year.

Blood Orange Marmalade Cocktail

2   ounces preferred spirit, such as gin or tequila

2   tablespoons Blood Orange Marmalade with Campari

¼   ounce fresh lemon juice

   Club soda (desired amount)

   Lemon slice

Add the spirit, marmalade, and lemon juice to a cocktail shaker over ice. Shake ingredients vigorously to make sure the marmalade is combined well. Pour into an old-fashioned glass and add club soda to fill. Garnish with a slice of lemon.

APRICOT BUTTER

MAKES 4 (8-OUNCE) JARS

Fruit butters contain no actual butter, but are concentrated fruit spreads that have an incredibly rich, silky texture. They call for less sugar than jams and jellies and require long, slow cooking. Many people make the mistake of pulling the pot off the heat too soon. It is important to let the butter cook down until the color is deep and it is very thick and spreadable — to the point that it is actually hard to pull a spoon through. You don't need to hover over the pot, but you do need to keep an eye on the butter and stir every few minutes to prevent scorching.

While apple butter may be the most traditional variety, stone fruits like apricot and peaches make amazing fruit butters. In addition to being wonderful on toast or spooned into yogurt, apricot butter makes a delicious and unusual filling for a layer cake or sandwich cookies.

3   pounds pitted, halved apricots (from 2 dry quarts)

3   cups sugar

3   tablespoons bottled lemon juice

½   teaspoon cinnamon

⅛   teaspoon ground cloves

1. Put the halved apricots in a wide, deep saucepan with ¼ cup water.

2. Bring the mixture to a boil, then reduce the heat and simmer the apricots, covered, until soft, about 10 to 15 minutes.

3. Purée the apricots and any remaining liquid in a high-speed blender, food processor, or food mill until smooth but not liquefied.

4. Return the purée to the saucepan and add the sugar, lemon juice, cinnamon, and ground cloves.

5. Bring the mixture to a boil, then reduce the heat to low and simmer, stirring frequently to prevent scorching.

6. Simmer the butter until very thick and concentrated. This could take as long as 2 hours.

7. If not processing, store the butter in the refrigerator and note on your swap sheets that it is perishable and should be refrigerated.

CANNING FOR SHELF STABILITY

The apricot butter can be processed for shelf-stability in a boiling- water bath. To do so, prepare a water-bath canner and heat four 8-ounce jars while the butter is thickening. (See Safe Water-Bath Canning Procedures, page 198.)

Ladle the butter into the jars, leaving ¼ inch headspace. Bubble the jars and wipe the rims with a damp cloth.

Place the lids on the jars and screw on the rings just until you feel resistance.

Process the jars in the boiling-water bath for 15 minutes. Allow the jars to cool in the water for 5 minutes before removing to a towel to cool completely.

Store in a cool, dark place for up to 6 months. (Fruit butters have a shorter shelf life than jams and jellies because they contain less sugar.)

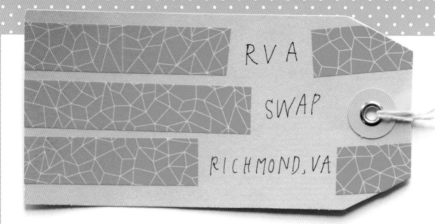

ANDREA BUONO HAD ATTENDED FOOD SWAPS in Brooklyn before moving back to her hometown of Richmond, Virginia. One night, while out for a drink, she struck up a conversation with the woman behind the bar, a veteran of the hospitality industry named Beth Dixon. The two women discovered that they shared a passion for home food preservation. When Andrea mentioned food swapping, Beth was intrigued. Andrea knew how food swapping worked, and Beth knew everyone in the local food world. Within a week, they had launched the RVA Swappers, and held their first event in August 2012.

The RVA Swappers meet monthly all over Richmond. Word spread quickly about RVA Swappers after the group was profiled in a local magazine and was featured on the Southern Foodways Alliance website. Their events regularly fill to capacity.

The swap draws college students, twenty-something city dwellers, and older people from the surrounding county. Most swappers bring prepared foods, not as much garden produce or backyard eggs. Because putting up food is a Southern tradition, Beth and Andrea see a lot of preserves and pickles. But Richmond is also keeping up with the times: fermented foods have become quite popular at the swaps.

Being the organizers of the RVA Swappers has opened doors for Beth and Andrea in the Richmond food scene. When the Southern Foodways Alliance met in Richmond for a symposium on "Women at Work," the organizers asked Beth, as one of the city's best-known female craft bartender, to make cocktails for event; when they heard about RVA Swappers, they also asked Beth if she would be willing to make preserves for a dinner attended by famous chefs and editors of food magazines. A local greengrocer has asked Beth and Andrea to teach canning classes at her store. Andrea, who was anxious about finding like-minded people on her return to Richmond, has made many friends through the swap that share her interest in local foods, creating recipes, and sharing skills.

Richmond is keeping up with the times: fermented foods have become quite popular at the swaps.

Andrea points out that while food swaps promote a way of living, the sense of community is critical to their continued success. In this age of social media, a food swap remains a face-to-face activity. Swappers develop relationships with other people in their community that fall outside of their regular groups. Andrea also feels strongly about being part of a national food swap movement. Just as she brought the food swap concept to Richmond from Brooklyn, Andrea wants the RVA Swappers to know that if they move away, they can find a swap, or start one, in their new city.

VANILLA PEAR SAUCE

MAKES 3 (8-OUNCE) JARS

Once summer turns into fall, you begin to see more apple and pear concoctions at the food swap. While applesauce is a favorite with everybody, I almost prefer the delicate taste of pear sauce. I don't add very much in the way of spices or flavorings here because I want to highlight the taste of the pears. A little vanilla is all that is needed to flavor this ethereal sauce.

Suggest to potential trading partners that they spoon this pear sauce into yogurt or use it as a topping for pound cake or ice cream. I think it is sublime straight out of the jar.

4   pounds ripe pears
    (a variety that will break down
    easily, such as Bartlett)

3   tablespoons freshly squeezed
    lemon juice

1   cup sugar

1   vanilla bean

1. Peel and core the pears and chop them into a small dice. You should have around 8 cups of diced pears.

2. Combine the diced pears, lemon juice, and sugar in a large saucepan. Use the widest pot that you can, because the wider surface area will allow the sauce to cook down and thicken more quickly.

3. Split the vanilla bean down the middle and scrape the inside into the pot with the pears. Add the outside of the bean as well.

4. Bring the pear mixture to a boil over high heat. Reduce the heat to medium and boil gently, stirring frequently, until the pears are tender and beginning to break down, about 10 minutes.

5. Meanwhile, prepare a boiling-water-bath canner and heat three 8-ounce jars. (See Safe Water-Bath Canning Procedures, page 198.)

6. Mash the softened pears to break them down further, using a potato masher. (If you prefer a smoother consistency for your sauce, you can use an immersion blender or food mill.)

7. Continue to boil the sauce gently, stirring constantly to prevent scorching, until thickened, about 15 minutes.

8. Ladle the sauce into the clean, warm jars, leaving ½ inch headspace. Bubble the jars and wipe the rims with a damp cloth. Place the lids on the jars and screw on the rings just until you feel resistance.

9. Process the jars in the boiling-water bath for 10 minutes. Allow the jars to cool in the water for 5 minutes before removing to a towel to cool completely.

10. Store in a cool, dark place for up to 1 year.

APPLESAUCE
WITH QUATRE ÉPICES
MAKES 3 PINTS

Homemade applesauce, a favorite with everyone, is just the thing to make when you come home from an outing to the apple orchard and ask yourself the inevitable question: "What am I going to do with all these apples?" Feel free to double this recipe if you have a true glut. Depending on where you live, you may find that applesauce, a traditional accompaniment to potato latkes, is a popular swap item as Hanukah nears.

Quatre épices, which simply means "four spices," is a French spice blend made of equal parts white pepper, cinnamon, cloves, and ginger. I find it to be the perfect flavoring for applesauce. If the idea of pepper is off-putting to you, you can replace it with allspice. Quatre épices, which is typically used to flavor charcuterie and soups, makes a lovely food swap item in its own right.

5   pounds apples
(10–12 apples)

3   tablespoons bottled
lemon juice

½   cup water

½–1   cup sugar to taste

1½   teaspoons quatre épices
(see note)

1. Peel, core, and roughly chop the apples.

2. Combine the apples, lemon juice, and water in a large saucepan. Bring the liquid to a boil, reduce the heat to low, and simmer the apples, covered, stirring occasionally.

3. Meanwhile, prepare a boiling-water-bath canner and heat three pint jars. (See Safe Water-Bath Canning Procedures, page 198.)

4. When the apples are tender enough to mash by hand, about 10 to 20 minutes depending on the varieties you use, remove from the heat. Mash the apples with a potato masher or, for a smoother texture, use an immersion blender.

5. Taste the apple purée and add sugar to taste. Add the quatre épices. Bring the mixture back up to a simmer, stirring to dissolve the sugar and distribute the spices.

6. Ladle the sauce into the clean, warm jars, leaving ¾ inch headspace. Bubble the jars and wipe the rims with a damp cloth. Place the lids on the jars and screw on the rings just until you feel resistance.

7. Process the jars in the boiling-water bath for 15 minutes. Allow the jars to cool in the water for 5 minutes before removing to a towel to cool completely.

8. Store in a cool, dark place for up to 1 year.

Note: *To make the quatre épices, combine equal amounts finely ground white pepper, cinnamon, ground ginger, and ground cloves in a small bowl and stir with a fork to combine. (Do not be tempted to use black pepper, because black specks in your applesauce are not very appealing.) Make a large batch and package the mixture in 2-ounce spice bottles for an easy swap item.*

ORANGE-GINGER
CRANBERRY SAUCE

MAKES 4 PINTS

Bring this orange-and-ginger-flavored cranberry sauce to a food swap in late October or early November, and people will line up to trade with you. Who doesn't want to get an early start on Thanksgiving or Christmas menu planning? I usually make this recipe twice so that I have two pints of cranberry sauce for my own Thanksgiving and enough to swap or give to friends.

I buy fresh cranberries at my farmers' market, where they come in from nearby Wisconsin, one of the largest cranberry-growing states in the country. Cranberries freeze like a dream, so I stock up during the last few weeks of the market and use my stash of cranberries all winter long in preserves and baked goods, such as the Mini Cranberry-Orange Quick Breads on page 118.

2   cinnamon sticks

10   whole cloves

6   whole allspice berries

4   cups sugar

4   cups water

8   cups fresh or frozen cranberries

1   tablespoon ground ginger

¼   cup orange-flavored liqueur, such as Grand Marnier (optional)

Zest of 1 orange

1. Prepare a boiling-water-bath canner and heat four pint jars. (See Safe Water-Bath Canning Procedures, page 198.)

2. Combine the cinnamon sticks (breaking them in half if necessary), cloves, and allspice berries in a spice bag or square of cheesecloth, and tie it closed.

3. Combine the sugar and water in a large, deep stockpot and add the spice bag. Bring the mixture to a boil over high heat, stirring to dissolve the sugar.

4. Boil the sugar syrup for 5 minutes. Add the cranberries and return to a boil.

5. Reduce the heat and simmer, stirring frequently, until the cranberries have broken down and the liquid has thickened, about 15 minutes. Do not be concerned if the sauce appears to be somewhat liquid — cranberries are high in pectin and the sauce will gel when it cools.

6. Add the ginger, orange liqueur (if using), and zest, and remove from heat. Skim off any foam that has accumulated and discard the spice bag.

7. Ladle the sauce into the clean, warm jars, leaving ¼ inch headspace. Bubble the jars and wipe the rims with a damp cloth.

8. Place the lids on the jars and screw on the rings just until you feel resistance.

9. Process the jars in the boiling-water bath for 15 minutes. Allow the jars to cool in the water for 5 minutes before removing to a towel to cool completely.

10. Check the seals and store in a dark, cool place for up to 1 year.

RHUBARB CHUTNEY

MAKES 3 PINTS OR 6 (8-OUNCE) JARS

One way to make a distinctive swap item is to use a familiar ingredient in an unfamiliar way. In this recipe, I take the beloved early spring fruit, rhubarb, which we usually see alone or paired with strawberries, and use it to make a sweet and tangy chutney. Despite the long cooking time, the chutney retains some of the rhubarb's pleasing color and turns a deep crimson. The dried cranberries plump up nicely and add to the visual appeal. This recipe is a little time-consuming, but it is basically foolproof. Just be sure to let the chutney simmer long enough to really thicken.

Because people may have never heard of rhubarb chutney, I highly recommend offering samples and serving suggestions to wary swappers. Pour the chutney over some cream cheese or other soft cheese like brie, put out some crackers, and encourage people to take a taste.

3½ cups distilled white vinegar

6 cups chopped rhubarb (about 3 farmers' market bunches or 12–15 stalks)

3 cups chopped yellow onion (about 2 medium onions)

3 cups brown sugar

1½ cups dried cranberries

2 tablespoons minced garlic (5–6 cloves)

2 tablespoons minced fresh ginger (2-inch piece, peeled)

1 tablespoon mustard seeds

1 teaspoon salt

1 teaspoon cinnamon

½ teaspoon ground cloves

½ teaspoon allspice

½ teaspoon red pepper flakes

1. Combine the vinegar, rhubarb, onion, brown sugar, cranberries, garlic, ginger, mustard seeds, salt, cinnamon, cloves, allspice, and pepper flakes in a large Dutch oven or stockpot. (The wider the pot, the faster the chutney will thicken.)

2. Bring the chutney to a boil over high heat.

3. Reduce the heat to medium-low and simmer, stirring frequently to prevent scorching, until the chutney has thickened. This can take between 45 minutes and an hour and a half, depending on the size of your pot.

4. While the chutney is simmering, prepare a boiling-water-bath canner and heat three pint or six 8-ounce jars. (See Safe Water-Bath Canning Procedures, page 198.)

5. Ladle the chutney into clean, warm jars, leaving ½ inch headspace at the top of each jar. Bubble the jars and wipe the rims with a damp cloth.

6. Place the lids on the jars and screw on the rings just until you feel resistance.

7. Process the jars in the boiling-water bath for 15 minutes. Allow the jars to cool in the water for 5 minutes before removing to a towel to cool completely.

8. Store in a cool, dark place for up to 1 year.

SOUR CHERRY PIE FILLING

MAKES 5 QUARTS

As a swap item, homemade pie filling has all the advantages of jams and jellies, but you see it far less frequently. I make this pie filling every summer and swap it months later when sour cherries are a novelty, and people line up to trade with me. Pie fillings are extremely useful items to have in your pantry, because they can be pressed into service for a last-minute dessert using store-bought pie crust or puff pastry, or even as a topping for ice cream.

You can use fresh or frozen pitted sour cherries for this recipe. If using frozen cherries, you will need to thaw and drain them first. You can use the drained liquid for the cherry juice called for in the recipe. If using fresh cherries that you pit yourself — hats off to you — use bottled cherry juice.

3   cups sugar

¾   cup Clear Jel (see note)

4   cups cherry juice

½   cup lemon juice

1   teaspoon cinnamon

¼   teaspoon salt

¼   teaspoon allspice

¼   teaspoon ground cloves

8   pounds pitted sour cherries, fresh or frozen

1. Prepare a boiling-water-bath canner and heat five quart jars. (See Safe Water-Bath Canning Procedures, page 198.)

2. Whisk together the sugar and Clear Jel in a medium bowl.

3. In a large stockpot, combine the sugar and Clear Jel mixture with 3 cups of the cherry juice and bring to a boil over medium-high heat, stirring constantly to dissolve the dry ingredients and to prevent scorching. The mixture will thicken quite quickly.

4. When the mixture is boiling, add the lemon juice, cinnamon, salt, allspice, and ground cloves, and return to a boil. Boil for 1 minute.

5. When the mixture is boiling again, add the cherries all at once and the remaining cup of cherry juice.

6. Stirring constantly to prevent scorching, bring the pie filling to a boil. Boil for 1 minute.

7. Remove the pie filling from the heat and ladle it into the jars, leaving 1 full inch of headspace. Bubble the jars and wipe off rims with a damp cloth. Place the lids on the jars and screw on the rings just until you feel resistance.

8. Process the jars in the boiling-water bath for 30 minutes. Make sure the water is covering the jars and watch for boiling over, because the quart jars are tall. Allow the jars to cool in the water for 5 minutes before removing to a towel to cool completely.

10. Check the seals and be prepared for leakage. Store in a cool, dark place for up to 1 year.

Note: *Clear Jel, a modified form of cornstarch, is the only thickener that the USDA approves for home canning, because it is designed to maintain its integrity in a high-acid environment and will not interfere with the heat absorption necessary to kill bacteria during processing. While Clear Jel is not readily available in grocery stores, you can find it online, and one bag should last you quite a long time.*

PEACH-HABANERO SALSA

MAKES 4 PINTS

While berries are always quite pricey at the farmers' market, you can usually find good deals on peaches when they are in season. The peach season is long, so sometime in September, I will buy yet another 2 quarts of peaches only to realize that I have canned enough peach jam and peach butter to get me through the winter. That is when I turn to this peach salsa recipe.

This sweet and fiery peach salsa works beautifully as a dip with tortilla chips, but that is merely the beginning. Pour some over cream cheese and serve with crackers for a quick appetizer. Or use it as a braising sauce for chicken thighs. To enhance the flavor and visual appeal of this salsa, I like to stir in some chopped fresh herbs, like basil or cilantro, prior to serving. If added during the cooking process, however, these herbs turn brown and lose their potency.

6   cups peeled, diced yellow peaches (about one dozen peaches)

1¼   cups diced onion

1   cup diced red pepper

2   habanero peppers, seeded and diced

2   tablespoons minced garlic

½   cup sugar

1   cup apple cider vinegar

¼   cup freshly squeezed lime juice

½   teaspoon salt

Note: Use caution when working with hot peppers and wear gloves.

1. Prepare a boiling-water-bath canner and four pint jars. (See Safe Water-Bath Canning Procedures, page 198.)

2. Combine the peaches, onion, red pepper, habanero peppers, garlic, sugar, vinegar, lime juice, and salt in a large stockpot and bring to a boil over high heat.

3. Reduce the heat to medium and boil the salsa for 5 minutes, until the ingredients begin to break down.

4. Ladle the salsa into the clean, warm jars, leaving ½ inch head-space. Bubble the jars and wipe the rims with a damp cloth. Place the lids on the jars and screw on the rings just until you feel resistance.

5. Process the jars in the boiling-water bath for 15 minutes. Allow the jars to cool in the water for 5 minutes before removing to a towel to cool completely.

6. Check the seals and store in a dark, cool place for up to 1 year.

QUINCE PASTE

MAKES 16 (2½-INCH) SQUARES

Also known as membrillo, quince paste is an ancient sweet that is experiencing a resurgence, thanks to the popularity of tapas restaurants and cheese courses. Indeed, the most common use for quince paste is as an accompaniment for hard cheeses such as manchego, but it also works well as a filling for pastries or as a spread for toast.

This recipe is one of the more involved in the book, but quince paste is a worthwhile project with which to challenge yourself. I brought quince paste to the November 2013 Chicago Food Swap, which was one of our biggest events ever and happened to take place on my 40th birthday. People went mad for it, and every fall, swappers ask when I am bringing it again.

3 pounds ripe quinces (6 or 7 fruits), peeled

1 lemon

4–5 cups sugar

1. Cut the quinces into quarters and remove the cores, reserving a large handful of cores and seeds.

2. Place the quinces into a large, wide saucepan and cover with water, 3 or 4 cups. Tie up the reserved seeds and cores in cheesecloth and add them to the pan. (These will add additional pectin to the mixture so the quince paste will set.) Using a vegetable peeler, remove several long strips of peel from the lemon and add them to the pot with the quince.

3. Bring the mixture to a boil, turn down the heat, and simmer, covered, until the quinces are tender, about 20 minutes. Drain and discard the cheesecloth with the seeds and cores.

4. Purée the quince pieces until smooth.

5. Weigh or measure the amount of purée. Return the purée to the saucepan and add an equal amount of sugar by weight or, if going by measurements, add 2 ¼ cups of sugar for every 2 cups of purée. Add 2 to 4 tablespoons of juice to taste from the lemon.

6. Bring the quince-and-sugar mixture to a boil, then reduce the heat to low and simmer, uncovered. Stir occasionally at the beginning, and then almost constantly toward the end to prevent scorching.

7. Once the paste has deepened in color to a rosy pink and thickened to the point that a spoon drawn through the middle will leave a clear path, 1 to 1 ½ hours, remove it from the heat.

8. Preheat your oven to its lowest setting, 150 to 170°F (65 to 75°C).

9. Line a 9-inch square cake pan with parchment paper or spray with a nonstick cooking spray. Pour the paste into the pan and spread it in an even layer, making sure to fill in the corners, and smooth the top with a spatula.

recipe continued on next page

Packaging

I like to wrap the paste in 7-inch squares of parchment paper and tie with bakers' twine.

10. Place the pan in the oven for 1 to 2 hours until the paste is firm to the touch. To test for doneness, cut a small square out of the corner and place it in the refrigerator until cool. If it is firm enough to slice, then it is done. If your test square is not firm enough, leave the quince paste in the warm oven or another warm place for several more hours, or even a day, until fully dry and firm.

11. Line a baking sheet with parchment paper and turn the quince paste out onto it so that the bottom of the paste has an opportunity to dry out as well. Allow it to rest in a warm place for several hours until firm to the touch.

12. When firm and dry, cut the paste into 16 squares.

13. Wrap each square and store in the refrigerator until ready to use or swap.

Note: *Although somewhat obscure these days, fragrant, pear-shaped quince have been cultivated since ancient times. Too firm and tart to eat out of hand, quince becomes soft when baked or poached and palatable when sweetened with sugar or honey. Because of its high pectin content, quince was one of the first fruits to be used to make jam and jelly.*

You can usually find quinces at better grocery stores such as Whole Foods in the late summer and fall, although they are quite dear. I buy my quinces from the farmers' market, where there is one vendor who carries them in September and October and charges the same price for them as he does for apples. I suggest that you ask around at your farmers' market for a local source. Quinces are quite firm, so be careful when cutting them.

PRESERVED VEGETABLES

PICKLES, SALSA, AND RELISHES are clever ways to make use of the summer and fall vegetable harvest, whether you garden, frequent the farmers' market, or pick your own at a farm. All of these products make outstanding food swap items. Artisanal versions are often very pricey in stores, making homemade varieties seem like a bargain.

The comedy show *Portlandia* once featured a hilarious sketch called "We Can Pickle That," which poked fun at the nation's pickling craze. For those of us who have uttered the sentence "you can pickle anything" in all seriousness, that sketch hit very close to home. While most people think of pickles as pickled cucumbers, any vegetable — and some fruits — can be pickled, with delicious results. At a food swap, you are likely to see an enormous variety of pickles, from beets to fennel, that surpasses anything you will find in stores.

Relishes, salsas, and savory jams are also outstanding ways to preserve summer vegetables and are very handy for gardeners facing a glut of zucchini or green tomatoes. One tip: Consider making these preserves when the vegetables are in season but swapping them a few months later, in winter, when fresh local vegetables may be a distant memory.

PICKLED FENNEL

MAKES 4 PINTS

I adore fennel, the anise-flavored bulb with the long green stalks. It is in season in the autumn, which explains why the first time I saw pickled fennel was at a food swap in October. At that swap, the pickled fennel was my must-have item. I have since created my own version of this elegant pickle, and it makes a wonderful addition to a relish tray or fall salads. This is one of my favorite recipes in the book.

I take particular care when packing these jars because, when done correctly, it makes for a beautiful presentation. Be sure the fennel fronds, lemon peel, and red pepper are placed on the outer edge of the jars to add visual interest.

6	fennel bulbs, stalks and root end removed, about 2½ pounds (reserve several of the best-looking fronds for garnish)
2	cups white wine vinegar
2	cups distilled white vinegar
⅔	cup water
1⅓	cups sugar
2	teaspoons pickling salt
4	dried red chile peppers
8	pieces of lemon peel, each 2–3 inches in length and ½–1 inch wide
2	teaspoons fennel seed

Note: *I recommend using widemouthed pint jars for this pickle because of the large size of the fennel slices.*

1. Prepare a boiling-water-bath canner and heat four pint jars. (See Safe Water-Bath Canning Procedures, page 198.)

2. Slice the fennel bulbs ¼ inch thick.

3. Combine the vinegars, water, sugar, and salt in a large saucepan, and bring to a boil over high heat, stirring to dissolve the sugar. Remove from the heat.

4. Pack the fennel slices tightly into the warm jars. Add several fennel fronds, 1 dried chile pepper, 2 slices of lemon peel, and ½ teaspoon fennel seeds to each jar.

5. Ladle the brine into the filled jars, leaving ½ inch headspace at the top of the jars. Bubble the jars and wipe off the rims with a damp cloth.

6. Place the lids on the jars and screw on the rings just until you feel resistance.

7. Process the jars for 15 minutes in the boiling-water bath. Allow the jars to cool in the water for 5 minutes before removing to a towel to cool completely.

8. Allow the fennel to cure for at least 1 week before opening.

9. Check the seals and store in a dark cool place for up to 1 year.

WHAT'S SPECIAL ABOUT PICKLING SALT?

Pickling salt, or canning salt, is pure sodium chloride without any iodine or anti-caking agents, which, when used in preserving, can result in a cloudy brine. Pickling salt is also more finely ground than kosher salt so it dissolves easily. You can make pickles and other preserves using other salts — so long as they do not contain any additives — but the measurements may be different. If you plan to do a lot of canning, it is probably worth buying a box of pickling salt. You should be able to find it in grocery stores with good canning sections, or online.

GARLICKY DILLY BEANS

MAKES 8 PINTS

Pickled green beans, known as dilly beans, make a forgiving first project for a novice canner, and the results are exceptionally tasty. An old-fashioned pickle, dilly beans have become trendy in recent years, and a jar of artisanal dilly beans sells for anywhere from $8 to $10. For the same money, you could easily buy enough green beans to make the 8 pints that this recipe yields. Save a few jars for yourself and swap the rest. If this quantity is intimidating, however, feel free to halve the recipe.

Dilly beans, like most pickles, need several weeks to cure for the flavors to develop fully. You can certainly swap pickles before they are ready to eat, but be sure to mark the date that you made the pickles and advise your trading partner when to open the jar.

6 pounds green beans

4½ cups distilled white vinegar

4½ cups water

½ cup pickling salt

1 head garlic, separated into cloves and peeled

8 teaspoons dill seeds

1 teaspoon red pepper flakes

1. Prepare a boiling-water-bath canner and heat eight pint jars. (See Safe Water-Bath Canning Procedures, page 198.)

2. Trim the ends off the green beans, and cut the longer beans to a uniform length so that they will fit in a pint jar, leaving at least ½ inch headspace.

3. Combine the vinegar, water, and pickling salt in a saucepan and bring to a boil. Remove from the heat.

4. Pack the green beans tightly into the warm jars. Add 2 cloves garlic, 1 teaspoon dill seeds, and ⅛ teaspoon red pepper flakes to each jar.

5. Ladle the brine into the filled jars, leaving ½ inch headspace at the top of the jars. Bubble the jars and wipe off the rims with a damp cloth.

6. Place the lids on the jars and screw on the rings just until you feel resistance.

7. Process the jars for 10 minutes in the boiling-water bath. Allow the jars to cool in the water for 5 minutes before removing to a towel to cool completely.

8. Check the seals and store in a dark, cool place for up to 1 year.

Dilly Beans

apples
for
eggs

GREAT BRITAIN

TO:

FROM:

GREAT BRITAIN'S CENTURIES-LONG tradition of people growing food on small individual plots known as allotments shows no sign of abating. Indeed, while the available land for allotment gardens declines, demand for these plots — driven by rising food prices, a desire for greater self-sufficiency, and concerns over large carbon footprints — continues to increase, causing long waiting lists.

In 2011, Vicky Swift was faced with the usual glut of seasonal produce from her garden allotment and a love of making bread that had long ago outstripped the size of her freezer. Suspecting that others faced some of the same challenges and knowing that still others longed for homegrown produce but had no allotment of their own, she decided to create a produce exchange in her town of Altrincham, outside Manchester. Internet research led her to the LA Food Swap, and Vicky soon realized that food swapping was an international phenomenon.

Vicky held the first Apples for Eggs event in 2011. Sue Jewitt started a second Apples for Eggs in York the following year, and a third popped up in Ormskirk, near Liverpool, in 2013. Apples for Eggs swaps have now been established in a total of seven towns.

Edible gardening remains the focus of Apples for Eggs. But Vicky reports that there is always a good selection of prepared foods like jams and pickles, baked goods, dips, soups, and sauces.

Once someone asked if he could bring a cockerel, but the organizers decided that nothing more alive than a sourdough starter is allowed.

By all being under the umbrella of Apples for Eggs, the swaps have greater reach than any single swap would on its own. Although they share a name, each Apples for Eggs swap has its own unique identity, determined by the hosts, venues, and swappers who attend.

Once someone asked if he could bring a cockerel, but the organizers decided that nothing more alive than a sourdough starter is allowed.

Vicky, Sue, and the other Apples for Eggs organizers are proud to be connected to a worldwide movement that is bringing like-minded people together around food. They would like to continue to develop Apples for Eggs as a social enterprise, further developing their blog and website as a resource, and offering support to community groups to help them get their own food swaps established. The ultimate goal? For food swapping to become part of a new mainstream.

ZUCCHINI RELISH

MAKES 4 OR 5 PINTS

It is a cliché that vegetable gardeners are overrun with zucchini in the summer months. I do not garden, but I nevertheless end up with a lot of zucchini in August because it is one of the cheapest things to buy at the farmers' market. Zucchini are so versatile that there is no reason to resist stocking up.

A big batch of zucchini relish is easy to make and is a terrific way to use a lot of late-summer produce. This zucchini relish is my family's favorite condiment for hot dogs or grilled chicken sausage. I actually like to mix it with canned tuna and mayonnaise for a unique take on tuna salad.

6	cups diced zucchini (about 2 pounds)
2½	cups diced yellow peppers (about 2 peppers)
½	cup diced jalapeño peppers (about 2 peppers)
4	cups diced yellow onions, (about 2 onions)
2½	cups distilled white vinegar
1	cup sugar
2	tablespoons pickling salt
1	tablespoon brown mustard seeds
1	teaspoon celery seeds
1	teaspoon turmeric
½	teaspoon red pepper flakes

Note: *Red peppers would work as well, but the yellow ones look best with the zucchini.*

1. Prepare a boiling-water-bath canner and heat five pint jars. (See Safe Water-Bath Canning Procedures, page 198.)

2. Combine the zucchini, yellow peppers, jalapeño peppers, onions, vinegar, sugar, pickling salt, mustard seeds, celery seeds, turmeric, and red pepper flakes in a large, deep saucepan. Bring the mixture to a boil over high heat, stirring to dissolve the sugar.

3. Reduce the heat to low and simmer, stirring occasionally, until the vegetables have cooked down and the mixture has begun to thicken, about 30 minutes.

4. Ladle the relish into the clean, warm jars, leaving ½ inch headspace. Bubble the jars and wipe the rims with a damp cloth.

5. Place the lids on the jars and screw on the rings just until you feel resistance.

6. Process the jars in the boiling-water bath for 15 minutes. Allow the jars to cool in the water for 5 minutes before removing to a towel to cool completely.

7. Check the seals and store in a dark, cool place for up to 1 year.

GIARDINIERA

MAKES 5 PINTS

Giardiniera is a Chicago thing. A spicy mixed vegetable pickle, giardiniera is the required topping for Chicago's iconic Italian beef sandwich. A milder version made with olives appears in New Orleans's muffuletta. But giardiniera's uses do not stop at sandwiches. Chicagoans add it to their pizza, toss it onto salads, and eat it straight out of the jar.

As a swap item, giardiniera boasts a lot of curb appeal. The colors of the mixed vegetables look beautiful behind glass. No need to add more than a simple label. As with all pickles, giardiniera needs a few weeks to cure after being jarred, so be certain to mark the date that you made it and suggest an opening date.

1	head cauliflower, cut into small florets
4	stalks celery, trimmed and sliced
3	carrots, peeled and cut into rounds
3	red peppers, diced
3	jalapeño peppers, ribs and seeds removed and minced
¼	cup sliced garlic cloves
2	cups water
4	cups distilled white vinegar
2	cups sugar
1	tablespoon pickling salt
1¼	teaspoons red pepper flakes
1¼	teaspoons celery seeds
2½	teaspoons black peppercorns

1. Combine the cauliflower, celery, and carrots in a large bowl. Prepare the red and jalapeño peppers and garlic, and set aside.

2. Prepare a boiling-water-bath canner and heat five pint jars. (See Safe Water-Bath Canning Procedures, page 198.)

3. Bring the water, vinegar, sugar, and pickling salt to boil in a large saucepan, stirring to dissolve the sugar.

4. When the brine is boiling, add the cauliflower, celery, and carrots. Return to a boil. Add the peppers and garlic and remove from the heat.

5. Ladle the vegetables into the prepared jars using a slotted spoon. Add to each jar ¼ teaspoon red pepper flakes, ¼ teaspoon celery seeds, and ½ teaspoon black peppercorns. Top with brine, leaving ½ inch headspace. Bubble the jars and wipe the rims with a damp cloth.

6. Place the lids on the jars and screw on the rings just until you feel resistance.

7. Process the jars in the boiling-water bath for 10 minutes. Allow the jars to cool in the water 5 minutes before removing to a towel to cool completely.

8. Check the seals and store in a cool, dark place for up to 1 year.

SPICY GREEN TOMATO SALSA

MAKES 3 PINTS OR 6 (8-OUNCE) JARS

When cold weather threatens, gardeners rush to pick all their green tomatoes off the vine before the first frost comes and they turn to mush. What to do with a bumper crop of green tomatoes? Certainly you should make at least one batch of fried green tomatoes. I recommend preserving the rest. Pickled green tomatoes are a Jewish deli classic and very easy to make. You can also make green tomato relish — delicious on hot dogs and sausage — or this green tomato salsa.

Preserving green tomatoes allows you to take full advantage of a seasonal fruit that is often seen as something to get rid of. And while maybe your family does not want to eat jar upon jar of green tomato pickles or salsa, you can be sure that the participants in your local food swap will be delighted to trade you for a jar.

5 jalapeño peppers

7 cups cored and diced green tomatoes (about 6 medium to large tomatoes)

2 cups diced red onion (about 1 large onion)

3 cloves garlic, minced

½ cup bottled lemon juice

1 teaspoon pickling salt

1 teaspoon ground cumin

1 teaspoon ground coriander

1. Prepare a boiling-water-bath canner and heat three pint jars or six half-pint jars. (See Safe Water-Bath Canning Procedures, page 198.)

2. Heat a large skillet over high heat. Add the jalapeño peppers to the skillet and cook until charred on all sides, turning as necessary. Remove the charred jalapeños to a heatproof bowl and cover. When cool enough to handle, slide the skins off the peppers, wearing rubber gloves to protect your skin. Remove the tops, ribs, and seeds and mince the peppers. Set aside.

3. In a large stockpot, combine the diced green tomatoes, minced jalapeños, diced onion, minced garlic, and lemon juice. Bring the salsa to boil over high heat, stirring frequently.

4. Add the salt, cumin, and coriander, and reduce the heat to medium. Gently boil the salsa until it thickens and the ingredients begin to break down, about 15 minutes.

5. Ladle the salsa into the warm jars, leaving ½ inch headspace. Bubble the jars and wipe the rims with a damp cloth.

6. Place the lids on the jars and screw on the rings just until you feel resistance.

7. Process the jars in the boiling-water bath for 15 minutes. Allow the jars to cool in the water for 5 minutes before removing to a towel to cool completely.

8. Check the seals and store in a dark, cool place for up to 1 year.

COUNTRYSIDE
LOCAL FOOD SWAP

akron·ohio

WHEN HEATHER ROSZCZYK left Portland, Oregon, to move back to northeast Ohio, it felt like a foodie death sentence. Now, she says, the area's culinary scene is exploding and she could not be happier.

Heather is the education and marketing manager for Countryside Conservancy, a nonprofit focused on local food and farming that operates the Countryside Local Food Swap. With its farmers' markets, sustainable farms located in the Cuyahoga Valley National Park, and educational programs, Countryside Conservancy plays a significant role in the Northeast Ohio local food movement. Indeed, many swappers are involved with Countryside in multiple ways.

The Countryside Conservancy staff were inspired to start the Countryside Local Food Swap after reading an account of the From Scratch Club food swap by blogger Alana Chernila, author of *The Homemade Pantry*. Countryside held its first swap in January 2013.

Countryside Local Food Swap meets on the third Tuesday of each month and regularly draws upwards of 40 swappers. Heather rotates the location because, in addition to keeping things fresh, it introduces people to various businesses and attractions around Akron. She is always on the lookout for interesting locations, whether it is a Countryside Initiative farmer's barn, a local art gallery, or a pavilion in Cuyahoga Valley National Park.

Why is running a food swap important to Countryside Conservancy's mission? To Heather, food swaps are all about cooking from scratch, an activity that has implications far beyond the kitchen. When people cook from scratch, they gain appreciation for the work that others — farmers, chefs, bakers, brewers — do. They are more likely to be mindful about what they put in their bodies, and in turn, to care about where food comes from. While technology and social media are helpful in many ways, they can also leave us wanting authentic interaction and community. Heather believes that people are seeking those in-person connections more than ever, and for people who love food, there are few better places to find it than a food swap.

When people cook from scratch, they gain appreciation for the work that others — farmers, chefs, bakers, brewers — do. They are more likely to be mindful about what they put in their bodies, and in turn, to care about where food comes from.

Heather notes with pride that two additional food swaps started in neighboring counties after people attended a Countryside Local Food Swap and wanted one closer to home. Heather hopes to organize a large joint swap between Countryside and other neighboring swaps in the future.

SAVORY TOMATO JAM

MAKES 5 (8-OUNCE) JARS

Another way to use up a glut of backyard tomatoes, tomato jam is a revelation to the uninitiated. It concentrates the sweet flavor of the tomatoes without the vinegar tang of a ketchup. Spread your tomato jam on sandwiches or serve it as an accompaniment to a cheese plate. Your fellow swappers will appreciate this new take on a familiar summer crop.

Remove the tomato seeds because they make the jam watery. It is a bit of extra work, but the final result is worth it. Be sure to cook the tomatoes down until they are thick, glossy, and spreadable, not thin or watery like a sauce or ketchup.

6 pounds slicing tomatoes, such as Early Girl or Beefsteak (10 to 12 tomatoes, depending on size), cored, seeded, and diced

4 cups sugar

¾ cup bottled lemon juice

1 tablespoon pickling salt

1 teaspoon red pepper flakes

1 teaspoon cinnamon

1 teaspoon ground ginger

½ teaspoon ground cloves

½ teaspoon ground allspice

1. Combine the tomatoes, sugar, lemon juice, pickling salt, red pepper flakes, cinnamon, ginger, cloves, and allspice in a large, deep saucepan or stockpot. (The jam will splatter when cooking, so select a deep pot to save your arms and countertops.)

2. Bring the mixture to a boil over high heat, stirring occasionally.

3. Reduce the heat to medium and boil until thickened, about 45 minutes. Stir frequently, particularly as the jam gets thicker, to prevent scorching.

4. While the jam is boiling, prepare a boiling-water-bath canner and heat five 8-ounce jars. (See Safe Water-Bath Canning Procedures, page 198.)

5. If there are still visible pieces of tomato in the jam, break them down using an immersion blender or by transferring the jam in batches to a food processor and pulsing several times. Do not purée the tomatoes, however.

6. Continue to boil until the jam is very thick and spreadable.

7. Ladle the jam into the prepared jars, leaving ¼ inch headspace. Bubble the jars and wipe the rims with a damp cloth.

8. Place the lids on the jars and screw on the rings just until you feel resistance.

9. Process the jars in the boiling-water bath for 10 minutes. Allow the jars to cool in the water 5 minutes before removing to a towel to cool completely.

10. Check the seals and store in a cool, dark place for up to 1 year.

TOMATILLO SAUCE

MAKES 7 OR 8 PINTS

Many people confuse tomatillos and green tomatoes, but tomatillos are actually a different member of the nightshade family. They are related to gooseberries and ground cherries, both of which also have papery husks that must be removed prior to eating. Tomatillos have a tart flavor and are used frequently in Mexican and Central American cuisine. Most salsa verdes are made with tomatillos.

I can large batches of tomatillo sauce in the summer because it helps me to make Mexican-inspired dishes all year long. I like this sauce on enchiladas, chicken tinga, and my favorite Mexican dish, chilaquiles, which combines leftover tortillas with eggs for a hearty brunch dish or a quick weeknight dinner. Because not everyone is familiar with tomatillos, when bringing this sauce to a swap, be certain to offer samples and recipe suggestions. The most straightforward use for this sauce is as a dip with tortilla chips, but that is merely one of many possibilities.

5 jalapeño peppers

6 pounds tomatillos, husks removed

2 large yellow onions, diced

4 cloves garlic, minced

1 tablespoon pickling salt

1½ cups bottled lemon juice

1. Roast the jalapeño peppers in a dry skillet over high heat, turning as necessary until the skins are charred all over. When cool enough to handle, remove the skins and cut the peppers in half, wearing gloves to protect your skin. Remove the veins and seeds and chop.

2. Bring a large pot of water to boil. Working in batches if necessary, blanch the tomatillos for 5 minutes just until softened. Drain.

3. Again, working in batches if necessary, transfer the blanched tomatillos to a food processor and process until finely chopped but not puréed.

4. Combine the chopped tomatillos, onions, garlic, chopped jalapeños, salt, and lemon juice in a large stockpot and bring to a boil. Reduce the heat and simmer the sauce until the ingredients have broken down, about 20 minutes.

5. While the sauce is simmering, prepare a boiling-water-bath canner and heat eight pint jars. (See Safe Water-Bath Canning Procedures, page 198.)

6. When the sauce is ready, ladle it into the prepared jars, leaving ½ inch headspace. Bubble the jars and wipe the rims with a damp cloth.

7. Place the lids on the jars and screw on the rings just until you feel resistance.

8. Process the jars in the boiling-water bath for 15 minutes. Allow the jars to cool in the water for 5 minutes before removing to a towel to cool completely.

9. Check the seals and store in a cool, dark place for up to 1 year.

HALIFAX
• FOOD SWAP •
NOVA SCOTIA

NOVA SCOTIA IS A SMALL Canadian province, and Halifax is a small Nova Scotian city. But when the Ecology Action Centre, a local nonprofit, and *Rustik* magazine brought Kate Payne, the founder of the modern food swap movement, to Halifax, 45 people came to hear her speak. Perhaps given the history of the area, this kind of enthusiasm for food swapping is not surprising. Nova Scotia's Annapolis Valley is home to some of the best growing soil in the world. The landscape is dotted with small and medium-size farms that raise meat, grain, and vegetables. While the growing season may be short, farmers can grow a lot in that short time, and more and more farms now boast greenhouses to extend the season.

Food swap co-organizer Aimee Carson is the food coordinator at Ecology Action Centre, which receives funding from the Public Health Agency of Canada to build capacity for regional food systems in Nova Scotia. Aimee's role, in part, is to develop food infrastructure by helping to establish and promote farmers' markets and CSAs, community gardens, greenhouses, and root cellars.

The Halifax food swap group is small and informal, meeting at private homes and drawing from friends and acquaintances of the organizers. It does not even have a formal name. That is fine for right now. But one day, Aimee hopes to bring a large public food swap to Halifax through her work at Ecology Action Centre.

The regulars who attend the Halifax food swap bring foods, especially preserves and ferments, that reflect Nova Scotia's food culture. A short growing season necessarily means a rich preserving tradition. Local ingredients, such as apples, blueberries, peaches, and tomatoes, are used wherever possible. Bakers bring breads and pastries made with flour from local grains.

. . . when food is the centerpiece of an activity, it connects people like nothing else. After all, every culture has a food tradition, and everyone enjoys eating good food.

Food swaps encapsulate everything that Aimee holds most dear. She believes that when food is the centerpiece of an activity, it connects people like nothing else. After all, every culture has a food tradition, and everyone enjoys eating good food. Our abilities to connect to local food systems and to prepare our own food are critical for self-sufficiency and good health. Food swaps promote local foodways, cooking, and skill-sharing, all while building community. No wonder the people of Halifax have embraced this trend.

RESOURCES

Food Swaps around the World

FOOD SWAP NETWORK
www.foodswapnetwork.com
Lists food swaps around the world organized by region and offers resources for food swap hosts and participants
Many food swaps do not maintain their own website but rely on Facebook and other social media sites to share information. Here is a list of those food swaps that have a dedicated website.

United States

EAST

BK SWAPPERS
Brooklyn, New York
http://bkswappers.tumblr.com

BOSTON FOOD SWAP
Boston, Massachusetts
www.bostonfoodswap.com

FROM SCRATCH CLUB
Albany, New York
http://fromscratchclub.com

VALLEY FOOD SWAP
Northampton, Massachusetts
http://valleyfoodswap.tumblr.com

SOUTH

ATLANTA FOOD SWAP
Atlanta, Georgia
www.thehomesteadatl.com/swap

MIDLANDS FOOD
SWAPPERS
Columbia, South Carolina
http://midlandsfoodswappers
.wordpress.com

MIDWEST

CHICAGO FOOD SWAP
Chicago, Illinois
www.chicagofoodswap.com

COUNTRYSIDE LOCAL
FOOD SWAPS
Akron, Ohio
http://countrysideconservancy
.businesscatalyst.com/learn
-countryside-local-food-swaps.htm

INDY FOOD SWAPPERS
Indianapolis, Indiana
www.indyfoodswappers.com

MID-MITTEN HOMEMADE
Mason, Michigan
www.mid-mittenhomemade.com

NWI FOOD SWAP
Northwest Indiana
www.nwifoodswap.com

ST. LOUIS FOOD SWAP
St. Louis, Missouri
www.stlfoodswap.com

WEST

LA FOOD SWAP
Los Angeles, California
www.lafoodswap.com

MILE HIGH SWAPPERS
Colorado
http://milehighswappers.com

PDX FOOD SWAP
Portland, Oregon
www.pdxfoodswap.com

Outside the United States

APPLES FOR EGGS
FOOD SWAPS
Great Britain
http://applesforeggs.com

HOME GROWN EXCHANGE
Great Britain
http://homegrownexchange.org.uk

Pantry and Kitchen Equipment

Some of the recipes in this book call for specialized kitchen equipment. You should be able to find almost of all the equipment mentioned without difficulty at big-box stores like Target or Bed, Bath and Beyond or specialty kitchenware stores like Williams-Sonoma and Sur La Table. For canning supplies, many grocery stores and hardware stores now carry canning jars, lids, and rings. These are often the most economical source for these items because their weight makes shipping from online retailers prohibitive.

Most of the ingredients called for are readily available at large grocery stores, specialty food retailers, such as Whole Foods, or ethnic markets. Some of the fruits and vegetables I mention may only be available at farmers' markets in season; where that is the case, I make a note of it.

Because the spirit of a food swap is about building community and promoting sustainability, I encourage you to shop at local food and kitchenware retailers whenever possible.

Other sources for ingredients, kitchen tools, and canning equipment:

CANNING PANTRY
888-858-1602
www.canningpantry.com
Canning supplies

FILLMORE CONTAINER
866-345-5527
www.fillmorecontainer.com
Glass containers and closures, canning accessories

FRESH PRESERVING STORE
855-813-9352
www.freshpreservingstore.com
Canning supplies

KING ARTHUR FLOUR
800-827-6836
www.kingarthurflour.com
Specialty flours, baking supplies, and kitchen tools

KITCHEN KRAFTS
563-535-8000
www.kitchenkrafts.com
Specialty baking, canning, and candy-making supplies

PENZEYS SPICES
800-741-7787
www.penzeys.com
Spices and extracts

SAVORY SPICE SHOP
303-297-1833
www.savoryspiceshop.com
Spices, herbs, and extracts

Food Packaging

THE CONTAINER STORE
888-266-8246
www.containerstore.com
Gift tags and labels, some gift and food packaging, especially around the holidays

COST PLUS WORLD MARKET
877-967-5362
www.worldmarket.com
Paper baking pans, spice jars, bottles, gift tags, and labels, especially around the holidays

MICHAELS
800-642-4235
www.michaels.com
Cellophane bags, muffin wrappers, bakery boxes, ribbon, twine, cardstock, craft punches, and more

NASHVILLE WRAPS
800-547-9727
www.nashvillewraps.com
Packaging wholesaler with a wide variety of boxes, bags, and ties but only sells in large quantities

ORIENTAL TRADING
800-875-8480
www.orientaltrading.com
Surprising source for inexpensive cellophane bags, bakery boxes, takeout containers, and paper goods

PAPER SOURCE
888-727-3711
www.papersource.com
Expensive but beautiful paper goods, ribbons, tags, and food packaging kits

PICK YOUR PLUM
855-506-7586
www.pickyourplum.com
A daily deal website for craft supplies and food packaging

SPECIALTY BOTTLE
206-382-1100
www.specialtybottle.com
Glass bottles, jars, and tins with no minimum purchase

WEBSTAURANT STORE
717-392-7472
www.webstaurantstore.com
Restaurant supply wholesaler with low prices on packaging and disposable containers for baked goods but high shipping costs for individuals

METRIC CONVERSION CHARTS

Unless you have finely calibrated measuring equipment, conversions between US and metric measurements will be somewhat inexact. It's important to convert the measurements for all of the ingredients in a recipe to maintain the same proportions as the original.

Weight

TO CONVERT	TO	MULTIPLY
ounces	grams	ounces by 28.35
pounds	grams	pounds by 453.5
pounds	kilograms	pounds by 0.45

US	METRIC
0.035 ounce	1 gram
¼ ounce	7 grams
½ ounce	14 grams
1 ounce	28 grams
1¼ ounces	35 grams
1½ ounces	40 grams
1¾ ounces	50 grams
2½ ounces	70 grams
3½ ounces	100 grams
4 ounces	112 grams
5 ounces	140 grams
8 ounces	228 grams
8¾ ounces	250 grams
10 ounces	280 grams
15 ounces	425 grams
16 ounces (1 pound)	454 grams

Volume

TO CONVERT	TO	MULTIPLY
teaspoons	milliliters	teaspoons by 4.93
tablespoons	milliliters	tablespoons by 14.79
fluid ounces	milliliters	fluid ounces by 29.57
cups	milliliters	cups by 236.59
cups	liters	cups by 0.24
pints	milliliters	pints by 473.18
pints	liters	pints by 0.473
quarts	milliliters	quarts by 946.36
quarts	liters	quarts by 0.946
gallons	liters	gallons by 3.785

US	METRIC
1 teaspoon	5 milliliters
1 tablespoon	15 milliliters
¼ cup	60 milliliters
½ cup	120 milliliters
1 cup	230 milliliters
1¼ cups	300 milliliters
1½ cups	360 milliliters
2 cups	460 milliliters
2½ cups	600 milliliters
3 cups	700 milliliters
4 cups (1 quart)	0.95 liter
4 quarts (1 gallon)	3.8 liters
8¾ ounces	250 grams
10 ounces	280 grams
15 ounces	425 grams
16 ounces (1 pound)	454 grams

Acknowledgments

Writing this book was a dream come true for me and something that I could not have achieved without the help of many people.

Thanks first to Marisa McClellan for introducing me to our shared agent, Clare Pelino. Enormous thanks to Clare for believing in this first-time author and for answering all my anxious questions with humor. I want to thank the team at Storey Publishing, including Margaret Sutherland, Lisa Hiley, and Michaela Jebb, for making my cookbook-writing dream come true and for being such delightful collaborators.

To Vanessa Druckman, thank you for starting the Chicago Food Swap with me all those years ago. Thanks to the many businesses who have hosted the Chicago Food Swap over the years. A special thank you to LaManda Joy and Lindsay Shepherd for offering the Chicago Food Swap a permanent home at the exact moment it needed one. To the members of the Chicago Food Swap community, thank you for your enthusiasm, creativity, and input over the years. You make all the work of running the swap worthwhile.

I would also like to acknowledge the food swap organizers around the country, and indeed around the world, who took the time to speak with me and share their thoughts for this book, including Mandy Andree, Tara Bellucci, Andrea Buono, Aimee Carson, Chris Dean, Beth Dixon, Aimee Goggins, Stephanie Hibbert, Emily Han, Lyn Huckabee, Georgia Kirkpatrick, Suzanne Krowiak, Elizabeth Kruman, Jane Lerner, Eve Orenstein, Maria Ortado, Heather Roszczyk, Bethany Rydmark, Kate Payne, Michelle Richards, Melissa Smith, and Danielle Welke. Kate Payne, Megan Paska, Emily Han, and Bethany Rydmark deserve special recognition for their work in launching the food swap movement.

Beth Dixon, MaryBeth Jirgal, Laura Gladfelter, Patty Heinze, and Paddy Meehan all contributed recipes to this book, for which I am very grateful.

I would like to thank everyone who tested recipes, including Maureen Collins-Kolb, Jennifer Gilbert Gebhardt, Jacky Hackett, Sandy Johnson, and Julie King. Lori Buerger gave me the structure for the subsection on packaging. Genevieve Boehme, in addition to providing two recipes, tested almost every recipe and shared her tips on creative food packaging. Her contribution was enormous and I cannot thank her enough.

Thanks to Elizabeth Kregor for her help with legal issues surrounding food swapping. To Maris Callahan and Sara Fisher, a special thanks for their input on how to craft a press strategy.

I wrote much of this book at the River Forest Public Library, a cozy place where the only distractions are shelves of glossy cookbooks and neighbors who stop by periodically to check on my progress. Thanks to the staff there for fielding my frequent interlibrary loan requests and providing such a delightful place to work.

Love and thanks to my mother, Gail Kern Paster, the best example of a working mother I can imagine. To my aunt, Ann Brody Cove, thanks for being my culinary role model.

All my love and gratitude to my husband, Elliot Regenstein, for his unwavering support of me and my midlife career change. Love and thanks to my children, Zoe and Jamie Regenstein, for letting me go to the food swap every month — as long as I come home with cupcakes, of course.

The joy of writing this book and seeing it published is diminished only by the fact that my beloved father, Howard Paster, is not here to enjoy it with me. I dedicate it to his memory.

INDEX

241

INDEX

Other Storey Books You Will Enjoy

Valerie Peterson and Janice Fryer

Whether you want to decorate themed cookies for a baby shower, a birthday party, or a wedding, you'll find everything you need in this beautiful and inspiring guide. Learn foolproof methods for rolling, baking, piping, flooding, and other key techniques.

Kirsten K. Shockey & Christopher Shockey

Get to work making your own kimchi, pickles, sauerkraut, and more, with this colorful and delicious guide. With beautiful photography, learn methods to ferment 64 vegetables and herbs, along with dozens of creative recipes.

Jennifer Trainer Thompson

Feel the burn by making with your own hot sauce! With 32 recipes for creating your own signature blends, plus 60 more recipes for cooking with home-made or commercial versions, treat your taste buds to a delicious wallop.

Maggie Stuckey

Bring the neighborhood together with your own soup night and 90 crowd-pleasing recipes for hearty chowders, chili, and vegetable soups for every time of year. Additional recipes for salads, breads, and dessert round out the soup night experience.

These and other books from Storey Publishing are available wherever quality books are sold or by calling 1-800-441-5700. Visit us at *www.storey.com* or sign up for our newsletter at *www.storey.com/signup*.

Food Swap Card

WHO *Your Name*

WHAT *Your Item*

NOTES *What's in it · How to prepare it ·*
What to pair it with · Vegan · Gluten-free · Vegetarian

OFFERS *Name & Item*

....

....

....

....

....

....

....

....

....

Food Swap Card

WHO *Your Name*

WHAT *Your Item*

NOTES *What's in it · How to prepare it ·*
What to pair it with · Vegan · Gluten-free · Vegetarian

OFFERS *Name & Item*

....

....

....

....

....

....

....

....

NOTES

NOTES

Food Swap Card

WHO *Your Name*

WHAT *Your Item*

NOTES *What's in it · How to prepare it ·*
What to pair it with · Vegan · Gluten-free · Vegetarian

OFFERS *Name & Item*

....

....

....

....

....

....

....

....

....

Food Swap Card

WHO *Your Name*

WHAT *Your Item*

NOTES *What's in it · How to prepare it ·*
What to pair it with · Vegan · Gluten-free · Vegetarian

OFFERS *Name & Item*

....

....

....

....

....

....

....

....

....

NOTES

NOTES